The Sharp Edge of Educational Change

D0143641

Despite a generation of educational policy and research, most current reform efforts fail to understand the depth, range and complexity of what educators do. Furthermore, these reforms rarely recognize that what must be changed is an interconnected, highly complex and profoundly political system which shapes and constrains both the work of teaching and efforts to improve or transform it.

The Sharp Edge of Educational Change brings together the evidence of recent educational research to convey the realities of reform as they affect educators' practice. It deals with how educational change is, not how it should be, or how we would like it to be. The collected chapters each focus on particular, current reform strategies as they actually unfold in schools, including: assessing student learning; school restructuring and detracking; increasing the racial diversity of the teaching population; and parental involvement.

Each chapter illustrates the technical difficulties, political dynamics, intellectual challenges, and emotional demands of reform. In so doing, the book provides new and rich perspectives on the nature of teachers' and administrators' work.

Nina Bascia is Associate Professor of Theory and Policy Studies at the Ontario Institute for Studies in Education (OISE), University of Toronto.

Andy Hargreaves is Co-Director and Professor in the International Centre for Educational Change, also at the OISE.

WITHDRAWN

Educational Change and Development Series

Series Editors: Andy Hargreaves, Ontario Institute for Studies in Education, Canada and
Ivor Goodson, Warner Graduate School, University of Rochester, USA and Centre for Applied Research in Education, University of East Anglia, Norwich, UK

Re-schooling Society
David Hartley

The Gender Politics of Educational Change
Amanda Datnow

The Rules of School Reform
Max Angus

Whose School is it Anyway? Power and Politics
Kathryn Riley

Developing Teachers: The Challenges of Lifelong Learning
Chris Day

Change Forces: The Sequel
Michael Fullan

The Color of Teaching
June Gordon

The Sharp Edge of Educational Change: Teaching, Leading and the Realities of Reform
Edited by Nina Bascia and Andy Hargreaves

The Sharp Edge of Educational Change

Teaching, leading and the realities of reform

Edited by
Nina Bascia and Andy Hargreaves

London and New York

First published 2000
by RoutledgeFalmer
11 New Fetter Lane, London EC4P 4EE

Simultaneously published in the USA and Canada
by RoutledgeFalmer
29 West 35th Street, New York, NY 10001

RoutledgeFalmer is an imprint of the Taylor & Francis Group

Typeset in ITC Garamond by
The Running Head Limited, www.therunninghead.com
Printed and bound in Great Britain by St Edmundsbury Press,
Bury St Edmunds, Suffolk

British Library Cataloguing in Publication Data
A catalogue record for this book is available from the British Library

Library of Congress Cataloging in Publication Data
The sharp edge of educational change: teaching, leading and
the realities of reform/
    edited by Nina Bascia & Andy Hargreaves.
    p. cm. (Educational change and development series)
    Includes bibliographical references and index.
    1. School improvement programs — United States. 2. School improvement
programs — Canada. 3. Educational change — United States. 4. Educational
change — Canada. I. Bascia, Nina. II. Hargreaves, Andy. III. Series.
LB2822.82. S42 2001
371.2'07—dc21   00-036634

ISBN 0–750–70865–4 (hbk)
ISBN 0–750–70864–6 (pbk)

Contents

Acknowledgements   vii
The Editors   viii
List of Contributors   ix

I Introduction   **1**
1 Teaching and Leading on the Sharp Edge of Change   3
   Nina Bascia and Andy Hargreaves

II Courses of Change   **27**
2 The Attrition of Educational Change over Time: The Case of
   "Innovative," "Model," "Lighthouse" Schools   29
   Dean Fink

3 Leadership Succession, Cultures of Teaching and
   Educational Change   52
   Robert B. Macmillan

4 Change Agentry and the Quest for Equity: Lessons from
   Detracking Schools   72
   *Jeannie Oakes, Amy Stuart Wells, Susan Yonezawa and
   Karen Ray*

5 Changing Classroom Assessment: Teachers' Struggles   97
   Lorna Earl and Steven Katz

6 The Impact of Mandated Change on Teachers   112
   Beverley Bailey

III Contexts of Change   **129**
7 Gender Politics in School Reform   131
   Amanda Datnow

8 In the Margins: The Work of Racial Minority Immigrant
   Teachers   156
   Nina Bascia and Dennis Thiessen

Contents

9   Changing Schools in a Changing World   178
    Benjamin Levin and J. Anthony Riffel

IV Prospects for Change   195
10 Inside–Outside Change Facilitation: Structural and Cultural
    Considerations   197
    Wayne Seller and Lynne Hannay

11 Professionals and Parents: A Social Movement for
    Educational Change?   217
    Andy Hargreaves

    Index   236

Acknowledgements

This book was first conceived, and many of the chapters first presented, at a conference we organized at the Guild Inn Hotel in Scarborough, Ontario in November 1995. The conference was part of the initiative to support a research network on Changing Teachers in a Globally Changing World, funded by the Social Sciences and Humanities Research Council of Canada (SSHRC). Andy Hargreaves and Ivor Goodson were coordinators of the network. Many of the research projects reported on in this volume were also funded by the SSHRC.

In addition to the hard work of all the contributors in this book, we want to acknowledge the characteristically superb support of Leo Santos in preparing and organizing the manuscript for publication.

All chapters are original to this volume, excepting Chapter 4 by Jeannie Oakes and her colleagues which was first published in the 1997 *ASCD Year-book, Rethinking educational change with heart and mind*, Alexandria, VA, ASCD, edited by Andy Hargreaves and reprinted with permission from the Association for Supervision and Curriculum Development.

Nina Bascia and Andy Hargreaves
International Centre for Educational Change
Toronto, Ontario

The Editors

Nina Bascia is Associate Professor and Associate Chair of the department of Theory and Policy Studies, and a member of the International Centre for Educational Change, at the Ontario Institute for Studies in Education of the University of Toronto. Her research focuses on the policy, social and organizational contexts of teachers' work, with particular emphasis on teachers' unions and teacher leadership roles. She is author of *Unions in teachers' professional lives* (1994) and co-editor of *The contexts of teaching in secondary schools: teachers' realities* (1990) and of *Making a difference about difference: the lives and careers of racial minority immigrant teachers* (1996).

Andy Hargreaves is Professor of Education in the department of Theory and Policy Studies, and co-director of the International Centre for Educational Change, at the Ontario Institute for Studies in Education of the University of Toronto. He is Editor-in-Chief of the *Journal of Educational Change* and the author and editor of many books in the field of educational change including *Learning to change* (with Lorna Earl) (in press), *Changing teachers, changing times* (1994) and *What's worth fighting for out there?* (with Michael Fullan) (1998).

Contributors

Beverley Bailey is an Associate Professor at Brandon University. Her area of research is focused on the change process in both schools and universities. Currently her research is directed toward the problems of multicultural education and the impact that lack of change has on that population. Her teaching areas are educational psychology and counseling. Her recent publications concern university change and the problematical area of the education of aboriginal students.

Amanda Datnow is an Assistant Professor in the department of Theory and Policy Studies at the Ontario Institute for Studies in Education of the University of Toronto. Her research focuses on the politics and policies of school reform, particularly as they relate to the professional lives of teachers and issues of equity. Within her broader research agenda, her major areas of focus are the intersection of gender and school reform and the scaling up of externally developed school reform models in urban schools. She is the author of *The gender politics of educational change* (1998), co-author of *Scaling up school reform* (forthcoming), and author of numerous research articles on school reform and gender and education.

Lorna Earl is an Associate Professor in the department of Theory and Policy Studies and Associate Director of the International Centre for Educational Change at the Ontario Institute for Studies in Education of the University of Toronto. Her research focuses on large-scale educational reform, with particular attention to the role that assessment plays in school improvement. As an applied researcher and evaluator, her primary interest is the wise application of research, assessment and evaluation knowledge to the realities of schools and classrooms. Recent publications include *Schooling for change* with Andy Hargreaves and Jim Ryan (1997); *Assessment and accountability in education: improvement of surveillance* (1999); *Developing indicators: the call for accountability* (1999); *Education for the middle years: the paradox of hope* (1999); and *The evaluation of the Manitoba School Improvement Program* (1998).

Dean Fink is an international educational development consultant and an associate of the International Centre for Educational Change at the Ontario

Institute for Studies in Education of the University of Toronto. A former principal and superintendent with the Halton Board of Education in Ontario, he is co-author of *Changing our schools* (1996) and author of *Good schools/real schools: why school reform doesn't last* (2000).

Lynne Hannay is Associate Professor in the Curriculum, Teaching and Learning Department as well as Head of the Midwestern Field Centre and a member of the International Centre for Educational Change at the Ontario Institute for Studies in Education of the University of Toronto. She has two parallel focuses in her field development work with schools and in her research. One interest concerns professional learning practices including action research. The other research program involves the process of organizational change in secondary schools. In both lines of inquiry, she has conducted longitudinal studies as well as published in professional and refereed journals. She is also a co-author of *Reconceptualizing school-based curriculum development: decision-making at the school level* (1990).

Steven Katz is a doctoral candidate and preservice instructor in the department of Human Development and Applied Psychology, and a member of the International Centre for Educational Change at the Ontario Institute for Studies in Education of the University of Toronto. His research focuses on the epistemological foundations of teachers' instruction and assessment practices, and proceeds in contexts delimited by broader policy initiatives. Recent publications include *Substituting the symbol for the experience: exposing a fallacy in mathematics education* (1999) and *Competency, epistemology and pedagogy: curriculum's holy trinity* (2000).

Benjamin Levin is Deputy Minister of Education and Training for the Province of Manitoba. He is on leave from his position as Professor of Educational Administration at the Faculty of Education of the University of Manitoba. He is the co-author of *Understanding Canadian schools* (1994 and 1998) and *Schools and the changing world* (1997), and co-editor of *Organizational influences on organizational productivity* (1995). His research interests are in education policy and economics, and he is working on a new book on international education reform slated for publication in 2001.

Robert B. Macmillan is Associate Professor in the Department of Education at St. Francis Xavier University in Nova Scotia, Canada. His research focuses on the changing nature of the principalship and on the role of schools in their communities. He has written about changes in principals' and teachers' work caused by the creation of school advisory councils and by the introduction of computer technology into the curriculum. He is currently working on an edited volume entitled *Theory and inquiry in educational administration: the Greenfield legacy.*

Jeannie Oakes is Professor and Associate Dean of the Graduate School of Education at the University of California, Los Angeles. She is perhaps best known for her work on the implications of tracking and ability grouping for the learning opportunities of low-ability, poor and ethnic minority students, reported first in *Keeping track: how schools structure inequality* (1985). Her most recent book, *Becoming good American schools: the struggle for civic virtue in education reform* (2000), investigates state and local efforts to implement "equity minded" education reform, including alternatives to tracking and ability grouping.

Karen Ray received her doctorate in Education from the Graduate School of Education at the University of California, Los Angeles in 1999. She has most recently worked as a child care center licensor for the state of Washington. She currently lives in Olympia, Washington, with her husband and two children.

J. Anthony Riffel is Professor Emeritus in the Department of Educational Administration, Foundations and Psychology at the University of Manitoba. Most recently he is the co-author of *Schools and the changing world: struggling toward the future* (1997).

Wayne Seller is Associate Professor in the department of Curriculum, Teaching and Learning, and a member of the International Centre for Educational Change at the Ontario Institute for Studies in Education of the University of Toronto. As Head of the OISE/UT Northwestern Field Centre, his research and field development focuses on the interrelationship of change in schools and effective professional development and the development of leadership for schools and school systems. He is co-author of *Curriculum: perspectives and practice* (1990).

Dennis Thiessen is Professor in the department of Theory and Policy Studies at the Ontario Institute for Studies in Education of the University of Toronto. His research focuses on curriculum and school change and teacher development. He is co-author of *Getting into the habit of change in Ohio schools: the cross-case study of twelve transforming learning communities* (1999) and co-editor of *Making a difference about difference: the lives and careers of racial minority immigrant teachers* (1996), *Children and their curriculum: the perspectives of primary and elementary school children* (1997), and *Agents, provocateurs: reform-minded leaders for schools of education* (1998).

Amy Stuart Wells is a Professor of Educational Policy at UCLA's Graduate School of Education and Information Studies. She is a sociologist of education whose research and writing has focused broadly on issues of race and education and more specifically on educational policies, such as school desegregation, school choice, charter schools, vouchers and tracking, and how they shape and constrain opportunities for students of color. She is the author and editor of numerous books and articles, including *The multiple meanings of charter school reform: lessons from ten California school districts* (forthcoming), *Stepping over the color line: African American students in white suburban schools* (1997), and *The politics of culture: understanding local political resistance to detracking in racially mixed schools* (1996).

Susan Yonezawa is partnership coordinator for the University of California, San Diego Center for Research in Educational Equity, Assessment, and Teaching Excellence. Her areas of research interest include equity-minded educational policies such as tracking and detracking, with a particular interest in students' course placements and pathways to college-readiness. Currently, she is working on developing educational reform-minded partnerships between the university and low-income, high-minority schools in San Diego as part of the post-affirmative-action UC outreach initiative.

I   INTRODUCTION

1 Teaching and Leading on the Sharp Edge of Change

Nina Bascia and Andy Hargreaves

In Montreal, English artist Raymond Mason has erected a sculpture, "Illuminated Crowd," the leading members of which appear drawn, enthralled, toward a bright light. Moving back through the crowd, however, as the light begins to fade, one encounters darker human conditions: anxiety, anger, sickness, death. Mason's sculpture is meant to represent the flow of human emotions through space. It could just as easily represent flows of human responses to change.

Change puts some people in the limelight and others in the shadows. Some are keen to be on the leading edge of change; others find themselves more on the sharp edge. While many books illuminate the leading edge of educational change, this one deals with the equally important topic of educators, especially teachers, who experience its darker side.

This book brings together the evidence of recent educational research to convey how the sharp edge of change affects teachers' practice. It is an antidote to celebratory views of change where

- lighthouse schools are erected as beacons for others to follow
- large injections of venture capital or resources from foundation projects infuse success into special clusters of schools
- triumphal claims are made about the power of standards-based reform or large-scale educational changes to raise the achievement results of entire nations and
- reform is hailed as the savior of all society.

These optimistic claims persist despite our understanding that, as the chapter by Fink in this collection shows, lighthouse schools are often voracious consumers of human energy and other resources that leave other schools in the shadows (Lortie, 1975); and their light quickly dims to the point where they become indistinguishable from other schools around them (see Sarason, 1982). We know that corporate- or foundation-funded improvement projects may create temporary or localized success but are difficult to sustain beyond the initial investment, if government underfunds education or imposes contradictory reform demands. As for large-scale reform, the grandiose claims made for it are too often contradicted by precipitous falls in teacher morale and recruitment as reform agendas are implemented too swiftly, on too many fronts and with little consideration of teachers' concerns (e.g., Woods *et al.*, 1997). The claim that educational reform is a special agent of social redemption is an historically repetitious one containing few precedents for success — and little cause to believe that this millennial moment of educational reform will be any less disappointing than previous ones (McCulloch, 1997; Popkewitz, 1999).

Why does educational reform so often fail? Why does so much of it wash over or weaken the very people whose commitment is essential to implementing it? There are two key factors which underpin what Sarason (1990) depressingly calls "the predictable failure of educational reform." The first is that most reform efforts fail to understand the depth, range and complexity of what teachers do. They approach teaching in a largely one-dimensional way as a set of skills, beliefs and behaviors that can and must be changed — and in doing so fail to grasp what teachers need to help them to change. They fail to understand the good reasons why many teachers persist with what they already do, or change in ways that reformers do not acknowledge. Second, reformers rarely recognize that what must be changed is an interconnected, highly complex and profoundly political system which shapes and constrains the work of teaching and efforts to improve or transform it.

Four Dimensions of Teaching

Educational change efforts are always underpinned by particular theories or assumptions about what teaching is like and what principles or activities comprise it. These different conceptions of teaching become especially apparent when teaching is compared across different countries, regions or communities (Broadfoot and Osborn, 1993; Coulter, 1996; Louis, 1990) or over different periods of time (Hamilton, 1989; Tyack, 1991; Werner, 1991). Assumptions about teaching are also brought to the surface and questioned when society is changing quickly, when educational practice is under pressure to respond, and differing reform ideologies compete with each other for influence (Darling-Hammond, 1992; Hargreaves, 1994). Four different conceptions of teaching are activated, but usually overlooked, in different instances of educational reform: technical, intellectual, socio-emotional and socio-political ones.

1 Technical

A technical view of teaching has prevailed across much of the world since the establishment in the West of large bureaucratic school systems a century or more ago (Carlson, 1992; Larson, 1977). Central to this notion of teaching is the belief that if procedures are correctly defined, clearly detailed and carefully monitored, most major teaching decisions can and should be prescribed through policy mandates that alter school schedules, programs, assessment and teaching responsibilities. Teachers are viewed as technicians whose job is to implement relatively uniform "treatments" for students, who are "processed" by schools as if they are all roughly the same (Darling-Hammond, 1992; Hargreaves, 1994). When a technical view of teaching is influential, reformers assume that educators have the capacity and ability to teach in different and more effective ways but are either lazy, unknowledgeable, unfocused or resistant to change (Earl and LeMahieu, 1997).

In the technical approach, pedagogies are sometimes prescribed on the basis of scientific evidence about which practices best lead to desired goals for learning, but they are also often mandated on the basis of unexamined "common-sense" or hierarchical judgements about what works best in classrooms. In the scientific case, educational researchers and the policymakers they influence lay claim to studies that demonstrate how particular teaching strategies are effective in producing significant learning gains in areas such as literacy and numeracy (Reynolds, 2000). Researchers in the technical tradition argue that teachers should no more be allowed to choose or invent their own methods based on intuitive or experiential judgements than doctors or other professionals should be allowed to treat patients in defiance of the evidence. Advocates of the technical view argue that to allow teachers to teach in ways that demonstrably offer lesser benefit to students, especially the most disadvantaged ones, is educationally and morally irresponsible (Reynolds, 2000).

Examples of the technical perspective at work include the implementation of Madeline Hunter's "direct instruction" methods in many US school districts in the 1980s (Hunter, 1984) where teachers' compliance was secured through inservice training, administrative supervision and teacher evaluation systems. Today, many US schools and districts subscribe to Robert Slavin's *Success for All* program because it shows strong evidence of positive effects on achievement results, compared to other less prescriptive strategies (American Institute for Research, 1999). In England and Wales, national policy has mandated hours for numeracy and literacy in primary schools, with accompanying texts of scripted and timed teaching performance that teachers are required to follow (Galton, 2000).

Adherents to the technical perspective are not confined to advocating "conventional" teaching strategies. Proponents of innovative methods based on the latest research in cognitive science may also be drawn to changing teachers' practices by requirement and compulsion. The Kentucky Education Reform Act exemplifies this view. Believing that fundamental change was long overdue, the Kentucky legislature conceived a statewide, systemic approach to school reform, including changes in curriculum and teaching strategies toward an emphasis on higher-order thinking and performance-based assessment. School improvement was measured using an "accountability index," and every two years schools were rewarded for meeting their thresholds or sanctioned for not. Rewards meant financial bonuses for "good" teachers, with sanctions including state takeover of the school and dismissal for "bad" ones (Whitford and Wong, 2000).

Whatever the scientific merits of particular practices, the strategy of trying to bring them about merely by mandate or compulsion has limited effectiveness. Reform strategies that specify required changes in teaching practices tend to be effective only with regard to learning basic skills — missing out on the higher-order learning that is essential for young people's successful participation in the economies and societies of the new century (Hallinger and Murphy, 1987). Indeed, concentration on lower-order teaching and learning can lead teachers to de-emphasize more complex and sophisticated educational work elsewhere in the curriculum. Mindful of these more complex aspects of their work, teachers may endure prescriptions about how they teach literacy or numeracy, for example, for limited periods of the school day, but they will resist attempts to extend such prescription across broader areas of their work (Datnow *et al.*, 1998). Indeed, Galton (2000) argued that, even if the scientific case about effective teaching practice is strong, changing teachers' practices by force lessens teachers' professionalism and their deeper commitments to their work.

The reality is that prescribed pedagogical change acts on a narrow, restricted view of teaching and learning. As Sergiovanni (1999) notes, changes like standards-based reform attend only to the technical aspects of teaching and learning and neglect the complex, human lifeworld of schooling. A technical conception views teaching as predominantly entailing working with students in classrooms. Anything else — developing curriculum, working with other teachers, meeting with students or parents — is not considered "real teaching" at all (Bascia, 1994; Darling-Hammond, 1992). Yet attending to and activating these wider aspects of the lifeworld of teaching is essential to successful reform, especially for those who work with disadvantaged students (Bascia, 1996). Among poor and marginalized groups, for example, the teaching of literacy is more likely to be effective where, through critical literacy, it engages with the cultural realities of students' lives (Lankshear, 1997; Weiler, 1998) and where it is supplemented by other community-based strategies that directly attack the damaging effects of poverty and marginalization on students' learning. Yet worldwide, program initiatives and resources directed at the full scope of disadvantage are being redirected to more specific preoccupations with developing the technical skills of literacy as if they occur in isolation (Thomson, 1999). Indeed, in some cases, such as our own province of Ontario, legislated time commitments have tied teachers even more exclusively to the classroom with less time to devote to these other important aspects of their work (Bascia, 1998; Hargreaves, 1998c).

Of course, it is disturbing that many teachers persist with existing practices or develop new ones with scant regard for relevant research evidence.

In any other profession, this failure to keep current with recent research would be unconscionable. Yet prescribing pedagogical change does nothing to develop a stronger professional learning culture among teachers. Indeed, by undermining teachers' morale, distracting them from more complex aspects of their work, and creating a bureaucratically unwieldy and politically volatile apparatus of enforcement (Whitford and Wong, 2000), the technical approach, pursued alone, may do more harm to teaching and learning than good.

2 Intellectual

An intellectual conception views teaching as complex work requiring sophisticated professional judgement that draws on deep intellectual resources of knowledge, expertise, reflection, research and continuous learning. Comparing teaching to other professions, Rowan (1994) found that educators' work ranks highly in task complexity.

All teaching requires an intellectual grasp of subject matter and some sort of reflective relationship to practice. In recent years, changing social conditions and research developments on children's processes of cognitive understanding have led to dramatic changes in expectations regarding what teachers should achieve with their students. Increased cultural diversity, informational technology, changing families, a more service-oriented economy and in some places growing preoccupations with national identity have required teachers to respond to constant shifts in how policy-makers and administrators define curriculum, pedagogy and assessment.

In addition to mastering the traditional intellectual foundations and processes of teaching, teachers today are also being challenged to have the following attributes.

- They must *master new content knowledge* and meet increasingly demanding content standards (Shulman, 1986).
- They must *learn to plan* their teaching differently around what students must know, not what teachers prefer to teach. These new forms of planning are highly complex. Even the best teachers need considerable time and support to become expert in them (Hargreaves and Earl, in press).
- They must develop knowledge of and expertise in a rapidly expanding range of *assessment and accountability* strategies (Earl and Katz, in this volume; Stiggins, 1995; Wiggins and McTighe, 1998).
- They must become critical consumers of and respondents to externally driven change as well as acting as their own self-initiating *change agents* with others around them (Fullan, 1999).
- They must commit to *continuous professional learning* of formal and informal kinds as they respond to the rapidly changing worlds of their students and the demands of policy for ever improving standards

(Cochran-Smith and Lytle, 1992; Day, 1999). A high-quality teaching profession must also be an active learning profession.

- They must be able to *inquire into their own practice* and collect as well as evaluate student achievement data, so they can pinpoint evidence about where their practice may be problematic and what may need to be improved (Hargreaves and Fullan, 1998; Lieberman and McLaughlin, 2000; Newmann and Wehlage, 1995).
- They must have the desire to know how to learn from and *collaborate effectively with others around them* — colleagues, parents and students themselves. Increasingly, teachers need to draw on every source of learning and assistance available so they do not become overwhelmed by facing the increasing demands of their job alone (Hargreaves, 1994; Talbert and MacLaughlin, 1994).

All people, Antonio Gramsci (1971) said, are intellectuals; but only some have the *function* of intellectuals. Teachers are one such group (Aronowitz and Giroux, 1991). Teachers help to create the generations of the future. Their work, as such, cannot and must not be reduced to skill and technique alone. Teaching that is worthy of the name is visionary work, imbued with moral purpose that ultimately develops the citizens of tomorrow. Teaching is therefore profoundly intellectual in its underpinning purposes as well as in its complexity.

Supporting and fulfilling the intellectual dimensions of teaching so that teachers reach their potential is no mean feat. Among other things, an intellectually enriched teaching professional requires:

- *time* aside from classroom responsibilities, within and outside the regular school day, to plan and think through the complexities of change together; engage in inquiry; look at and learn from each other's practice; and reflect on and redesign what they do (Cochran Smith and Lytle, 1992; Fullan with Stiegelbauer, 1991)
- *access* to ideas, information and expertise through the provision of high-quality professional development; the availability of skilled support from consultants and staff developers; the provision of computer access to networks of professional learning, support and problem-solving; and a supply of relevant resources during and beyond the initial period of new program implementation (Hargreaves and Earl, in press)
- *leaders* who themselves model effective professional learning by examining their own practice and working alongside staff as they puzzle their way through improvement efforts together (Little, 1984).

Reform strategies predicated on this intellectual conception of teaching require a substantial resource environment; a belief that teachers have important contributions to make to curriculum development because of their special knowledge of students and their grasp of the immediate realities of practice; and a ready acknowledgement that teachers' work today extends far beyond the classroom.

Reforms rooted in voluntary initiatives, in corporate- or foundation-funded improvement projects, or in partnerships between school districts and universities (Seller and Hannay, in this volume) for example, often embody these intellectually driven principles and practices of change — but their effects are often temporary or localized. Government policies tend to favor short-term behavioral compliance rather than long-term intellectual investment in teachers (Hargreaves and Fullan, 1998); they have tended to minimize professional development provision and to focus it on short-term implementation of government priorities (Helsby, 1999); they have turned visionary leaders into performance managers as well as separating their professional associations from the unions of their teaching staff (Bascia, 1998); and instead of giving teachers increased preparation time in the school day, they have in some cases scaled it back so that virtually all of a teacher's working day is spent in front of students, totally absorbed in the pressing immediacy of the work.

While the evidence repeatedly points to the importance of supporting the intellectual work of teaching and the intellectual development of teachers, few governments have incorporated this intellectual conception of teaching and its resource implications into their political reform efforts. Indeed, they have often actively undermined it, either by default or by design. This has been the unfortunate state of affairs, for example, in Ontario during much of the 1990s. Provincial curriculum changes have required teachers to develop school-based plans, but resources for professional development have been reduced. Curriculum development sessions must occur at lunch, after school and on weekends, outside of regular school time — in fragments rather than in longer blocks, in and around teachers' already complex and exhausting work schedules. Rapidly deteriorating working conditions have also led to polarized relationships between government and teacher unions, with unions discouraging teachers from working outside the contractually specified day, and many districts reducing or entirely eliminating professional development days that had previously been used for planning, meeting, reflecting and other collegial work.

With decreased educational funding and government policies that have become more technical in their orientation, opportunities for teachers to engage directly in curriculum development have been replaced by detailed "teacher-proof" curricula (comparable to political trends elsewhere — as, for example, the English National Curriculum) that leave little time, scope or opportunity for intellectually informed professional judgement and reflection. In many parts of the world, in other words, governments have sought to raise student standards by dumbing down their teachers.

3 Socioemotional

More innovative, often voluntary or entrepreneurial approaches to educational change typically acknowledge and improve the intellectual dimensions of teaching, not least by actively involving teachers in the change and development process. Yet even such reform movements can miss vital aspects of what it means to be a teacher and to improve over time. One of the most overlooked dimensions of the educational change process is the socioemotional one.

Even and especially at its best, teaching is more than an intellectual and cognitive activity. A socioemotional conception of teaching includes but also extends far beyond cognitive standards, content knowledge, intellectual mastery, deliberative judgement, rational planning, critical reflection and systematic problem-solving.

One of our current research programs is investigating the emotions of teaching in a changing world (Hargreaves, 1997b, 1998a, 1998b, 1999, 2000; Hargreaves and Fullan, 1998; Hargreaves and Lasky, 2000). At the core of this program is the recognition that, in Denzin's (1984) terms, teaching (like learning and leading) is always (although not solely) an *emotional practice*, both by intention and neglect. Teaching arouses and colors feelings in teachers themselves, in students and in others. It engages students or bores them, connects with parents or keeps them at a distance, builds trust and co-operation among colleagues or generates jealousy and suspicion. This socioemotional work of teaching manifests itself in a number of areas that all have implications for educational change.

First, most teachers' goals for their students are at least partly social and emotional. Teachers of younger children often see themselves as developing citizens who can participate in public life (Woods, 1993). Many want their students to develop commitments to their communities, and tolerance and respect for others in a multicultural society. These socioemotional goals of teaching are perhaps most evident among teachers who have special responsibility for socializing students who are recent immigrants, as Bascia and Thiessen show in their chapter, but many other teachers also embrace these goals (Hargreaves, 1998b). In a rapidly changing world of unstable relationships, transformed family structures and constantly shifting work requirements, many teachers want to educate their students to be much more than productive workers in a knowledge society (Schlechty, 1990). They want to build stronger self-esteem and self-confidence in young people (Elkind, 1997); develop what Goleman (1995, 1998) calls key emotional intelligences of self-awareness, self-regulation, empathy, motivation and a wide variety of social skills (Fullan, 1997); and cultivate stronger dispositions to care for and build relationships with others (Noddings, 1984). These essential goals are absent from many official government reform agendas (though this is not so much the case in a number of predominantly Catholic countries such as Ireland, Spain, Portugal and much of South America).

Second, attending to students' emotional lives is necessary to provide a safe, orderly and supportive climate in which cognitive and academic learning can take place. While this is a key finding and implication of the school effectiveness literature (e.g., Mortimore *et al.*, 1988), and is even acknowledged in school inspection and evaluation in the UK, many reform strategies actively perpetuate the fragmented nature of secondary schools where teachers are divided by subjects, students are scattered across courses, and teachers teach too many students to know them well (Meier, 1998; Sizer, 1992). Students who drop out of high school regularly complain that not one adult there knew them well (Hargreaves *et al.*, 1996). Reform strategies that are primarily content-driven and standards-based perpetuate structures that serve content rather than children; and when teachers' efforts are focused on implementing detailed curriculum requirements, they are distracted from maintaining core continuous relationships with students, colleagues and communities that are foundational to all high-quality teaching and learning.

Effective teaching, learning and leading all involve what Denzin (1984) calls emotional understanding — the ability to read and respond quickly to others' moods and feelings. Without this understanding, teachers can misconstrue their students' boredom as studiousness, and leaders can misread their teachers' anxieties and stresses about change efforts as resistance directed at them. Emotional understanding is threatened when policies, structures and change practices create excessive distance between teachers and those around them. This occurs:

• when school structures and reform strategies restrict and rationalize the relationships between teachers and students
• when, in culturally diverse societies, the still scarce resource of minority teachers tends to be shunted into specialized sidings of second language or special education teaching (although minority teachers can and should also contribute to relationships in the school community as a whole) (Bascia, 1996; Bascia and Thiessen, in this volume; Foster, 1994)
• when staffrooms and change efforts are colored by gender influences among teachers that are not explicitly addressed as such by policy or leadership efforts (Datnow, in this volume; Robertson, 1992)
• when administrators stereotype and misread changes in their community (for example, misconstruing problems of poverty as ones of single-parenthood) (Levin and Riffel, in this volume)
• when policies of regularly rotating principals between schools, or inadequate policy supports that create chronic principal turnover in innercity schools, prevent school leaders from understanding and working effectively with the culture of their staffs over time (Macmillan, in this volume)
• when teachers construct their professionalism in insular and exclusive ways that place them on inaccessible pedestals above parents and their wider communities, intensifying anxiety levels in relationships between them (Hargreaves, in this volume; Zeichner, 1991).

Teaching and leading involve what Hochschild (1983) terms *emotional labor.* This is the labor that people in service and caring professions perform to manage or mask their own emotions so they can produce desired or required emotional states in others. At its best, emotional labor is a positive force in teaching and leading where teachers infect students with their own enthusiasm; resist being provoked by tense or angry colleagues who are experiencing problems at home; or are able to charm, persuade and otherwise move corporate benefactors to provide financial support for educationally desirable initiatives that benefit students.

Such emotional labor is an energizing labor of love that represents great skill, competence and maturity. But in unsupportive work contexts, educators experience emotional labor as draining and exhausting — leading to feelings of alienation, selling out and loss of the self. Such feelings are, importantly, linked to senses of reduced self-efficacy among teachers that lead in turn to poorer results with students (Ashton and Webb, 1986; Rosenholtz, 1989). Contemporary reform efforts increasingly engender negative emotional labor that repeatedly puts teachers at the sharp end of change. For example,

- where teachers' own purposes are overridden or pushed aside by exclusively cognitively driven reform agendas (e.g., Bailey, in this volume; Nias, 1991); where frantic, volatile and capricious change agendas scatter teachers' efforts to the winds as they try to respond to multiple purposes (Helsby, 1999); where educators are provided with insufficient time and resources to meet the increasingly high expectations demanded of them; or where teachers see groups such as parents or colleagues as emotional distractions rather than as core to their purposes and worthy of their emotional investment (Hargreaves, in this volume)
- conditions that create feelings of powerlessness (Ball, 1987; Datnow, in this volume; Kemper, 1995): as in fear-laden processes of inspection and supervision (Jeffrey and Woods, 1996; Waite, 1995); guilt-oriented strategies for bringing about anti-racist and anti-sexist education (Troyna, 1995); political and media-based discourses that shame and blame teachers for educational failure (Scheff, 1994; Stoll and Myers, 1998); and wilful exclusions of teachers and their expertise from the change and improvement process (Bailey, in this volume)
- conditions that prevent, destroy or poison relationships: reform strategies that draw teachers away from their students, divide them from administration, put them under excessive pressure from parents, and isolate them from each other.

Sadly, these are the very conditions in many politically driven reform efforts that repeatedly put teachers at the sharp edge of change.

4 Sociopolitical

A sociopolitical conception of teaching views teachers, individually and collectively, as political actors working in contexts that are inescapably political. The sociopolitical work of teaching takes place inside classrooms; within schools and other educational settings more widely; as well as in and with communities, the media and various areas of formal decision-making. This conception of teaching emphasizes the impact of teachers' choices and actions on others, especially students; differences in power, status and authority among teachers; and teachers' power, status and authority relative to others (Ball, 1987; Bascia, 1994, 1998; Blase, 1991; Ginsburg *et al.*, 1992; Siskin, 1994; Smaller, 1991, 1998). Policies and practices predicated on a political model of teaching encourage teachers' involvement in making decisions about educational issues through school-based decision-making, curriculum development, teacher leadership positions, teacher union involvement, and participation in advisory groups to policy-makers; and they attempt to recognize and instigate enduring power imbalances between different individuals and groups.

Political action is often perceived as being antithetical to "good" teaching, and politically active teachers can sometimes seem to care more about their own work preferences and conditions than about students or classroom practice (Bascia, 1997; Hargreaves, 1995; Siskin, 1994) — as in the resistance of many teachers to mixed ability teaching that Oakes describes in her chapter; or in the gendered politics of school change described in Datnow's chapter, where older male teachers resist and ridicule the innovative efforts of their younger female colleagues. Yet, there is growing acceptance of counter-arguments. Many of the issues over which teachers try to exert some degree of control and influence, such as preparation time, resource levels, class sizes and implementation timelines, represent important conditions for quality teaching and learning. Moreover, teachers have a grasp of the front-line realities of teaching that can make important contributions to educational decision-making (Bascia, 1994, 1998; National Commission on Teaching and America's Future, 1996; Talbert and McLaughlin, 1994).

Yet government driven reform strategies often create conditions of professional powerlessness among teachers. They exercise "power-over" teachers rather than building "power-with" them (Blase and Anderson, 1995). "Power-with" strategies are more common in the kinds of joint-planning activities, collaborative action research projects and professional community building efforts in more local and voluntary change initiatives that Seller and Hannay describe in their chapter. When clearly connected to teaching and learning, such efforts make a demonstrable difference in the improvement of learning standards (Newmann and Wehlage, 1995). In this sense, politics is not an interference with or distraction from learning, but a vital part of its improvement.

At the same time, the increased power and status that teachers want for themselves in their relations with governments and administrators is the very thing they frequently deny to the students and parents with whom they work. Students have rarely been consulted about educational changes (Levin, 2000; Rudduck *et al.*, 1997); teachers' assessment judgements and criteria have been a mystery to them (Earl and LeMahieu, 1997); learning and achievement targets have mainly been developed for students and seldom developed with them. Parents, meanwhile, have been kept at a distance, often seen as adversaries more than allies (Hargreaves, in this volume), and informed about changes that affect them and their children only once professional decisions have been made (Fink, in this volume). Micropolitical relationships among teachers — differences in power, status and perspective such as those identified by Datnow and by Bascia and Thiessen in this volume — can have strong effects on the nature and quality of school programs. In terms of its benefits for students, therefore, the political perspective is a challenge not only for governmental and administrator change-makers, but also for teachers themselves.

Trajectories and Tragedies of Change

Many of the reforms investigated in this book are rooted in conceptions of teaching and educational practice that challenge the dominant technical model. Their intentions are for a more dynamic educational system, and a teaching force that has a greater capacity to respond effectively to a range of local (and changing) conditions, and that is more committed to its continuing improvement and satisfied with its work. Yet despite a generation of educational policy and evaluation research that has repeatedly demonstrated the inadequacy of technically based reform (e.g., Fullan with Stiegelbauer, 1991; McLaughlin, 1987; Sarason, 1990), the evidence in this book suggests that educational reform in the 1990s has persisted, at root, as being disturbingly simplistic and functionalist in its assumptions and approaches. The fundamental question is "why"?

The problem is certainly not a shortage of research on how to manage educational change. There is now an extensive knowledge base on the stages of concern through which people move as they adopt educational change (Hall *et al.*, 1975); on how change is experienced by teachers at various points in their lives and careers (Huberman, 1993; Sikes *et al.*, 1985); on the major characteristics that comprise effective schools (Reynolds, 1985); the key components of successful school improvement (Hopkins, 2000; Newmann and Wehlage, 1995; Stoll and Fink, 1996); the leadership qualities needed to foster successful change (Leithwood *et al.*, 1999); and on lessons and guidelines that can steer schools through the process of developing and implementing complex reforms (Fullan, 1993; Louis and Miles, 1990). With such a rich knowledge base on the technical aspects of change management, as well as on the human, culture-building processes of suc-cessful school improvement, why do reform efforts repeatedly fail to engage teachers' commitments and expertise, or fade from the limelight after their early promise?

Answers to these questions lie in deeper, more critical understandings which probe beneath the technical and human aspects of educational reform — recognizing that the historically ingrained patterns of failed educational change are more than matters of technical mismanagement or breakdowns in human communication and understanding. They reside, rather, in the sys-temic, contextual and political nature of public education and people's attempts to control and change it. In this respect, context clearly matters (McLaughlin and Talbert, 1993), and a more critical literature of educational change and reform is beginning to examine why (Hargreaves *et al.*, 1998).

The foundational research of Milbrey McLaughlin and her colleagues has persuasively shown that there are enormous variations in school ex-perience and quality between districts, individual schools and even sepa-rate subject departments (Little and McLaughlin, 1993; McLaughlin *et al.*, 1990; Siskin, 1994). Differences of leadership or of strength in the profes-sional cultures or communities of teaching shape and redefine reform and improvement initiatives according to the particular district, school or depart-ment in which they are developed or implemented.

> The parameters or configurations of the workplace are not the same for all . . . teachers, nor is the salience of a given parameter the same for all teach-ers in similarly configured settings. This is because the . . . contexts of . . . teaching have different landscapes as one moves between national systems and cultures, across state [or provincial] and local educational systems, across parent communities within the same system, between public and private sectors, or across subject-area departments. Thus, teachers' con-struction of their workplace and the significance of any particular context for their work will necessarily be conditioned by its relevance and char-acter and by its meaning in the context of other salient workplace condi-tions. (McLaughlin and Talbert, 1990: 7–8)

If context clearly makes a difference to change and reform efforts, how best can we understand that context? Following Smith and his colleagues (1987), Talbert and McLaughlin (1994) see the contexts of teaching and change as a set of "nested" or "embedded" layers or levels of influence, extending from nations to states, districts, schools and departments, that all affect the nature of teaching and learning at the center. While this expla-nation usefully differentiates between different policy approaches, its functionalist, systems-theory conception of distinct layers in an embedded system does not easily account for the highly complex, spatially penetrat-ing and rapidly shifting patterns of influence in today's informational society. It does not explain why, in political terms, contexts repeatedly have the same perverse characteristics of, for example, overstandardization, restricted approaches to inservice training, and pitifully inadequate levels of government funding for public education in poor communities. At the same time, the "nested system" explanation does not address how and why contexts change, as, for example, in relation to the emergence of charter schools or the impact of informational technologies on schooling.

Recent studies of in-school interaction have begun to develop more sensitive and sophisticated approaches to understanding the social context of schooling, making the context as well as the school the focal point for empirical inquiry. These more sophisticated views of micro–macro relationships avoid drawing conceptual boundaries between what is inside the classroom and what is "out there" in the world beyond (Hargreaves and Fullan, 1998). Acker (1999), for example, has described how streams of people are forever moving in and out of the schools today and how educators have to deal with all of them.

> There was a constant interchange of people who went in and out of the school. It is important to note their presence, because it contradicts that a school is an isolated society. Although each school has its own culture, it is formed in contact with the wider society, in the particular local context. (p. 125)

At the same time, context is not so complex that it can only be explained (or explained away) as an unpredictable, ineffable process of chaos. Drawing on theories of "new science" which describe the physical and natural worlds as chaotic systems that defy predictability and control (Gleick, 1987), organizational and educational theorists have sought to explain organizational and educational change as chaotic systems that cannot be managed by standard procedures and tight control (Fullan, 1993; Gunter, 1997; Wheatley, 1994). While their acknowledgement that today's organizations are highly complex and not amenable to standardized regulation is to be welcomed, these theories of chaos are themselves functionalist. They compare human societies and organizations to physical and biological systems. Wheatley (1994), for example, argues that there is no reason to assume that complex human systems are fundamentally different from complex natural ones. In relying on this naturalistic analogy, such theorists still explain change as a process without human will, devoid of politics. But as Anthony Giddens (1995) has implied, the chaos we experience in our lives and organizations is not just "natural" or accidental — it is often wilfully and politically manufactured by governments that want to intensify the productivity of teachers and other state employees, introduce change at an excessive pace, and keep everyone off-balance (Hargreaves, 1997a).

Jan Nespor (1997) argues for an alternative approach that explains contextual influences on education in terms of "questioning conventionally defined boundaries, looking for flows rather than states, focusing on networks and the layered connections that knot them together rather than on simpler linear histories of circumscribed events or settings" (p. xiv). Flows and networks can be considerably more methodologically challenging for theorists to trace than causal pathways. But this task has been made somewhat easier in recent years because of the greater politicization and therefore transparency of schooling. School councils, charter schools, and the public listing of schools in comparative performance tables are redefining the relationships between parents and professionals and making them more volatile and visible. The corporate world is becoming more involved in defining the curriculum, sponsoring new technologies, and setting the basic agendas and terms of educational discourse through which reform is debated and decided (e.g., value-added achievement, high-performance learning communities, total quality management). The boundaries around public schooling that gave it at least an appearance of autonomy as an agent for the general public good have been weakened by the wilful intrusions of commercial and market forces. There is a new terrain here for educational study, and while research on schools and communities, education and enterprise, or computers in the classroom already exist, few studies explore how all these forces and influences interconnect in specific sites.

This task is a demanding one, calling for multiple forms and sites of data collection, but the challenge is achievable. For example, Nespor (1997) shows how portfolio innovation in one elementary school is occasioned and shaped by a whole range of forces in complex, interactive ways. He describes how the school's principal gained permission from the authoritarian district superintendent to deviate from standard procedures by gaining his ear; how the superintendent's appointment followed on from a mandate to clean up the city; how parents' objections to the new assessment were assuaged by linking portfolios to business discourses of skill development that were circulating as a result of corporate interventions in education; and how, when the school's teachers could not develop their expertise in portfolio assessment sufficiently well, they became uncertain and defensive about it, assailed as they were by multiple school and district innovations and separated from each other by classroom isolation. As a result, teachers used the complex language and representation of portfolio assessment to obscure grading hierarchies and communicate with fellow teachers rather than communicating clearly with the working-class parents of the students they were supposed to serve.

It is these more complex, politicized aspects of the contexts of educational change, in which human will and powerful social interests are clearly at work, that explains why teachers are so often on its sharp edge. This is evident in several ways.

First, the scale of the problems that schools are expected to address just cannot be solved easily by teachers if at all. Ultimately, in the classic words of Basil Bernstein (1970), "education cannot compensate for society," yet teachers and schools are repeatedly burdened with the expectation that they can save and redeem society (Popkewitz, 1999). Schools are expected to save children from poverty and destitution; to rebuild nationhood in the aftermath of war; to develop universal literacy as a platform for economic survival; to create skilled workers even when little skilled employment beckons them; to develop tolerance amongst children in nations where adults are divided by religious and ethnic conflict; to cultivate democratic sentiments in societies that bear the scars of totalitarianism; to keep developed nations economically competitive and help developing ones to become so — essentially, to make restitution for all the sins of the present generation by how educators prepare the generations of the future (Hargreaves and Lo, 2000).

Many of the contemporary reforms described in this book, despite their increased conceptual sophistication, focus on relatively circumscribed changes in practice and cannot effectively combat the large, pervasive and intractable social problems they are intended to solve. Bascia and Thiessen, for example, reveal how and why, despite goodwill and hard work, the (small) presence of racial minority teachers is unable to bring about the magnitude of changes in school practices necessary to ensure diverse students' social, emotional and academic well-being. Similarly, Hargreaves indicates that larger transformations in public education can only occur if teachers begin working with parents and communities to create a broader social movement for educational change.

Second, the context of change operates as a complex and interrelated system where everything depends on (or undermines) everything else. In this sense, most chapters here suggest that when a reform addresses one dimension of teaching, the others cannot be held in abeyance. The chapters contain many examples of reforms that trigger unanticipated or unintended consequences in other parts of the system. Educational practice is *simultaneously* an intellectual, socioemotional and sociopolitical as well as a technical enterprise. Political power differences, emotional costs, intellectual demands and logistical factors are *always* involved, in ways that are too complex to be predicted and regulated by policy fiat. Datnow's analysis reveals the micropolitical conflicts that can arise between female and male teachers, or any group of educators who differ in ideology and relative power, when they attempt to engage in what is intended as an intellectual or emotionally (morally) based change. Macmillan's chapter on principal succession describes how the strategy of rotating principals to change and improve school cultures actually has the opposite effect of keeping them the same. Oakes shows how initiatives to introduce mixed ability learning immediately challenge every other aspect of teachers' practice — in terms of their pedagogical approach, their beliefs about ability, their ways of organizing the curriculum, and their own subject attachments and identities. Bailey's teachers testify how these contradictory pressures and seemingly capricious shifts of policy emphasis scatter them in so many directions that they ultimately decide not to move at all. Fink describes how the innovative efforts that lead to early glory in one "model" school create ensuing suspicion in the community and jealousy in the system that undermines its chances of sustaining long-term success. And Levin and Riffel show

how a range of administrative responses to societal change have little impact on the core activities of teaching and learning.

Third, even the most creative reform efforts are essentially undermined by logics of political control which lead to excessive standardization, regulation and inflexibility that stifle teachers' intellectual involvement, emotional engagement and political empowerment as effective change agents. Our chapters clearly show that technical conceptions of teaching and schooling are alive and well in educational policy, and tend to cancel out many of the promises that reform holds to improve teachers' intellectual, social, emotional and political capacities. Earl and Katz report how the teachers they studied had to juggle requirements for more authentic assessment with a new standardized reporting form. Bailey's teachers face repeated mandates to be more caring (or less caring) by administrative fiat that takes its position of authority for granted. Many of the teachers described in Bascia and Thiessen's chapter seem to view immigrant students as aberrations from a norm, a norm that many of Oakes' and Datnow's teachers feel drawn back to as they struggle with the complexities of diverse, mixed ability settings.

Fourth, the contextual influences on teachers and teaching are increasingly intrusive. The greater politicization and transparency of schooling cannot buffer educators from the "outside" world. What is "out there" is also "in here" in terms of the diversity of students, in the technological world of "real virtuality" (Castells, 1996) through which students live their lives and which they bring to school, in the ways that the passions and desires of many students are relegated from the curriculum and regulated within the classroom by a Eurocentric tradition of rationalized control, and so on (Hargreaves and Fullan, 1998). Developments such as school councils and charter schools are redefining relationships between parents and educators and making them more visible and more volatile. The corporate world is becoming more involved in defining the curriculum, in sponsoring new technologies, and in setting the basic agendas and terms of educational discourse (e.g., value-added achievement, high-performance learning communities, total quality management) through which reform is debated and decided (Robertson, 1998). Bascia and Thiessen chart the impact of diversity issues on minority teachers in schools; and Hargreaves documents how increasing parental demands on schooling are creating heightened teacher anxiety. These complexly interacting influences cannot be explained through the linear logic of discrete variables or causal pathways. Context is too complex for that.

Fifth, the chapters in this book confirm that the massive informational base as well as fiscal and moral supports required to sustain reforms effectively are rarely available. Seller and Hannay's model of sustained technical support seems the rare exception rather than the rule. Bailey and also Earl and Katz indicate that teachers' experience of waves of reform as "flavor of the month" eventually leads them to lose their enthusiasm and/or their ability to sustain changes in practice. Levin and Riffel reveal how insufficient information and limited "systems thinking" among administrators restrict their capacity to respond in an intellectually informed way to societal changes or educational policy decisions.

These are not idiosyncratic or isolated stories. These chapters are evidence of disturbing, recurring and perverse patterns. The revelations will come as no surprise to anyone who has been living and working in educational settings over the last several decades. The surprise, if there is one, is that educational policymakers have not learned anything from these decades of research, whose recurring theme has been the complexity (if not outright failure) of educational change and the inadequacy of so many reform ideas — that despite changes in the work and relationships among teachers, parents, students and administrators we have so little evidence that anyone has learned anything new about the processes of teaching and schooling beyond the confines of their own personal locations.

Conclusion

Educators find themselves working in a deeply paradoxical profession where, on the one hand, they are hailed as the catalysts of change, the harbingers of the new informational society, the creators of the knowledge and learning on which success in this society will depend. This is why so much is expected of them and why so much change is demanded from them. On the other hand, teachers are also casualties of the informational society with its commitment to individual skilling, personal lifestyle, consumer preference, market driven influences, and the accompanying shrinking of the state and collapse of public commitment and public life (Hargreaves and Lo, 2000). At the very same time as they are expected to work better and harder, teachers also find themselves more restricted, more regulated and less supported to do their work. This paradox is the most crucial context of teaching of all. If change is not to remain transient and localized, and if other reforms are not to destroy and diminish the very teachers on whom the future of quality public education for all depends, it is about time that teachers were pulled back from the sharp edge of change and moved toward its leading edge — intellectually, emotionally and politically. We hope this book will help stimulate that move.

The chapters in this collection offer some starting points for how that project might be achieved. They suggest that school changes cannot be disengaged from the context of their occurrence, and that schools and teachers cannot simply be objects of contextual change. Rather, educational change must connect teachers to the system and society in an activist way, where they can see themselves not just as effects of the context, but as part of the context, contributors to it, and as agents who can and must influence how others perceive, shape and support their work.

References

Acker, S. (1999) *Realities of teaching: never a dull moment.* London: Cassell.

American Institute for Research (1999) *An educator's guide to school-wide reform.* Washington, DC.

Aronowitz, S. and Giroux, H. (1991) *Postmodern education: politics, culture and social criticism.* Minneapolis: University of Minnesota Press.

Ashton, P. and Webb, R. (1986) *Making a difference: teachers' sense of efficacy.* New York: Longman.

Ball, S. (1987) *The micro-politics of the school.* London: Methuen.

Bascia, N. (1994) *Unions in teachers' professional lives.* New York: Teachers College Press.

Bascia, N. (1996) Inside and outside: minority immigrant teachers in Canadian schools. *Qualitative Studies in Education,* 9(2), 151–65.

Bascia, N. (1997) Invisible leadership: teachers' union activity in schools. *Alberta Journal of Educational Research,* 43(2/3), 69–85.

Bascia, N. (1998) Changing roles for teachers' federations. *Orbit,* 29(1), 38–40.

Bernstein, B. (1970) Education cannot compensate for society. *New Society,* 26 February, 344–7.

Blase, J. (ed.) (1991) *The politics of life in schools.* Newbury Park, CA: Sage Publications.

Blase, J. and Anderson, G. (1995) *The micropolitics of educational leadership.* London: Cassell.

Broadfoot, P. and Osborn, M. (1993) *Perceptions of teaching: primary school teachers in England and France.* London: Cassell.

Carlson, D. (1992) *Teachers and crisis: urban school reform and teachers' work culture.* New York: Routledge, Chapman and Hall.

Castells, M. (1996) *The rise of the network society.* Oxford: Blackwell.

Cochran-Smith, M. and Lytle, S. (1992) Communities for teacher research: fringe or forefront? *American Journal of Education,* 100(3), 298–324.

Coulter, R. (1996) Gender equity and schooling: linking research and policy. *Canadian Journal of Education,* 21(4), 433–52.

Darling-Hammond, L. (1992) Reframing the school reform agenda. *The School Administrator* (November), 22–7.

Datnow, A., Hubbard, L. and Mehan, H. (1998) *Educational reform implementation: a co-constructed process.* Research report 5. Santa Cruz, CA: Center on Education, Diversity and Excellence.

Day, C. (1999) *Developing teachers: the challenge of lifelong learning.* New York: Falmer Press.

Denzin, N. (1984) *On understanding emotion.* San Francisco: Jossey-Bass.

Earl, L. M. and LeMahieu, P. G. (1997) Rethinking assessment and accountability. In A. Hargreaves (ed.), *Rethinking educational change with heart and mind. The 1997 ASCD Yearbook,* pp. 149–68. Alexandria, VA: Association for Supervision and Curriculum Development.

Elkind, D. (1997) Schooling in the postmodern world. In A. Hargreaves (ed.), *Rethinking educational change with heart and mind. The 1997 ASCD Yearbook,* pp. 27–42. Alexandria, VA: Association for Supervision and Curriculum Development.

Foster, M. (1994) The role of community and culture in school reform efforts: examining the views of African-American teachers. *Educational Foundations*, 8(2), 5–26.

Fullan, M. (1993) *Change forces: probing the depths of educational reform.* New York: Falmer Press.

Fullan, M. (1997) Emotion and hope: constructive concepts for complex times. In A. Hargreaves (ed.), *Rethinking educational change with heart and mind. The 1997 ASCD Yearbook*, pp. 216–33. Alexandria, VA: Association for Supervision and Curriculum Development.

Fullan, M. (1999) *Change forces: the sequel.* New York: Falmer Press.

Fullan, M. with Stiegelbauer, S. (1991) *The new meaning of educational change.* New York: Teachers College Press.

Galton, M. (2000) "Dumbing down" on classroom standards: the perils of a technician's approach to pedagogy. *Journal of Educational Change*, 1(2), 68–74.

Giddens, A. (1995) *Beyond left and right.* Oxford: Blackwell.

Ginsburg, M., with Sknat, S., Raghu, R. and Weaver, J. (1992) Educators/politics. *Comparative Education Review*, 36(4), 417–45.

Gleick, J. (1987) *Chaos: making a new science.* Harmondsworth: Penguin.

Goleman, D. (1995) *Emotional intelligence.* New York: Bantam Books.

Goleman, D. (1998) *Working with emotional intelligence.* New York: Bantam Books.

Gramsci, A. (1971) *Selections from the prison notebooks.* London: Lawrence and Wishart.

Gunter, H. (1997) *Rethinking education: the consequences of Jurassic management.* London: Cassell.

Hall, G. E., Loucks, S. F., Rutherford, W. L. and Newlove, B. W. (1975) Levels of use of the innovation: a framework for analyzing innovation adoption. *Journal of Teacher Education*, 26, 52–6.

Hallinger, P. and Murphy, J. (1987) Instructional leadership in the school context. In W. Greenfield (ed.), *Instructional leadership: concepts, issues and controversies.* Boston, MA: Allyn and Bacon.

Hamilton, D. (1989) *Towards a theory of schooling.* New York: Falmer Press.

Hargreaves, A. (1994) *Changing teachers, changing times: teachers' work and culture in the postmodern age.* London and New York: Cassell and Teachers College Press.

Hargreaves, A. (1995) Development and desire: a postmodern perspective. In T. Guskey and M. Huberman (eds.), *New paradigms and practices in professional development*, pp. 9–34. New York: Teachers College Press.

Hargreaves, A. (1997a) Cultures of teaching and educational change. In B. Biddle, T. Good and I. F. Goodson (eds.), *The international handbook of teachers and teaching*, pp. 1297–1319. Dordrecht: Kluwer Academic Publishers.

Hargreaves, A. (1997b) Rethinking educational change: going deeper and wider in the quest for success. In A. Hargreaves (ed.), *Rethinking educational change with heart and mind. The 1997 ASCD Yearbook*, pp. 1–26. Alexandria, VA: Association for Supervision and Curriculum Development.

Hargreaves, A. (1998a) The emotional politics of teaching and teacher development: implications for leadership. *International Journal of Leadership in Education*, 1(4), 315–36.

Hargreaves, A. (1998b) The emotional practice of teaching. *Teaching and Teacher Education*, 14(8), 835–54.

Hargreaves, A. (1998c) Teachers' role in renewal. *Orbit Special Issue*, 29(1), 10–13.

Hargreaves, A. (1999) The psychic rewards (and annoyances) of classroom teaching. In M. Hammersley (ed.), *Researching school experience: ethnographic studies of teaching and learning.* London and New York: Falmer Press.

Hargreaves, A. (forthcoming) Beyond anxiety and nostalgia: building a social movement for educational change. *Phi Delta Kappan.*

Hargreaves, A. and Earl, L. (in press) *Learning to change.* San Francisco: Jossey-Bass.

Hargreaves, A., Earl, L. and Ryan, J. (1996) *Schooling for change: reinventing education for early adolescents.* Philadelphia: Falmer Press.

Hargreaves, A. and Fullan, M. (1998) *What's worth fighting for out there?* Toronto, New York and Buckingham: Elementary Teachers Federation of Ontario, Teachers College Press and Open University Press.

Hargreaves, A. and Lasky, S. (2000) The parent gap: the emotional geographies of teacher–parent relationship. Toronto: OISE/UT, unpublished manuscript.

Hargreaves, A., Lieberman, A., Fullan, M. and Hopkins, D. (eds.) (1998) *The international handbook of educational change.* Dordrecht: Kluwer.

Hargreaves, A. and Lo, L. (forthcoming) The paradoxical profession: teaching at the turn of the century. *Prospects* (a UNESCO Journal), 167–80.

Helsby, G. (1999) *Changing teachers' work.* Buckingham: Open University Press.

Hochschild, A. (1983) *The managed heart: the commercialization of human feeling.* Berkeley: University of California Press.

Hopkins, D. (forthcoming) Powerful learning, powerful teaching and powerful schools. *Journal of Educational Change*, 1(2), 1–20.

Huberman, M. (1993) *The lives of teachers.* London and New York: Cassell and Teachers College Press.

Hunter, M. (1984) Knowing, teaching and supervising. In P. Hosford (ed.), *Using what we know about teaching*, pp. 19–37. Alexandria, VA: Association for Supervision and Curriculum Development.

Jeffrey, B. and Woods, P. (1996) Feeling deprofessionalized: the social construction of emotions during an OFSTED inspection. *Cambridge Journal of Education*, 126(3), 235–343.

Kemper, T. (1995) Sociological models in the explanation of emotions. In M. Lewis and J. Haviland (eds.), *Handbook of emotions.* New York and London: The Guilford Press.

Lankshear, C. (1997) *Changing literacies.* Buckingham: Open University Press.

Larson, M. S. (1977) *The rise of professionalism: a sociological analysis.* Berkeley: University of California Press.

Leithwood, K., Jantzi, D. and Steinbach, R. (1999) *Changing leadership for changing times.* Buckingham: Open University Press.

Levin, B. (2000) Putting students at the centre in educational reform. *Journal of Educational Change*, 1(2), 21–39.

Lieberman, A. and McLaughlin, M. (2000) Professional development in the United States: policies and practices. *Prospects* (a UNESCO Journal), 225–36.

Little, J. W. (1984) Seductive images and organizational realities in professional development. *Teachers College Record*, 86(1), 84–102.

Little, J. and McLaughlin, M. (eds.) (1993) *Teachers' work.* New York: Teachers College Press.

Lortie, D. C. (1975) *Schoolteacher.* Chicago: University of Chicago Press.

Louis, K. S. (1990) Social and community values and the quality of teachers' work life. In M. McLaughlin, T. Talbert and N. Bascia (eds.), *The contexts of teaching in secondary schools: teachers' realities*, pp. 17–39. New York: Teachers College Press.

Louis, K. S. and Miles, M. (1990) *Improving the urban high school.* New York: Teachers College Press.

McCulloch, G. (1997) Marketing the millennium: education for the twenty-first century. In A. Hargreaves and R. Evans (eds.), *Beyond educational reform*, pp. 19–28. Buckingham: Open University Press.

McLaughlin, M. (1987) Learning from experience: lessons from policy implementation. *Educational Evaluation and Policy Analysis*, 9(2), 171–8.

McLaughlin, M. and Talbert, J. (1990) The contexts in question: the secondary school workplace. In M. McLaughlin, J. Talbert and N. Bascia (eds.), *The contexts of teaching in secondary schools: teachers' realities*, pp. 1–14. New York: Teachers College Press.

McLaughlin, M. and Talbert, J. (1993) *Contexts that matter for teaching and learning.* Stanford University: Center for Research on the Context of Secondary School Teaching.

McLaughlin, M., Talbert, J. and Bascia, N. (eds.) (1990) *The contexts of teaching in secondary schools: teachers' realities.* New York: Teachers College Press.

Meier, D. (1998) Authenticity and educational change. In A. Hargreaves, A. Lieberman, M. Fullan and D. Hopkins (eds.), *The international handbook of educational change.* Dordrecht: Kluwer.

Mortimore, P., Sammons, P., Stoll, L., Lewis, D. and Ecole, R. (1988) *School matters.* Beverley, CA: University of California Press.

National Commission on Teaching and America's Future (1996) *What matters most: teaching for America's future.* New York: Teachers' College, Columbia University.

Nespor, J. (1997) *Tangled up in school: politics, space, bodies and signs in the educational process.* Hillsdale, NJ: Lawrence Erlbaum Associates.

Newmann, F. and Wehlage, G. (1995) *Successful school restructuring.* Madison, WI: Center on Organization and Restructuring of Schools.

Nias, J. (1991) Changing times, changing identities: grieving for a lost self. In R. G. Burgess (ed.), *Educational research and evaluation: for policy and practice*, pp. 47–62. London: Falmer Press.

Noddings, N. (1984) *Caring: a feminine approach to ethics and moral education.* Berkeley: University of California Press.

Popkewitz, T. (1999) The culture of redemption and the administration of freedom as research. *Review of Educational Research*, 68(1), 1–34.

Reynolds, D. (ed.) (1985) *Studying school effectiveness.* New York: Falmer Press.

Reynolds, D. (2000) Can and should pedagogical change be mandated at times? *Journal of Educational Change*, 1(2), 61–7.

Robertson, H.-J. (1992) Teacher development and gender equity. In A. Hargreaves and M. Fullan (eds.), *Understanding teacher development.* New York: Teachers College Press.

Robertson, H.-J. (1998) Public education in a corporate-dominated culture. In A. Hargreaves, A. Lieberman, M. Fullan and D. Hopkins (eds.), *The international handbook of educational change*, pp. 396–417. Dordrecht: Kluwer Academic Publishers.

Rosenholtz, S. (1989) *Teachers' workplace*. New York: Longman.

Rowan, B. (1994) Comparing teachers' work with work in other occupations: notes on the professional status of teaching. *Educational Researcher*, 23(6), 4–17.

Rudduck, J., Day, J. and Wallace, G. (1997) Students' perspectives on school improvement. In A. Hargreaves (ed.), *Rethinking educational change with heart and mind. The ASCD Yearbook*. Alexandria, VA: Association for Supervision and Curriculum Development.

Sarason, S. (1982) *The culture of the school and the problem of change* (2nd edn). Boston: Allyn and Bacon.

Sarason, S. (1990) *The predictable failure of educational reform*. San Francisco: Jossey-Bass.

Scheff, T. J. (1994) *Bloody revenge: emotions, nationalism and war*. Boulder, CO: Westview Press.

Schlechty, P. (1990) *Schools for the twenty-first century: leadership imperatives for educational reform*. San Francisco: Jossey-Bass.

Sergiovanni, T. (1999) *The lifeworld of leadership*. San Francisco: Jossey-Bass.

Shulman, L. S. (1986) Those who understand: knowledge growth in teaching. *Educational Researcher*, 15(2), 4–14.

Sikes, P., Measor, L. and Woods, P. (1985) *Teachers' lives and careers*. Milton Keynes: Open University Press.

Siskin, L. (1994) *Realms of knowledge: academic departments in secondary schools*. London: Falmer Press.

Sizer, T. (1992) *Horace's School*. Boston: Houghton Mifflin.

Smaller, H. (1991) "A room of one's own": the early years of the Toronto Women Teachers' Association. In A. Prentice and R. Heap (eds.), *Gender and education in Ontario*, pp. 103–24. Toronto: Canadian Scholars' Press.

Smaller, H. (1998) Canadian teacher unions: an international perspective. *Contemporary Education*, 69(4), 223–7.

Smith, L. M., Dwyer, D. C., Prunty, J. J. and Kleine, P. F. (1987) *The fate of an innovative school*. London: Falmer Press.

Stiggins, R. (1995) Assessment literacy for the 21st century. *Phi Delta Kappan*, 77(3), 238–45.

Stoll, L. and Fink, D. (1996) *Changing our schools*. Buckingham: Open University Press.

Stoll, L. and Myers, K. (eds.) (1998) *No quick fixes: perspectives on schools in difficulty*. London and New York: Falmer Press.

Talbert, J. and MacLaughlin, M. (1994) Teacher professionalism in local school contexts. *American Journal of Education*, 102, 123–53.

Thomson, P. (1999) Doing justice: stories of everyday life in disadvantaged schools and neighbourhoods. Unpublished Ph.D. thesis. Australia: Deakin University.

Troyna, B. (1995) *Racism and education: research perspectives*. Buckingham: Open University Press.

Tyack, D. (1991) Public school reform: policy talk and institutional practice. *American Journal of Education*, 99, 1–19, November.

Waite, D. (1995) *Rethinking instructional supervision*. London and New York: Falmer Press.

Weiler, K. (1998) *Country schoolwomen: teaching in rural California, 1850–1950*. Stanford: Stanford University Press.

Werner, W. (1991) Curriculum and uncertainty. In R. Ghosh and D. Ray (eds.), *Social change and education in Canada* (2nd edn). Toronto: Harcourt Brace Jovanovich.

Wheatley, M. J. (1994) *New science: learning about organization from an orderly universe* (1st edn). San Francisco: Berrett-Koehler Publishers.

Whitford, B. L. and Wong, K. (2000) Between centralization and decentralization: two views on school reform. *Journal of Educational Change*, 1(1), 106–12.

Wiggins, G. and McTighe, J. (1998) *Understanding by design*. Alexandria, VA: Association for Supervision and Curriculum Development.

Woods, P. (1993) *Critical events in teaching and learning*. London: Falmer Press.

Woods, P., Jeffrey, B., Troman, G. and Boyle, M. (1997) *Restructuring schools, reconstructing teachers*. Buckingham: Open University Press.

Zeichner, K. (1991) Contradictions and tensions in the professionalization of teaching and the democratization of schools. *Teachers College Record*, 92(3), 363–79.

II   COURSES OF CHANGE

2 The Attrition of Educational Change over Time: The Case of "Innovative," "Model," "Lighthouse" Schools

Dean Fink

Introduction

This chapter examines the long-term fate of one of the most widely used approaches to educational reform — the creation of new, "model," "innovative," "exemplary," "beacon" or "lighthouse" schools, as they are variously called. What happens to these schools, not in the first flurry of interest, hope and excitement, but in the long run where their sustainability is at stake, is an important question not merely for these innovative schools themselves, but also for the wider systems in which they are embedded. What do innovative schools tell us? Do they last? What contribution do they make with respect to the "scaling up" of systemic educational reform and the sustainability of educational change? These are the questions that this chapter addresses, based on the evidence of one particular case of "break-the-mold" innovation, which I have analyzed for more than a quarter-century.

Slavin (1998) identifies two types of "systemic" reform movements. The first has been initiated by governments throughout the western world and reflects a deep pessimism that education can reform itself. These legislated, "systemic" changes are characterized by alterations in governance, accountability systems and mandated standards. Implicit in many of these reforms is the notion that the system is irremediably broken and requires either totally new types of schools or the reinvention of traditional schools. The desire to create new settings is reflected in the charter school movement and schools of choice in North America, and the preservation of selective grammar schools in the United Kingdom. Similarly, the trend in some American states and in the United Kingdom to close failing schools and reopen them with new leadership and a new staff reflects a hope that new beginnings will transform educational practice (Slavin, 1998; Stoll and Myers, 1998). In virtually all cases, these reforms are imposed by government mandate and involve limited consultation with the professional community.

Alternatively, scholars in many countries have rejected the pessimistic view and have initiated an approach to "systemic" change which attempts to develop "ambitious models for school reform" by "building networks of technical assistance, and school-to-school support to ever expanding numbers of schools that freely choose to implement the models" (Slavin, 1998: 1300). There are a number of examples, including Sizer's (1992) Coalition of Essential Schools, Levin's (1987) Accelerated Schools and the New American Schools network (Stringfield *et al.*, 1996) in the United States. The Learning Consortium (Fullan, 1991) and the Manitoba School Improvement Project (1997) in Canada, the Improving Quality Schools for All project (Hopkins *et al.*, 1994) in Britain and the National Schools Network (Ladwig *et al.*, 1994) in Australia are similar examples. In these cases, partnerships between university scholars and school personnel have worked to change structures, cultures and learning conditions of schools. These networks hope the more adventurous volunteer schools will serve as catalysts to "scale up" reform across other schools in the larger systems in which they are embedded. Despite their differences, mandated and "networking" approaches to educational change share a conviction that new and/or innovative alternatives to existing schools can promote substantive changes in other schools on a wider scale. This chapter asks whether such faith is justified.

The creation of alternatives to more conventional schools is not a new approach. Over the years, many "new" and innovative schools have been initiated. These "new" schools have usually begun life as places of hope, enthusiasm and creativity. Advocates proclaimed their excellence (Doremus, 1981). Popular educational journals extolled their virtues (Guernsey, 1970; Schwartz, 1971). Within a relatively short time, however, a significant number of these new schools evolve, indeed regress, into quite conventional schools. This loss of initial momentum and innovative direction by many newly established schools occurs because of what I call the "attrition of change," where the winds of certainty, tradition and nostalgia relentlessly wear away the face of change that these newly established schools represent. At the same time, innovative schools can paradoxically bring about change elsewhere in the system — also by attrition. By breaking precedents, innovative schools can open up opportunities for others. Moreover, they can foster cohorts of leaders who gradually carry innovative values, convictions and practices into other settings. This chapter explores these two complementary meanings of the "attrition of change" that innovative schools represent.

The Study

The study on which this chapter is based traces the twenty-five-year evolution of a new and purposefully innovative school, which I shall call Lord Byron High School in Ontario, Canada. Lord Byron opened in 1970, and quickly gained a reputation as one of Canada's most innovative schools. In its first three years of operation, 7000 visitors toured the school. Gradually, however, the school lost much of its innovative zeal and today it looks very much like other regular secondary schools. This school is of particular interest to me because I was an original staff member, its assistant (deputy) principal for a year, and later its district-office supervisor. I saw its attrition of change as an active participant and later as an interested observer. My personal history as both a participant in the school's early days and an observer and supervisor in more recent times presents unique opportunities as well as challenges for my research role.

My approach centered on three methodological components. First, the historical aspect of the case led to a search of relevant documents from the province of Ontario, from the South Board of Education of which Lord Byron was a part, and from the school itself. Second, I interviewed over seventy present and past Lord Byron staff members as well as key respondents from the South system to develop an oral history of the school's development. I selected my sample of respondents from among staff members from three different eras. I then randomly selected names from the staff lists for Lord Byron from 1975, 1984 and 1993.[1] In addition, all principals were interviewed in depth. My interviews focused on the changes in Lord Byron's purposes, culture, structure and leadership as well as the individual aspects of teachers' work and lives as they related to Byron's change agenda.

A third source of data was my personal involvement in and recollection of events at the school, in the South Board of Education and in the province of Ontario. As a practitioner researcher, I not only knew where to get important historical resources, but I also had participated in many of the school's and school board's significant events, and I was usually aware of most of the events reported by my respondents. This "inside-outside" relationship with the school enabled me to elicit in-depth answers to questions, and check on respondents' veracity (Hammersley, 1981; McNamara, 1980; Merton, 1970).[2]

The Life Cycle of Lord Byron

Evidence from Canada, the United Kingdom and the United States suggests that there is a characteristic life cycle to new schools. Many begin as places of creativity and experimentation, evolve though years of overreaching and entropy, and finally arrive at a state of survival and continuity (Fletcher *et al.*, 1985; Smith e*t al.*, 1987). Like most other societal institutions, schools contend with forces of both change and continuity. As the following narrative suggests, continuity is likely to win out.

Creativity and Experimentation: 1970–1975

The early 1970s was a unique era in the educational history of Ontario and the South Board of Education. For those of us who joined the staff of Lord

Byron with a view to effecting change in the "deep structures" of schooling (Cuban, 1988) the times could not have been more propitious. Education in Ontario was in the midst of a progressive era which created a context
for the South Board to initiate Lord Byron as an experimental "lighthouse"
school. It is difficult to trace the exact origins of the Byron concept but
certainly "the genuine interest" of the Director of Education was vital. Jim
Sizemore was a charismatic and powerful intellectual and political figure.
He established an Innovations Committee which provided the initial impetus
for the school. Perhaps unwittingly, however, by authorizing a fairly
elite group of South's staff to envision a school of the future, he created "a
group of people working on a common problem independently of the larger
community, tending to grow in a direction incomprehensible to their co-
workers and associates who had not experienced the learning process
undergone by the committee members" (Fullan and Eastabrook, 1977: 24).
Most of South's other employees, and virtually all of the potential parents
and students of Byron, had no idea what was being contemplated. Parents
found out about the school through a series of meetings conducted by the
school's first principal, Ward Bond, after many important decisions had been
made.[3]

The appointment of Ward Bond was such an important decision. By
giving Bond a year to plan, the opportunity to hire most of the staff, and
the ability to use a different staffing process, the system enabled him to
design what for the times was a radical alternative. He developed a timetable
which not only divided the school year into two semesters, but required
Byron teachers to be in class 66 per cent of the time compared to the
regional average of 60 per cent. This arrangement enabled Byron to staff
the school with fewer teachers than the regional average, and the Board
agreed to give the school the money left over. This Differentiated Staffing
Fund (DSF) was to be used to support the classroom through the provision
of teacher assistants, secretarial help and professional development
resources. The teachers' federation (union) worried that the move might
create a precedent for reducing teacher positions elsewhere but reluctantly
agreed to this arrangement as long as it was limited to one school.

Bond also challenged conventional thinking by setting up a leadership
structure with far fewer department heads than existed in other schools.
He invested much of the school's decision-making authority in the ten
department heads and the staff as a whole. During his tenure, Bond succeeded in ensuring a balance among potentially competing micropolitical
components of the school such as the school administration, the heads'
council and the staff as a whole. Under ensuing leaders, however, these
micropolitical rivalries would contribute to the "attrition" of change. At
various times, school administrators, the heads' council, and even the staff
as a whole expressed their belief that they had the right to a final say on
policy issues.

Bond's contribution to South Board leadership was profound. In its first five years the staff of Byron produced two directors of education (CEOs), three superintendents (inspectors), ten principals, four assistant principals, and a number of consultants and department chairs. In fact the rest of the South system often referred to the "Byron mafia." Virtually all of the "mafia" tended to lead in Bond's image. As one female respondent recalled, "I am not a hero worshipper but when I look back, he had a quiet leadership style rather than a really aggressive one, but I think his encouragement made people want to follow. In fact, he tended to make leaders rather than followers." He succeeded in defining the "meaning" of Lord Byron. As one teacher recalled, "Ward Bond would say, when you find them doing something wrong, pick them up, dust them off and start them out again, don't throw them out." While Bond articulated the original vision, it was shaped by the people he recruited as they tried to bring it to life in the school. The staff acted on the premise that most students were responsible, and adapted facilities and developed strategies to assist students on fulfilling this prophecy. An external evaluation report on Lord Byron published in 1975 stated:

> As well as observing those in formal positions (principal, vice principals, chairmen) exercise enlightened leadership, we noted that teachers are able to contribute significantly to the decision-making process, not only within the departmental structure. The administration has consciously provided opportunities for recognition of leadership among staff, other than those formally designated as chairmen. This approach has not only guaranteed high-quality leadership within the school, but has served as a training ground for an exceptional number of persons who have moved on to positions of leadership within the system.

Over the first five years of Byron's development, distinctive patterns of group behavior emerged among the staff members. Collegiality was not planned as separate projects or initiatives, but evolved almost spontaneously. Although the openness of the school building facilitated collaborative action to some extent, in many ways it occurred out of necessity. The size of the task of opening a new school, the urgency to get the operation running, and the considerable public scrutiny of other professionals outside, many of whom hoped the school would fail miserably, motivated the staff to collaborate if for no other reason than to survive. The staff dedicated itself to continuous improvement and rigorous evaluation of all aspects of the school's operations. In 1975, an external review committee, composed of well respected Ontario educators, commented that:

> the large amount of documentation produced by the Byron staff over the years attests to this commitment. At the same time this commitment caused our group serious concern. In essence we wonder if Lord Byron is "evaluating itself to death"? Evaluation consciousness is praiseworthy; too much may be counter productive.

Respondents who spoke about the early years described how their hard work and exhaustion were mitigated by the sheer exhilaration of doing exciting, meaningful work. "I worked like mad writing programs for five grades. I worked harder than I have ever worked — all departments did." Another teacher recalled that "the early years were inspiring. There was a lot of altruism. People came to work because they thought they were doing something for humanity — more than a job, it was a mission." Another teacher declared, "I became a teacher at Byron. I wrote more, I created from the ground up."

Unfortunately, the values espoused by the Lord Byron staff were clearly at odds with the administrative values which dominated Ontario and South's educational systems. The frustration expressed by many of the Byron respondents many years after the event was that they were certain they were moving in the right direction but could not prove it. Much of what went on at Byron was the product of people's experience, intuition, and trial and error, rather than "solid empirical" evidence. As in all schools, a few students skipped classes, some ignored homework, while others missed assignments. In other less visible settings, these transgressions would have been dealt with quietly and without fanfare. Byron tended to be so visible, public and open that its missteps were magnified and publicized. As one long-serving teacher recalled, "Being so open, the failures that kids had, and they probably would have failed in other schools, were quickly blamed on Byron."

Acting on a student-centered image in the early 1970s required a profound shift in thinking. While Bond and his colleagues succeeded within the school, they faced a wider educational community and a societal hegemony which was firmly rooted in maintaining continuity with what most people perceived to be "real school" (Metz, 1991). A fundamental principle of the school was not only to reach out to the community but also to include the community in the school. Byron had the first active parents' advisory committee in South, and adult participation as students in regular classes. In comparison to other secondary schools, Byron was much more open, inviting and parent-friendly, and it persisted in this policy throughout much of its history. Many members of the public, however, remained skeptical of this "lighthouse" school. Criticism was muted at first because of Bond's political skills and the smoothness with which the school operated in the first few years. Ironically, however, the very openness of the school invited criticism which "just never went away."

Perhaps the most disappointing aspect of the school's early days for former Byron staff members was the hostility they experienced from friends and colleagues in other schools in the South system. As a female teacher who was transferred to Byron in her second year of teaching explained,

> Because Byron was different and proud of being different, because it felt it was doing things for kids, the worst comments came from other schools.

When I would ask them, they had never been to the school, had really never talked to anybody in the school. Rumor and the sense that these people at Byron were doing something different, all they wanted to hear were the negatives. They never heard the positives.[4]

In some ways, Jim Sizemore and the South school district unwittingly contributed to these feelings. While there is no written record of Sizemore's hopes for Byron, former colleagues agreed that he viewed Byron as a way to "scale up" the newly created South system and particularly its secondary schools into more progressive educational directions and he hoped that as a result of Byron "the entire level of the system would be raised." Sizemore's forceful style, however, created enemies. Byron was seen by many South educators as part of the Sizemore agenda which threatened their values and beliefs, to say nothing of their organizational structures. Many South staff members shared the view that Byron enjoyed unique benefits from the newly created school district — a new building, unrestricted staff recruitment, and more resources than other schools. The reality was not quite like this: what Bond did was use the same resources as other schools in different ways. Unfortunately for Byron, a perception of special privilege became part of the regional folklore. This hostile reaction to Lord Byron from teachers and principals in other South schools was understandable, because the school was a threat to the "grammar of schooling" (Tyack and Tobin, 1994) which gave meaning to the careers of many system colleagues. A number of Byron respondents talked about how debilitating it was to be continually "fighting ghosts" — contending with "mindless" and "uninformed" criticism.

One and a half miles from Byron stood another secondary school, Roxborough (for a description of this school, see Hargreaves, 1994). Well respected in the community, Roxborough was a rather typical school of its times. Continuity and change sat uneasily side by side for everyone to see and compare. The staff members at Roxborough made no secret of their contempt for Byron and its innovativeness. What made the situation tense was the physical proximity of the two schools and Roxborough's reputation as the "academic" school. As a long-serving Byron teacher recalled, "It has always been a Byron–Roxborough comparison, not Byron and any other school." Like many schools in the 1960s and 1970s, Roxborough tended to sort and select its students on the basis of traditional notions of academic achievement. Underachievers or students with discipline problems were urged to go to other schools or find a job, which in the 1970s was still a possibility for school dropouts. Conversely, Byron's philosophy rejected this approach, and the school welcomed students who had not succeeded in other schools. Since most of these students were not high academic achievers, they contributed to Byron's reputation as a school for the non-academic students. In the early years, from 1970 to 1975, for the most part, the Byron staff was more worried about daily survival than a contest with other schools, but this insularity was often interpreted as arrogance.

In the minds of virtually all respondents, the early years of Byron under Bond's leadership were "the best of times." Ironically though, the seeds of "attrition" were already planted in those early days. The same forces which helped the school to experience great success in its first few years ultimately worked to effect its "attrition of change" in the long term. Sizemore's sponsorship, for example, helped the school grow and develop, but he also contributed to the ill-will which was directed toward Lord Byron by many in the South system. Bond's skill and popularity, indeed charisma, enabled the school to overcome early obstacles, develop a cohesive, collaborative staff, mute community concerns, and direct micropolitical tensions into productive avenues, but he was "a very hard act to follow." Some have even suggested that the school began its "attrition" of change the day the system promoted Bond in 1974.

An idea of an "innovative," "break-the-mold" school which had begun with a system-led Innovations Committee in 1969 had by 1975, in the view of an the external review committee, made "significant progress towards achieving the overall goal of creating a humane environment for students" (p. 11). Moreover, it suggested that "Lord Byron is a model worthy of study by other schools" (p. 27). Certainly, the extensive evaluation of the school, completed shortly after Bond's departure, declared Lord Byron to be a great success.

Overreaching and Entropy: 1975–1984

Bond's image pervaded the ensuing years and made succeeding him a difficult if not impossible job. As one Byron teacher of the 1990s stated:

> He still walked the halls when I got there. I never saw the man for years, but the way people talked about him and the references to what he had done that helped people be the way they were, they were legion. People were always turning to me in great shock and saying "Oh, you don't know him . . ."

Moreover, Bond's fostering of leadership meant that the critical mass of the original leaders in Byron received promotions and left the school. Some even departed the system. Over time, these lost leaders were replaced by people who had been followers in the early days. These new leaders brought with them a "golden age" mentality (Louis and Miles, 1990) which made the structures initiated by Bond for a different time and set of circumstances very difficult for subsequent principals and school leaders to change.

Overreaching. By 1976, at the provincial level events were moving in ways that threatened Byron's future. The governing party perceived the educational "pendulum" as having moved too far to the left in terms of student choices and teacher and school decision-making, and steps were taken to

redress the historical policy balance (Stamp, 1976). The South Board's political makeup increasingly reflected this provincial shift. Provincial and school
board policies increased the number of compulsory courses required for
graduation, dictated time allocations, altered role definitions for department
leaders, and forced experimental schools to conform to the organizational
structure of the majority. After Sizemore's retirement in 1975, the South
Board enacted policies based on the belief that schools should be more
similar than different. Policies on examinations, staffing, timetables and
leadership structures forced Byron to conform to regional requirements. By
the late 1970s, Byron staff members who had enjoyed the "golden years"
felt abandoned. As one teacher remembered, "I felt like nobody outside the
school at the Board level trusted what was going on in the school or supported it." This feeling of betrayal pervaded people's recollections of the
late 1970s and early 1980s.

Bond's replacement in 1974 was Bruce Grey. Only 34 years of age
when he became the principal of Lord Byron, he had been a successful vice
principal in a very large traditional school and he embraced his conception
of the Byron philosophy enthusiastically. His greatest difficulty was that he
was not Bond. Grey's appointment coincided with renewed aggressiveness
from the teachers' federation over the department chair structure which they
argued cost teachers jobs and opportunities. Inside the school, a few staff
members felt that Grey used the rhetoric of Byron but he did not really
believe in its philosophy because he was not a "Byron person."

Some people on staff felt that students' liberty had become license. Tendencies which were evident in the first four years became manifest in the
"Grey era." The halls were often littered. Students would sit in front of the
school smoking. Many changes could be traced to a doubling in student
enrollment from 900 in 1970 and to over 2000 in 1976. As the student population grew and the staff increased, communications tended to be through
department meetings as opposed to staff meetings. Some placed the blame
for problems at Grey's door; others more charitably saw school size, the
promotion of many of the key players, lack of regional support, and attacks
by other professionals in the system as factors. A few teachers specifically
attracted by Byron's "radical" reputation were hired. One former department
chair who moved to Roxborough reflected a widely held view in the professional community when he claimed that "left wingers gave the school a
bad name" and "mistakes were made and foolish things were done." In the
words of one respondent, a few teachers did "some dumb, dumb, things."
Stories abounded of teachers having students chant mantras in the classroom, not disciplining students who started a fire, using coarse language,
assigning make-work projects, and designing experiential courses of ques-
tionable academic validity. I recall a student who came to me to complain
about his advanced level course in history. The teacher had a component
in which the students were to emulate the Australian walkabout. Each
student was to devise an independent study activity. Since there were no

predetermined procedures, standards or indeed instructions, this student derisively described it as "walkabout, talkabout, fuckabout."

By 1977, when Grey received a promotion and moved to another school board, Byron was one of the largest schools in the school board. In addition to the problems of record growth, Grey felt that a number of people on staff had difficulty transferring their loyalty from Bond to the "Byron concept." As Grey said, for some people on staff, change got personified in the originating principal rather than becoming part of the structure and culture of the school. From his present perspective of senior leadership he said,

> Change has to be built into the processes. Change identified with a person has the roots of its own destruction. There has to be loyalty to broader issues. Life cycles of many "lighthouse" schools have been shortened because people could not shift loyalties from the individual to broader concepts.

The tremendous growth in enrollment during Grey's tenure meant that ten to twenty teachers were added each year. The careful selection which characterized the recruitment of initial staff was lost to the sheer urgency of adding staff. More teachers were "force transferred" from other schools which were declining in enrollment. As one female teacher explained:

> I think one of the things we didn't do well was we didn't pick up well with new teachers. We did not have any kind of mentoring program, what-ever, to sort of support these people in all the ways they needed to be supported both in the classroom and out. We got too big too fast. We didn't talk to staff.

Departments became large. Meaningful whole-staff meetings were out of the question. Communications within the school became an issue of major concern. The cross-school collegiality that characterized the Bond era began to disintegrate as people coalesced around their departments and subject groupings (Siskin, 1994). Each year, a host of new procedures or school policies was initiated to ensure liaison among staff and to maintain con-nections with students and their parents. Where flexibility and collaboration once reigned, rules and regulations crept in. Perhaps the most challenging aspect of size was the anonymity it created for many students and some teachers. With anonymity came concerns over student discipline, atten-dance, smoking, work completion and vandalism. At the same time, increased enrollment meant more teachers and more Differentiated Staffing Fund which enabled Byron to "throw money at problems" much to the chagrin of other schools and their principals. Creating cohesive staff action to attend to issues became an increasing problem. Specialization replaced cooperation as the way to solve school-wide problems.

When Grey left, Byron was a large, well-resourced and ostensibly suc-cessful school, but the seeds of its "attrition" were evident to people in the school. Grey had found himself in a "Catch 22." He could consolidate. To do so, however, would have alienated many of the staff who were hired because of the school's innovativeness. Conversely, he could continue to innovate, which would receive the enthusiastic support of the staff and was consistent with his own career ambitions, but which risked pushing the school and its staff too far and too hard. He therefore chose the latter alternative and expanded differentiated staffing, adding adult education, community outreach and outdoor education programs. Many of these programs were very successful and were copied by other schools. Unfortunately, these successes did not translate into a positive reputation for the school as a whole. Miles and Huberman (1984) describe a set of schools in their study that tried to do too much in too short a time and experienced problems resulting from policies which were a "poor fit with organizational norms and procedures" (p. 147). They call this phenomenon "overreaching." Byron pushed or was pushed too far, too fast. As one teacher saw it:

> Too many things were going on, without enough evaluation. Some people were doing things that were non-traditional even to the Byron philosophy. They carried them from the seventies to the utmost extreme. If I were a parent I would have felt the same way as a lot of other parents felt.

Initial structures and processes designed for a smaller school had not been consolidated or altered before new initiatives were undertaken. Like most innovative schools, Byron tended to operate on an intellectual paradigm of change, and its community on another paradigm that was based on continuity. Like other schools faced by demographic changes, shifts in leadership, the departure of key staff members and altered political circumstances (Fletcher *et al.*, 1985; Gold and Miles, 1981; Smith *et al.*, 1987), Byron continued to try to live up to its "innovative" past while social forces beyond the school's control were quickly moving in different directions. This collision resulted in miscommunication and misrepresentation. Many parents in the community "voted with their feet" by opting for Roxborough.

Entropy. After the 1977 school year, because of shifts in community demographics, enrollment began to decline, slowly at first and then dramatically. By 1984 Byron had bottomed at 970 students. The system's negotiated surplus procedures, which generally meant that the least experienced and younger staff members were the first to be transferred, significantly altered the staff composition. This compounded the "attrition of change" in the school. Not only were the staff members who remained from the early 1970s now getting older in ways that were starting to affect their energy and investment (Sikes *et al.*, 1985), but any opportunity to create age and gender balance was out of the principal's hands: staffing depended upon centralized procedures which were carefully scrutinized by the teachers' federation. Reduced enrollment meant contraction of program and the further loss of students to Roxborough, which did not experience the same kind of enrollment decline until the late 1980s. Since Byron had only known growth, this was an important psychological turning point for staff.

Compounding the problem was an exodus of students to Roxborough. Many of the exiting students were high performers who left to get more specialized courses or to participate in Roxborough's program for the gifted. In a sense, Byron suffered from the flight of the affluent middle class. As a result, the community came to perceive it as a "special education" or "experimental" school, long after its innovative days were over. This flow of optional attendance created great imbalances between Roxborough and Byron. This further erosion of the student base through optional attendance made public relations, not educational issues, the main school priority.

I became a superintendent in 1983 with Byron under my jurisdiction. The school was a shadow of its former self. The staff was disheartened. The innovative ethos I had experienced in the first few years had virtually disappeared. The principal was in ill health. Balkanization and individualism (Hargreaves, 1994) had replaced the collegiality of the formative years. As the school declined in numbers, departments competed for students because student enrollments in various courses protected teachers' jobs. Collaboration decreased not only across the school but also within departments because grades and subjects were often reduced to one or two classes which precluded internal department collaboration. As one teacher explained, "It can become difficult for people with low seniority when you bring in someone with higher seniority, then it can become competitive. Discussions go on behind people's backs: 'What's going to happen to me?' Coherence and team building within the school and within departments became increasingly difficult as teachers came and went in relatively short order. Teachers who knew their tenure at Byron would be short often found it difficult to do the extras that many other teachers have always done. The same teacher asked rhetorically, "How much interest were you going to put into the designing of new courses and being innovative when you knew that after one year you were going to be gone? It really has been in and out for many staff."

The staff who remained had aged considerably. In 1970 the average age of staff had been under 30, by 1985 it was approximately 47. The impact of declining enrollment had resulted in a complement of very few teachers with less than five years experience and a majority with over ten years of experience. One staff member stated that the staff got "older and more tired." Another teacher who had spent twenty-four years at Byron explained that:

> We don't run quite as fast and as far with it [new ideas] as we used to. When this staff was young, they didn't have kids and didn't have mortgages and they didn't have other domestic responsibilities. Their parents weren't aging, then they had more free time. The collegial relationship was more important so they had more time.

A constant theme of respondents, regardless of when they had worked at Byron, was how hard they worked. The words they used to describe this work differed. In the early days they talked of "exhilaration," "joy," "commitment," "dedication," "hope" and "fun." Teachers in the 1980s and 1990s employed words like "exhaustion," "frustration," "powerlessness" and "work." Certainly the changing context explains a great deal of this shift, but the aging of the staff, and the lack of infusion of new, young people in the 1980s, account for a large measure of the teachers' changing outlook.

The picture which emerges is of an aging, somewhat disgruntled staff which still worked hard and believed in Byron's student-oriented mission but felt overwhelmed by contextual conditions beyond its control (Huberman, 1993; Sikes *et al.*, 1985). For many in the early days, work was a source of personal and professional fulfilment. For most teachers at Lord Byron in the mid and late 1980s, it was just a job. As a teacher who came to Byron in the 1980s commented:

> Coming from the school that I taught at before, I have more behavioral problems in my classroom than I did at the other school so it is a different kind of work. I feel that I don't cover as much of the core content because I'm dealing with behavior. I don't have as much energy. It is more intense in the classroom than it used to be.

The on-going criticism, the contraction of program and the elimination of valued structures led to some staff members "just giving up," others departing for other schools, while many of those who stayed became more entrenched in the correctness of their version of the Byron philosophy, and refused to adjust to changing times and circumstances. As a principal who arrived at the school in the 1980s explained with regard to long-term staff members:

> There was probably greater reluctance to accept change and to incorporate it into their style. I don't know if that was a function of the school or of the leadership. I do know it is a function of the staff getting older. I think they had been at this for a long time. They had sort of done their thing for many years and got tired.

In a sense Byron closed in upon itself and dissipated what creative energy it had left in a fruitless effort to deal with the "reputation issue." Entropy had set in. Similar patterns have appeared in other innovative schools in North America and the United Kingdom (Fletcher *et al.*, 1985; Gold and Miles, 1981; Smith *et al.*, 1987) — initial creativity and experimentation, being followed by overreaching and entropy. Some schools never moved on from this stage and eventually closed their doors (Fletcher *et al.*, 1985; Riley, 1998).

Survival and Continuity

In 1984, a new principal, Patrick Garner, and vice principal, Betty Kelly, were assigned to the school. Neither had ever taught at the school, but both had requested this assignment. They admired Byron's innovative reputation and welcomed the opportunity to restore some of Byron's past "glory." Their major challenge was to restore public confidence and rebuild a demoralized teaching staff. To ensure the school's viability, the new principal agreed to add two regional special education programs to the school. Other schools also had space but Byron offered a caring philosophy which had persisted through good times and bad. The addition of special education programs, while laudable, did nothing to stem the outflow of the more academically talented students to Roxborough. Throughout their tenures as principal, Garner, and Kelly after him, sought to balance the traditional egalitarianism of Byron with the very real community and social pressures for excellence and elitism. To retain their higher-achieving students, they departed from the anti-elitism of the original Byron philosophy and convinced staff that it was necessary to add French Immersion and segregated gifted programs. Garner's and Kelly's approach to the community was to use every opportunity to say "Byron has changed." In practice, however, changes to the school's structures, curriculum and staff were minimal. They recognized that Byron's programs were still as good if not better than most schools and worked energetically to alter public perceptions of the school, which they achieved with considerable success. The flow of optional attendance to neighboring schools came to an end. As the school's supervisor I began to hear that "Byron used to have problems but now it has changed."

By the mid-1980s, the school was no longer considered the experimental, non-traditional school within the South Board. Byron's structure was similar to most other schools. Perhaps more significantly, enrollment had bottomed in 1984 and remained fairly stable for the next six years. School leaders did not have to face the frenetic addition and then disheartening reduction of staff of the previous decade. Indeed, they did have some opportunity to restructure their heads of department group and hire some younger teachers. In addition, the system had ensured the school's survival by increasing its enrollment by supporting new programs. Since many of the key people in senior administration were products of Byron, they were aware of the school's history and were prepared to provide support to the school. For example, a former Byron principal who was the system's special education supervisor arranged for the two new programs to be placed at Byron. At the same time, successive principals of Roxborough worked cooperatively with Byron's principals to reduce the debilitating features of the rivalry between the two schools. While the schools and the system worked to normalize the situation in the mid and late 1980s, some things remained unchanged — Byron's reputation as the "experimental" school had become part of the lore of South community and was still accepted as fact.

But reality is that the school has changed profoundly. One teacher captured the shift in meaning at the school in the mid-1980s when he stated, "Byron now is like a regular school. Its philosophy was to do anything that is good for the students. I don't think that philosophy has changed, but what people perceive is good for the student has changed." This definition of what is "good for the students" has gradually become the responsibility of the district and in more recent times that of the province.

With the appointment of the new leadership team in 1984 and a leveling off of the enrollment decline, the school moved through a third phase: in some ways more conventional and in some ways, by inviting regional programs to be housed in the school, ensuring some innovation. In this way the past reputation was merged with the conventional present to help create a more stable environment for succeeding years. The school was still changing, but changing toward the more normative pattern of secondary schooling in the system. In effect, it was changing toward system certainty, going "back to the future"!

The result of Garner's and Kelly's work was to place Byron very much into the mainstream of schooling in South. This pattern of stabilization also occurred in most other long-term change projects (Gold and Miles, 1981; Evans, 1983; Smith *et al.*, 1987). It retains some of its uniqueness in the way it treats its students, its inclusion of high-risk students in regular classes and the diversity of its programs. But in most other ways, it is more similar to than different from other schools in the district now.

Scaling Up

There is relatively little research literature about the effectiveness of "lighthouse" or "model" schools as vehicles or "catalysts" for change. Those who have commented on the phenomenon suggest that the strategy has limited utility for promoting change in the larger system (Goodlad, 1996; Prestine, 1998). Yet Hargreaves and his colleagues (1992) also argue that, while model schools cannot be replicated, they do:

> consciously break the paradigms of existing educational practice. At considerable risk to themselves, their staffs and their students, they create concrete examples of other ways of doing things. This paradigm-breaking function is the most important one that lighthouse schools perform . . . [Innovative] schools . . . break the paradigms of practice by creating living images of possibility, practicality and hope. (pp. 126–7)

Certainly, this belief underlies the "model" school approach to systemic reform (Barber, 1996; Manno *et al.*, 1998; Sizer, 1992; Stringfield *et al.*, 1996). The evidence of Byron's impact on the South Board supports this "paradigm-breaking" concept. Although it was never directly replicated, Byron made an immediate impression on the other schools in the system. Within five years of Byron's opening, all but Roxborough were semestered, and even Roxborough came very close to semestering in the late 1980s (the move being defeated by the vote of just one staff member!). Other structures and practices originating at Byron traveled to other sites throughout the system, albeit with modifications. A modified version of Byron's heads' structure was adopted by policy as the headship structure for all the schools in the Board. As a result of this and subsequent policies, department heads in the South Board continue to play a greater leadership and supervisory role than heads in many other school jurisdictions in Ontario. Byron's more humane approach to discipline is now enshrined in the policies of the Board, and through former Byron leaders, in other schools. Approaches to programming initiated at Byron, such as the focus on lifetime activities in physical education, individualized science curricula and multi-text English programs continue to influence schools in the district. As a Byron teacher who continues to have extensive contacts with his former Byron colleagues stated:

> We have sprinkled the Byron staff through many schools and I think they take with them the philosophy and innovativeness. I see Leanne Hubbs who is now at Seven Maples and changes have occurred there. They had become a little stagnated for a period of time. Those are the people who still have the philosophy that change is important and we must continue to be innovative and carry out new designs. We can't just say, well it's worked well for the past ten years so we'll just continue on for the next ten years. Those are the things Byron has instilled in people and those people who have left the school carry with them. If you wanted to go up through the system you should go to Byron.

Schools which have been physically designed on the lines of Byron provide flexibility in the use of space for large and small group instruction and personal counseling. Efforts to copy Byron's purposes, structures and culture directly in other schools, however, have met with resentment and ultimately rejection. While it is true that using Lord Byron to "scale up" the system had limited impact in the short range, from the perspective of twenty-five years the evidence suggests that it did have considerable influence.

As a "paradigm-breaker" in South, Byron's practices and purposes have over time contributed significantly to the development of a more student-centered secondary school philosophy in the South system. In its early days, the Byron approach was the central topic of the system's leadership program which trained many of the system leaders, at both the primary and secondary levels. Through his visits to schools, Sizemore challenged leaders to look at Byron as an alternative. This "challenging of conventional ideas" would appear to be Byron's most significant lasting legacy. Moreover, as described previously, many Byron people themselves moved into leadership roles and became part of the staffs of other schools. They literally embodied Byron's legacy in their leadership of other institutions. As they did so, they not only showed the system the possibilities for different organizational patterns, teaching approaches and relationships with students, but also worked with other teachers and managers to make these possibilities a reality. It is through these former Byron staff members as leaders that the Byron ideals have spread. My respondents spoke of an unwritten obligation, a mission, to carry the Byron message to other places. A woman who never taught at Byron but who presently holds a senior position in the school district described the influence of a Byron leader on her:

> Joan brought with her an attitude of experimentation with a view to the improvement of instruction that I had never experienced and she reveled in professional discourse as the bread of daily life . . . we would talk about what we had done in class that day, how it had gone, why it hadn't gone better . . . it was my first experience with that type of collaboration with a view to improving teaching.

As some of these leaders moved beyond the school level to senior positions with the Board, such as director and superintendent, regional policies also began to reflect the philosophy and policies of Byron. The inclusiveness of Byron is reflected in the special education programs initiated by a former Byron staff member. The significance of staff development in South as a key to educational change is attributable in large measure to leaders produced by Lord Byron. Byron, in its early days, was the first school in South to allocate significant amounts of school funds to professional development. Appraisal systems which focused on professional growth were championed in the system by Ward Bond (Fink and Stoll, 1997). It generally takes time for leaders to move into positions of influence within a school system. In my own case, it took three years from the day I left Byron to begin participating in regional educational discussions and eight years to be in a position to shape regional policies. This is one of the more important reasons that one must look at the impact of a model school over time to determine its influence on the larger system and upon other institutions.

A striking example of Byron's contribution to the erosion of barriers to change within the South Board was its contribution to women's leadership in the system. This began with a women's group encouraged by Bond in Byron's early days. This group of women has continued to meet on a regular basis for the past twenty-five years, even though none of them continues on the staff of Lord Byron. As one of the early members of the group explained:

> The women's group at Byron is not focused here but it is all over the county now, because many of those women, because of the peer support, and the advice and the information that they received, are now principals and vice principals and department heads and directors of education over the province. That came about because of this little nucleus of people who got together to talk about stuff. It was wonderful! Wonderful! It certainly changed the face of secondary education in South.

Before the Byron women's group, the management of South was "an old-boys network." When I was promoted to principal in 1975, there were no women secondary principals and only two secondary assistant principals. At present, women play a very significant leadership role at all levels of the South Board and its secondary school. The two senior academic superintendents, seven of the present seventeen secondary principals and thirteen of the twenty-five assistant principals are women.

One of the most important and controversial debates in educational reform concerns the "scaling up" of change (Cohen, 1995; Elmore, 1995; Reynolds, 1998). The problem of "scaling up" is essentially that of how to transfer successful programs or other innovations from individual schools or pilot projects, so that they can transform entire systems. Research on school improvement suggests that, while we know a great deal about how to create islands of change, there has been little success in creating archipelagos, and even less success in creating continents of change (Hargreaves *et al.*, 1996). How to "scale up" change becomes a significant challenge. Unfortunately, in practice the quest for "scaling up" has often amounted to research to find the *conditions* under which particular programs or innovations can get adapted more widely, rather than seeing how the *fundamental purposes* and *principles* underpinning these programs might be spread more diffusely, even if the programs themselves are not.

Thus the overt or high-profile approach to "scaling up" the successes of Byron involved the system and its Director, in the words of a retired secondary principal, "ramming the Byron model down our throats." Sizemore and others (Gold and Miles, 1981; Smith *et al.*, 1987) hoped that other schools would adopt the successful aspects of the innovative school. This "shock and copy" strategy was typical of the times in Ontario and in South, and created a backlash of distrust, suspicion, anger, entrenchment and jealousy — somewhat muted in Byron's early years but much more apparent as the school began to experience the "liabilities of newness" (Gold and Miles, 1981). This reactive response is common when valuable educational principles are wrapped up in what are seen as faddish, packaged, self-promoting programs. Byron's more subtle "scaling up" impact on the rest of the system was not by shock, blueprint or direct transportation but rather by the way it spawned influential teachers and leaders who, over time, carried the principles and practices of Byron in their work with other schools throughout the system. In effect, Byron changed the system by long-term "attrition." This sort of "scaling up" can only be identified and understood by studying schools over long periods of time. In sum, the creation of new school models can provide a catalyst for policy germination, opportunities for training in innovative practices and a seed-bed for the long-term development of innovative educational leaders. This suggests that for "scaling up" to work it must be more of a reculturing process than a strategic plan of transportation (Goodlad, 1996; Newmann and Wehlage, 1995).

Sustainability

Another important area of debate and inquiry in educational change concerns how far particular reforms can be *sustained* over time. What makes innovation and change sustainable (Fullan, 1991; Hopkins *et al.*, 1994; Louis and Miles, 1990; Slavin, 1998; Stoll and Fink, 1996)? How can innovations last beyond the first flurry of early success? Does successful change require a heavy consumption of resources and human energy that cannot be sustained over time? Lord Byron sustained its innovative character for less than ten years. Shifts in government policies, changes in the school's demographics, transitions in the school's leadership, resistance to change within the school's community and the erosion of a collaborative culture led to an "attrition of change" which resulted in its conforming to the purposes, principles and practices of other secondary schools in the system in order to survive as an institution.

The evidence of this study suggests that schools as separate organizations may not be the "centers" of change but rather the "objects" of change. Byron's creation, growth and long-term attrition were, in large measure, attributable to forces beyond its control. Byron's external contexts powerfully shaped its internal contexts. The Byron story further indicates that when educational authorities establish "model" schools to "scale up" larger systems, they inevitably undermine the sustainability of the school's innovative ethos. Conversely, when educational authorities take steps to protect the leadership, the teaching staff and the advantaged position and profile which sustain a model school, they invite overt and covert opposition from members of other school settings toward the model school's philosophy, policies and practices. These perceived threats to the "grammar of schooling" in other schools inhibit the possibility of "scaling up," and the criticism of staff members in these other schools fuels community opposition which affects the sustainability of the model school's innovative ethos.

Not only does the professional community present an obstacle to sustainability, but a model school's parent and larger communities can create an even thornier problem for the school (Fletcher *et al.*, 1985; Gold and Miles, 1981; Riley, 1998). If a "break the mold" school is to succeed, its staff must share an image or vision of a "good" school which is usually quite different from its community's conception of a "real" school (Metz, 1991). If these two images become too divergent then a school faces the kind of backlash which contributed to Byron's "attrition of change." The Byron case indicates that the professionals' image of a "good" school must and possibly should diverge somewhat from the community's conception of a "real" school in order to effect positive change, but it can't differ so much that the community loses confidence, undermines the sustainability of the school's changes, and in the process provides ammunition to those who would oppose the "scaling up" of the system.

These two interrelated dilemmas suggest that to sustain innovation in a model school while using it as a catalyst for change in the larger system, the system's leaders must adopt a very deliberate, low-profile, long-term "scaling up" strategy. As one of my respondents suggested, he would eliminate words like "innovative," "model," "new" and "lighthouse" from discussions of proposed "scaling up" schools. Leaders need to talk about pilot projects and experiments and allow the natural distribution of leaders and ideas to influence the system. Perhaps if the "lighthouse" doesn't burn as brightly in the beginning, its light will continue to burn longer, not only in the school but in the larger system. While organizational structures and accountability measures may well travel to other settings rather quickly, the Byron case provides further evidence that change in the things that count in education — teaching, learning and caring — require a reculturing process in schools (Hargreaves, 1994) which takes time, sensitivity to people's concerns, and leadership which invites change (Stoll and Fink, 1996).

The evidence of this study of the history of an innovative school points to the existence of an ironic change dynamic. On the one hand there is tendency for the school itself to experience attrition and over time to lose much of its early momentum and innovativeness. Exceptionally innovative schools are unlikely to meet the criteria of sustainability. On the other hand, the school can exert longer-term impact beyond its own walls through the rule-breaking precedents it sets that open up opportunities for others, and through the key leaders it spawns who take their innovative images of schooling to other parts of the system. Innovative schools, therefore, can have subtle long-term effects on the "scaling up" of system-wide change that otherwise might be difficult to detect using most conventional research strategies. In this scenario, sustainability of individual school change is the sacrifice paid to the scaling up of change across the system. Conversely, if local school systems try to protect the sustainability of the model schools by allocating scarce resources or assigning the system's best personnel to such schools, scaling up becomes the sacrifice to sustainability. In other words, the model schools' change strategy may contain a paradox of sustainability and scaling up, where "scaling up" and sustainability are actually inversely related to each other (A. Hargreaves, personal correspondence). The possible widespread existence of such a paradox most certainly merits further exploration and study.

Notes

1   This provided me with a minimum of fifteen subjects in each of the three years. Although this was not a random sample in the statistical sense, it was what Ball (1984: 75) would call "naturalistic coverage" because it approximated the diversity of people who were involved in Byron over the years.

2   McNamara argues that outsiders who observe classrooms do so selectively and

fail to comprehend the complexity of the situation. He suggests that outsiders to the classroom "invariably have a message for us; they have discovered situations in the classroom that need to be rectified . . . This might be possible to take if it were not so often coupled with an arrogant or patronising manner and naive view of classrooms and the problems faced by practising teachers" (1980: 115). In his response, Hammersley contends that the term "insider" is misleading because "it implies that those being studied constitute a single homogeneous group" (1981: 169). He challenges McNamara's view that the "outsider's" analyses are often invalid and of little use to teachers by asserting that carefully constructed research which employs observation in different contexts, and interviews with all types of participants, can deal with threats to validity claimed by the insider's doctrine. This debate highlights the insider's advantage of understanding the group from the inside and therefore the complexity of the situation. The outsider, however, can theoretically view the situation somewhat dispassionately, unaffected by the internal culture and micropolitics.

3   This narrative is based on the archival materials of the South Board of Education and Lord Byron High School, and the recollections of interview respondents, as well as my own memories as a participant in many of the events.

4   Other studies of "innovative" schools (Fletcher *et al.*, 1985; Gold and Miles, 1981; Smith *et al.*, 1987) depict the same kind of hostility faced by innovative schools from sources internal to the school system. Hargreaves (1984) describes the kind of "contrastive rhetoric" that critics in at least one other school used to demean a non-traditional British school, Countesthorpe. By being "high profile," schools like Byron, Thornlea (Fullan *et al.*, 1972), Bayridge (Fullan and Eastabrook, 1977), Lincoln (Hargreaves, 1994) and Beachside (Ball, 1981) often invite criticism by antagonizing colleagues in other schools by implying that the "new" way is the only way.

References

Ball, S. (1981) *Beachside comprehensive: a case-study of secondary schooling.* Cambridge: Cambridge University Press.

Ball, S. G. (1984) Beachside reconsidered: reflections on a methodological apprenticeship. In R. G. Burgess (ed.), *The research process in educational settings: ten case studies*, pp. 69–96. London: Falmer Press.

Barber, M. (1996) *The learning game: arguments for an education revolution.* London: Gollancz.

Bolman, L. and Deal, T. (1997) *Reframing organizations: artistry, choice and leadership.* San Francisco: Jossey-Bass.

Cohen, D. K. (1995) What is the system in systemic reform? *Educational Researcher*, 24(9), 11–17 and 31.

Cuban, L. (1988) A fundamental puzzle of school reform. *Phi Delta Kappan*, 70(5), 341–4.

Doremus, R. R. (1981) Whatever happened to: John Adams High School. *Phi Delta Kappan*, 63(3), 199–202.

Earl, L. and Lee, L. (1998) *Evaluation of the Manitoba School Improvement Program.* Toronto: Gordon Foundation.

Elmore, R. (1995) Structural reform in educational practice. *Educational Researcher*, 24(9), 23–6.

Evans, B. (1983) Countesthorpe College, Leicester. In B. Moon (ed.), *Comprehensive schools: challenge and change*, pp. 5–32. Windsor, UK: Nelson Publishing.

Fink, D. and Stoll, L. (1997) Weaving school and teacher development together. In T. Townsend (ed.), *Restructuring and quality: issues for tomorrow's schools*. New York: Routledge.

Fletcher, C., Caron, M. and Williams, W. (1985) *Schools on trial*. Milton Keynes: Open University Press.

Fullan, M. G. (1991) *The new meaning of educational change*. New York: Teachers College Press.

Fullan, M. and Eastabrook, G. (1977) *Bayridge Secondary School: case study of the planning and implementation of educational change*. Toronto: Ontario Institute for Studies in Education.

Fullan, M., Eastabrook, G., Spinner, D. and Loubser, J. J. (1972) *Thornlea: a case study of an innovative secondary school*. Toronto: Ontario Institute for Studies in Education.

Gold, B. A. and Miles, M. B. (1981) *Whose school is it anyway: parent–teacher conflict over an innovative school*. New York: Praeger.

Goodlad, J. (1996) Sustaining and extending educational renewal. *Phi Delta Kappan*, 78(3), 228–34.

Guernsey, J. (1971) Portland's unconventional Adams High. *American Education*, 6(5), 3–7.

Hammersley, M. (1981) The outsider's advantage: a reply to McNamara. *British Educational Journal*, 7(2), 167–71.

Hargreaves, A. (1984) Contrastive rhetoric and extremist talk. In A. Hargreaves and P. Woods (eds.), *Classrooms and staffrooms*, pp. 303–29. Milton Keynes: Open University Press.

Hargreaves, A. (1994) *Changing teachers, changing times*. London: Cassell.

Hargreaves, A., Earl, L. and Ryan, J. (1996) *Schooling for change*. London: Falmer Press.

Hargreaves, A., Fullan, M., Wignall, R., Stager, M. and Macmillan, R. (1992) *Secondary school work cultures and educational change*. Toronto: Ministry of Education.

Hopkins, D., Ainscow, M. and West, M. (1994) *School improvement in an era of change*. London: Cassell.

Huberman, M. (1993) *The lives of teachers*. London: Cassell.

Ladwig, J., Currie, J. and Chadbourne, R. (1994) *Toward rethinking Australian schools*. Sydney: National Schools Network.

Levin, H. (1987) Accelerated schools for disadvantaged students. *Educational Leadership*, 44(6), 9–21.

Louis, K. S. and Miles, M. B. (1990) *Improving the urban high school: what works and why*. New York: Teachers College Press.

McNamara, D. R. (1980) The outsider's arrogance: the failure of participant observers to understand classroom events. *British Educational Journal*, 6(2), 113–25.

Manno, B., Finn, C., Bielein, L. and Vanourek, G. (1998) How charter schools are different: lessons and implications from a national study, *Phi Delta Kappan*, 79(7), 489–98.

Merton, R. K. (1970) Insiders and outsiders: a chapter in the sociology of knowledge. *American Journal of Sociology*, 78(1), 9–47.

Metz, M. H. (1991) Real school: a universal drama amid disparate experience. In D. E. Mitchell and M. E. Goetz (eds.), *Education politics for the new century*, pp. 75–91. New York: Falmer Press.

Miles, M. B. and Huberman, A. M. (1984) *Innovations up close: how school improvement works*. New York: Plenum Press.

Newmann, F. and Wehlage, G. (1995) *Successful school restructuring*. Madison, WI: Center on Organization and Restructuring Schools.

Prestine, N. (1998) Disposable reform? Assessing the durability of secondary school reform. Paper presented at the annual meeting of the American Educational Research Association, San Diego, CA.

Reynolds, D. (1998) World class school improvement: an analysis of the implications of recent international school effectiveness and school improvement research for improvement practice. In A. Hargreaves, A. Lieberman, M. Fullan and D. Hopkins (eds.), *International handbook of educational change*, pp. 297–321. Dordrecht: Kluwer.

Riley, K. (1998) *Whose school is it anyway?* London: Falmer Press.

Schwartz, R. B. (1971) Profile of a high school: an introduction. *Phi Delta Kappan*, 52(5), 514–15.

Sikes, P., Measor, L. and Woods, P. (1985) *Teacher careers: crises and continuities*. Lewes: Falmer Press.

Siskin, L. (1994) *Realms of knowledge: academic departments in secondary schools*. London: Falmer Press.

Sizer, T. (1992) *Horace's School*. New York: Houghton Miflin.

Slavin, R. (1998) Sand, bricks and seed: school change strategies and readiness for change. In A. Hargreaves, A. Lieberman, M. Fullan and D. Hopkins (eds.), *International handbook of educational change*, pp. 1299–1312. Dordrecht: Kluwer.

Smith, L. M., Dwyer, D. C., Prunty, J. J. and Kleine, P. F. (1987) *The fate of an innovative school*. London: Falmer Press.

Stamp, R. (1976) *The schools of Ontario*. Toronto: Queen's Printers of Ontario.

Stringfield, S., Ross, S. and Smith, L. (eds.) (1996) *Bold plans for school restructuring: the new American schools design*. Mahwah, NJ: LEA Publishers.

Stoll, L. and Fink, D. (1996) *Changing our schools: linking school effectiveness and school improvement*. Buckingham: Open University Press.

Stoll, L. and Myers, K. (eds.) (1998) *Schools in difficulty: no quick fixes*. London: Falmer Press.

Tyack, D. and Tobin, W. (1994) The grammar of schooling: why has it been so hard to change? *American Educational Research Journal*, 31(3), 453–79.

3   Leadership Succession, Cultures of Teaching and Educational Change

Robert B. Macmillan

Introduction

Improving teaching and learning has become a priority of governments and policymakers (cf. Finn and Vanourek, 1998). However, creating more effective schools cannot be done simply by transposing seemingly successful strategies from one school context to another (Reynolds *et al.*, 1996). The process of school improvement is extremely complex. To be successful, it must take the specific context of each school into account (Creemers, 1996). To explain the complexity of these contextual differences between schools, researchers have drawn on and developed the concept of school culture, and have begun to explore how it influences students, teachers and school leaders as well.

Research on school cultures indicates that successful school change occurs when teachers develop shared beliefs of what ought to be, have a clear focus on improving teaching and learning, are involved collaboratively in decision-making (Hargreaves, 1994; Rosenholtz, 1989) and have a means to deal with issues openly (Darling-Hammond, 1995). To create effective schools, teachers must therefore have the opportunity to share ideas (Little, 1982) and must believe that colleagues can help them to resolve instructional issues (Beck and Murphy, 1996).

Successful implementation of educational change also requires effective leaders who are able to engage mindfully with the school's culture and its community, and who involve teachers integrally and meaningfully as team members in the implementation process (Carlson, 1996; Leithwood *et al.*, Steinbach and Ryan, 1997; Senge, 1990). In the case of implementing Site-Based Management, for example, Leithwood and Menzies (1996) found that school performance did not improve when leaders imposed initiatives in a top-down manner. Where initiatives were effective (measured in terms of outcomes), principals used a model of implementation which incorporated collective, organizational learning among all members of the school community. In summary, we now seem to have a clearer sense of what kind of leadership is required to introduce initiatives effectively, which characteristics of school cultures facilitate implementation, and which strategies leaders must use to foster effective school cultures (e.g., Dalin, 1993; Reynolds *et al.*, 1996).

School districts often provide policy structures and strategies to guide the implementation of initiatives at the school level. One strategy that some districts use is to identify effective principals, then move them to schools that need improvement. Such districts expect principals to institute changes and improvements in their new schools as part of their career trajectories (Ganz and Hoy, 1977). Some districts have suggested that rotating principals is an effective management strategy for principals, too, as it helps them to improve and upgrade their skills and abilities (Aquila, 1988; Boesse, 1991). However, the research on principal and leader succession does not indicate the optimum length of principal tenure (Hart, 1993).

Rotating principals between schools can be a politically and administratively attractive strategy. If leadership is a key to successful change, then rotating school leaders is a simple and decisive policy that promises swift improvements in troubled schools. But what really happens when leaders confront a new school culture? How receptive or resilient are particular cultures of teaching and schooling to change? Does nothing succeed like leadership succession? Or can some cultures of teaching endure and outlive the series of leaders who come through the revolving doors of their schools? Is leadership rotation, in other words, a powerful and underused lever for change, or does it simply amount to moving the deck chairs around on an educational Titanic?

This chapter addresses the phenomenon of leadership succession. It examines how teachers react to change agendas that result from leadership succession events, and it investigates how these reactions are expressed in the school's culture. The appointment of a new administrator creates potential for instability in a school because previously understood working relationships between teachers and administrators are opened up for inspection and validation (Miskel and Cosgrove, 1985; Macmillan, 1996). During the initial stages of succession, innovations that had already been started are often placed in temporary limbo or shelved entirely until teachers are able to determine how the new principal's agenda or mandate compares with his or her predecessor's (Macmillan, 1991). Until these issues are clarified, a new principal trying to implement initiatives or foster cultural shifts may not be able to do so without inviting suspicion.

Concerns of this kind may be typical of all incidents of leadership succession. When succession is frequent and predictable, however, teachers may react with more than customary caution and anxiety, for they learn to respond not just to one shift but to recurring shifts of direction; not to the enduring influence of one leader who will stay, but to the possibly ephemeral influence of waves of leaders who will all assuredly move on. In light of all these possibilities, it is important to know how teachers respond to leadership succession where it is a regular occurrence (either because of administrative policy, or because of the problems of retaining leaders in challenging urban or remote areas). In conditions of routinized succession, are leaders able to transform their schools' cultures, or do these cultures resist and outlast their leaders?

Boesse (1991) reports on the professional benefits for administrators when a systematic rotation policy is in place in a school system. Administrators stated that they felt rejuvenated when experiencing a new setting. As for the organization, a change in administration, particularly when an outsider is appointed, usually heightens the expectation in teachers that a change initiative will shortly be announced (Carlson, 1971). For these and other reasons, school districts may be tempted to institute a principal rotation policy as a way to encourage change within their schools. However, the time period for the rotation may be critical. Tenure of less than five years may be problematic because initiatives usually take longer than five years to become institutionalized (Fullan, 1993; Weindling, 1992). Further, while the rotation may be beneficial for principals, the long-term impact of regular principal turnover on teachers and on school culture is still unknown.

Methodology

The data on which this chapter draws were collected through semi-structured interviews in two phases. In the first or pilot phase, eighteen teachers in four secondary schools were interviewed; in Phase Two, a modified interview schedule incorporating new insights from Phase One was used with eleven teachers in a fifth secondary school. All five schools had had new principals appointed within the previous two years. The first four schools are from one district and are located in both urban and rural areas. The policy in both school districts is to rotate principals systematically every five years.

In order to allay principals' potential concerns during the sensitive early period of their tenure and to assist on access to their schools, principals were asked to select the teachers to be interviewed. Although this strategy posed risks to the representativeness of the sample and to the openness of teachers' responses, the teachers were actually quite frank in their assessments of their new principals. Moreover, with a sample such as this, any criticisms of principals or assessments of their limited impact are likely to be underestimates of the extent to which such critical views are held among staff as a whole. In most schools, principals used two main criteria for selection: the availability of individuals during the period of the researcher's visit; and each teacher's willingness to discuss his or her perceptions of the succession event.

Each interview lasted from twenty to forty-five minutes and was tape recorded after permission had been granted by the interviewee. During the analysis of each interview, the substance of responses to questions was noted, with specific phrases, sentences and/or paragraphs extracted and coded.

Hardening of School Culture

In all five schools, teachers described how having to adapt regularly to principal turnover impacted on their school's culture. The discussion here focuses on the comments from teachers in the first four pilot phase schools, where the teachers' notion of the school being greater than their principal first emerged. Indeed, when they described their schools, teachers discussed them in terms of teachers and students and often omitted reference to principals altogether unless they were asked specifically about the principal's place in it. This teacher's description of school culture is typical:

> There's a great deal of supportiveness among staff . . . Part of the established culture, I think, reflects that there's some very keen, dynamic active areas in this school that are very interdependent and very supportive. And there's some greyer areas that tend to plod and be very resistant, "Old Guardish."

When a colleague was asked whether the principal had any impact on the school, she said, "the basic running of the school carries on no matter who's here." Contrary to what the literature frequently states about the importance of the principal's influence on school culture, this statement suggests that teachers cope with change and with their new principals very differently when succession is a frequent and predictable occurrence. When asked the same question about school culture and the principal's influence, a teacher in another school stated that "this school is perceived not to be an easy school for an administrator to come into because of the school culture, like that it's a hard rock to crack."

Another teacher who, as a long-serving staff member, had substantial experience of the school district's policy for systematically rotating principals, explained that one cause of a school culture's "impenetrability" was the rotation policy itself. Asked whether a principal had much to do with the school's culture, he replied:

> *Teacher*: Our school, for whatever reason, they said you've got a lot of experience with principals, like you didn't have to move. You saw every type of principal you wanted because two years [one principal], two years [another principal], two years [a third]. So I would say that a principal has to be at a school quite a while to put his stamp on it. The ones that were [here only] for a couple of years, I mean, maybe a little bit as far as the staff's concerned we saw a difference, but I don't think any of the students really did, and certainly not the community. Principals who were in schools for a long time like [names principals and schools], there was a definite stamp on that school by those men because they were part of the school, part of the school community. It's very difficult here.
> *Interviewer*: If you have such rapid changeover of principals, how does the staff react? Does the staff actually say, "Oh, hohum, you know, we'll just wait two years and this guy will just disappear"?

> *Teacher*: Oh yeah, definitely! We felt that way for a time, oh yeah. If he was good, you know, too bad, [he was transferred,] if he wasn't a good principal, well . . .
> *Interviewer*: Only two years.
> *Teacher*: Only a couple of years. Oh, really, that's for sure, that's for sure, but [previous principal] was here five years, the person before [previous principal] was here maybe four, and [the current principal], now he is finishing his first [year] now. It appeared at other schools that changes were approximately five years. In our school, you know, it was a revolving door. [Here,] you get to know someone and they were gone.

For this teacher, the positive feelings of anticipation that might sometimes accompany the arrival of a new administrator are all too easily displaced by a sense of apathy toward successive administrators as they pass in waves through the school. When succession is frequent and predictable, the principal is treated as merely a temporary aberration.

Although this particular school staff is apparently apathetic to its administrators, teachers are strongly committed to the substance and form of cultural practices in their schools and to perpetuating such practices as a way of working together as a total community involved in education, even if this means excluding the principal. This solidarity of purpose provides cohesiveness at the school level and is held together by experienced teachers with a long tenure in the school.

> You're dealing with a school that although there is a turnover rate [among teachers], it's not anywhere near as high as a lot of schools. Because there's a lot of people who've been here since day one. A lot. They've never seen anything else. So therefore, they've built they're own little intrastructure (*sic*) and that is setting the tone for the school.

This "intrastructure" of interactions among teachers provides the common, enduring understanding of what is educationally appropriate for their own school's circumstances. This does not mean that the teacher culture is unified on all matters and purposes. As in most large secondary school organizations, there are differences and even disagreements within it. As one teacher puts it, "I like to refer to the school as an extremely caring, supportive organism, but I also know that within that caring, supportive organism, there are some parts that are really tough to care for." This combination of difference with acceptance was evident in another of the schools.

> I think that people have worked together a long time and that they have certain understandings and tolerances of each other that they might not have if they were a new group of people working together. I think that there are, sort of, definite expectations of people. For instance, one of the department heads is used to being able to say at staff meetings, sometimes, some quite cutting comments in response to things that happen, and it's taken in the context of "Well that's that person."

Thus, while secondary teachers may acknowledge the existence of an internally fragmented culture (Hargreaves and Macmillan, 1995), they also are able to function together informally as a federation when the whole school is affected (Sergiovanni, 1984). Even in the case of complex, differentiated secondary schools, longstanding working relationships among teachers help to forge a common understanding of the school in the face of new principals and change.

A teacher who had transferred into the "revolving door" school as a department head at the beginning of the year, explained how teachers responded in unity toward principal rotation.

> The vice-principal to whom I was speaking about coming here said that the staff is very jaded as far as administration is concerned, that they'd had so many administrators and different demands that they had kind of had gone into themselves and they had the attitude that, and I could even see it in some of my own department, administrators come, administrators go. There'll be changes of thrust, there'll be changes in vision, whatever, and we'll kind of keep on going and if we don't like it, it will pass and someone else will come.

In these four schools where regular administrative turnover occurred, principals were perceived as simply "passing through." They were tolerated temporarily, although not always silently. This was especially true where administrators diverged from teachers' normative expectations about how visible principals should be in the school. For example, one teacher said

> I know [the principal] is a very busy person and we called him the "Phantom" around here for the first two months . . . He was winding up a number of other, shall we say, "professional endeavors . . ." It wasn't totally well received by the staff and, like I say, he's been aware of this from a very honest form, in an open forum.

In another school, teachers were also very clear in letting the principal know that his limited presence in the corridors and classrooms did not live up to their expectations of visibility.

> This year he's not very visible. He spends a lot of time in his office and this was a subject of jokes and comments and so on that were made at the school PD [professional development] day . . . And people are quite forthright in stating that perception.

In these schools, teachers felt that when long-standing school cultures were confronted with a new administrator "the culture is more powerful than the effects of the administrator so far." As confirmation of the power of the culture and the maintenance of the school, another stated that,

> There are days when they take the principal and the vice-principals right out of the school and it still functions. But you really don't notice a heck of a difference except that the kids see a difference.

Each new principal is temporarily tolerated and accommodated without teachers agreeing to or complying with the leaders' change agendas. This cultural norm of tolerance and acceptance without agreement or compliance seems to be based on teachers' perception that they can manage the school without the administration. With this belief deeply ingrained in the identity of these schools, teachers anticipate and prepare for each new round of rotations.

Possible explanations for this cultural norm can be found in another school considered by teachers and its principal to be the school district's training ground for new principals. Teachers described this school as being both physically and professionally departmentalized. Yet with each new principal rotation, teachers coalesced around their common beliefs about their school, and worked closely together to develop their own sense of self-sufficiency in the face of inexperienced administrators. The result was a self-reliant staff who reduced the upheaval in their school's operation that was precipitated by each new appointment, by reducing the principal's role to that of manager.

> *Teacher*: This is a close-knit group. That in itself is a kind of a hypocritical statement in a sense because staff here, even though we are close-knit as knowing what's going on with each other, the staff are fragmented a lot during the day because of the work rooms they have so you don't get a lot of mixing as much as we used to . . .
>
> *Interviewer*: Do you see the principal having much to do with the school's culture? And if the principal has an influence, what is that influence?
>
> *Teacher*: I don't see [the principal] much in that regard. The history of principals in this area seems to be, you know, you don't see too much of them. They are always off at meetings and the board office . . . He does the paperwork. He tries to force it [chuckles] he tries to put his ideas on us and things like that.

This teacher's "chuckle" alludes to an unspoken assessment of the principal's limited success in imposing new ideas. When the staff could not influence the administrator's actions directly, teachers defended their established cultural norms by stonewalling or presenting obstacles to implementation. One such cultural norm emphasized spotlighting students' accomplishments at graduation ceremonies, while the new principal wanted teachers to wear academic gowns (thereby emphasizing teachers' status and accomplishments).

> Some people were uptight over that. They thought they were putting the staff on a pedestal rather than the kids. And there was a few bad feelings over that with some people . . . Most of us put the kids first.

Although this principal did not understand the magnitude of his error at the time, he did have to tread carefully with later initiatives. As another teacher said, "I would feel probably a barrier beginning to develop there if he was wanting to change things I felt were working well."

In summary, these schools' cultures appear to have "hardened" as a result of teachers' experiences with processions of leaders and their accompanying change agendas moving through their schools. This hardening is rooted in an internal strengthening of the common aspects of teacher culture, and an external presentation of a common front to the intruders, who are the schools' new principals. One explanation for this hardening of the schools' culture is the uncertainty that accompanies succession events: the threats they pose to teachers' routines, existing relationships and familiar roles.

> There's always uncertainty because you're familiar with one kind of person. You don't know what this person's really going to be like once they're there and how they're going to act and what kinds of decisions they're going to make and what kind of policy are they going to try and bring about in a school and so on.

Until teachers have met the new principal and are able to predict how he or she will react or how their role within the school will be defined, teachers must wait in anticipation.

> But it is exceptionally stressful because you've got to realize what is it going to be like when this man meets you. Are you going to change for him? That is, knuckle down is such a nice way of saying it.

Almost all change of any scale or significance provokes some anxiety. A certain amount of anxiety in response to change can actually be helpful, stimulating people to be creative and to redouble their efforts (Hargreaves and Fullan, 1998). But in the face of change that is ceaseless and capricious, where individuals are pushed in one direction then another, anxiety can disable people and reduce their effectiveness (Hargreaves, 1998). To avert such overwhelming anxiety, many individuals develop cooption strategies to manage, reduce or prevent its effects (Schön, 1971). One such cooption strategy is to develop and preserve a common culture of purposes and valued practices which is strong enough to resist the disturbing efforts and initiatives of intruders, and indeed to influence and socialize the intruder instead of the intruder influencing them. With the solidarity of such a common cultural front, teachers can work to reduce their anxiety at the time of a succession event by believing that they can positively influence the new principal's actions and practices.

Work and organizations also provide familiar structures through which individuals construct a sense of self and place (Giddens, 1991; Storr, 1994). Any prospect of school restructuring is therefore a threat not only to teachers' practices, to what they do, but also to their basic senses of self and identity. One way people reduce the sense of uncertainty resulting from shifting structures is to construct a concept of what workplace structures and relationships ought to be (Schön, 1971). The teachers in the schools in this study have done precisely this in the face of structural changes threatened by the existence of principal turnover.

In effect, with their experience of regular administrative turnover, teachers in the schools described here evolved a vision of their school's culture which placed themselves at the core and the principal on the periphery. By doing this, teachers spared themselves from having to reformulate their basic constructions of reality and senses of purpose and identity with each change of principal.

These findings stand in direct opposition to what has been written concerning the role of the principal in changing school culture. How can these findings be reconciled with the claims and evidence of some of the most influential research on leadership, culture and change in schools, such as Sergiovanni (1995) who asserts that "It is clear that when schools are functioning especially well and school achievement is high, much of the credit typically belongs to the principal?" (p. 83). Leithwood, Begley and Cousins (1994) even identify six strategies that principals use "to influence the culture of their schools and to foster greater collaboration" (p. 143).

What is different about the circumstances investigated in this study is the particular experience that teachers have had with principal rotation and the short time that each principal spent on site. Teachers would not invest time and effort in each new initiative when they knew that it would likely disappear with the next rotation sequence. To prevent the expenditure of scarce time and energy, and to preserve a stable sense of purpose and identity, they developed strategies to minimize the effect of each new succession event and its accompanying new initiatives. For the principals in this study, the culture of the schools that they entered strongly influenced how they administered those schools since they were told openly or through teachers' actions what was expected of them. Negotiating change and being a credible member of the instructional team in the face of such a solidarity of purpose is a formidable challenge for "revolving door" principals to confront.

Stages of Succession

The fifth school, called Brookdale, provided an opportunity to explore in more depth the stages through which teachers moved as they responded to succession events. In this school, as in the others, teachers also described how staff had come together to form a solid front in the face of new principals. They resented the district's policy of regularly transferring principals, particularly since they saw themselves as having to bear the brunt of the bumblings of novice administrators. As one teacher stated,

> Brookdale has been a training ground for vice-principals and principals because it is small and we're out here in the corner. And if you really screw up, who cares? It's just Brookdale. But "If you do a great job, then we can

promote you and give you a bigger test." And the staff at Brookdale are solid enough that no matter who is here, you are not going to wreck the school. It's really a strong staff.

Teachers said of many of the older staff and quite a few of those in mid-career that "[most] people come and retire here because it's such a nice school." Teachers took pride in their school and personally resented any real or perceived slight, including ones they claimed resulted from district policies aimed at the school — especially using the relatively small Brookdale school as a training ground for principals.

This does not mean that teachers rejected and resented all change. Innovation did occur here, but it was shaped by principles and purposes that were central to and valued by the teachers' culture. As one teacher stated, there were "a lot of traditions here that continue. And it's a place where innovation, if it's well done, can make things really happen." The key to implementing change meant matching the innovation to the cultural image of the school that had been established through tradition. Teachers guarded and perpetuated this image through legends, rituals and stories which provided the assessment framework to determine whether or not an innovation should or would succeed. For example, they described themselves as a relaxed school without a lot of the policy trappings and restrictions of larger schools. Although several of the senior male staff wore collars and ties by choice and habit, what teachers wore was seen as their choice; there was no dress code.

> I remember he [the principal] one time, he instituted this rule that all males would wear collars and ties. And guys that had been on staff for fifteen or twenty years all of a sudden said, "You can't tell us that we have to wear collars and ties!" And they started not wearing ties and [had] open collars.

When forced to do what they previously did voluntarily, these teachers rebelled and perversely did the opposite.

These defining images of who they were as a school helped teachers to face the prospect of regular principal turnover. This turnover was created by the school's status as a training ground for administrators in the expanding school district. This created unusual tensions as each new principal had not yet developed a predictable leadership style and had to be trained in the ways of administration. This is especially true where each new principal is not only new to the school, but new to the principalship itself. Brookdale's teachers' fears of and complaints about this phenomenon were not unfounded. As Day and Baioğlu (1996) have found in their research on the career stages of headteachers (school principals) in England, leaders in their first principalship are likely to be more enthusiastic about change, but also more uncertain and unskilled about implementing it than in successive principalships. Using schools as leadership training grounds, in contexts of regular principal rotations is therefore likely to subject their staffs and students to poorly managed, capriciously shifting and excessively advocated patterns of change. As one teacher said, "the most dangerous thing about a leader, I think, is unpredictability."

Faced with the instability created by the "revolving door" in the principal's office, teachers at Brookdale developed a system through which they could gauge how each new administrator would function and how acceptable his or her administration would be. Once they had gauged how the principal would lead or manage and developed some sense of how far the individual could be influenced, then they would decide whether to engage with or disengage from the principal's initiatives.

The more detailed conversations conducted with Brookdale teachers reveal some of the ways in which teachers made sense of each new principal's practices and coped with subsequent change initiatives. Their sense-making and coping strategies appeared to pass through several phases. First, they tried to educate the principal in the cultural norms, beliefs and expectations of the school so that initiatives would be congruent with the school culture. Next, if education was not successful, they tried to negotiate with the administrator in order to reduce the impact of proposed changes on the way the school operated. If all else failed and the principal was determined to proceed, they reduced their interaction with the principal and marginalized him or her until the individual had to admit defeat, use administrative authority or leave.

The principals discussed here are the predecessor, Gordon, and the incumbent, Jim.

Stage One — Education

Jim's arrival highlighted the educational process and the strategies teachers used to make the new principal aware of their expectations for him. Some tactics were subtle, some less so, but teachers understood the task at hand. One said, "I think we knew that he was a new principal, that we would probably have to sort of show him the ropes." One tactic they used was to talk within Jim's hearing about what was the expected norm of behavior that teachers had of Brookdale principals.

> When the new air conditioning system was installed in the main office, the doors had to be closed. The students saw this and got a message that the open-door policy had changed. Jim heard my comment about the doors, and, despite the air conditioning system, he left the door [to the hallway] open a crack.

This teacher stood outside of Jim's partially open office door and talked to the school secretary about students' reactions to the closed door, bringing to the fore the difficult experience that they had with Gordon's administration. Jim took the cue, which teachers noted.

I think we watched and saw how he responded to the kids. And unlike the previous principal, he actually talked *to* people. Talked to kids, talked with kids. Seemed to be very open and friendly and not someone who was going to impose his rule, but rather sort of work with other people.

The observations proved to teachers that Jim had learned from their attempts to educate him in the ways of the school and that he would try to incorporate this understanding into his practice. This gave them hope that initiatives would be consistent with the school's culture.

Stage Two — Negotiation

Although the culture in this school exhibited a robustness which helped teachers to survive the vision of each new principal, it also contributed to the difficulties staff experienced as they tried first to educate and then to influence and negotiate with new principals, especially those who did not "fit" their expectations. When Gordon was perceived not to have gained much from the education process, teachers moved into the second stage of negotiation, as they confronted his determination to proceed with unpopular decisions. For example, Gordon tried to institute new supervision policies, even when told openly by teachers that such changes were unnecessary given the student culture of the school. His actions contravened the one key image that they had of themselves — that of a small, community school without the problems of the larger, urban institutions. Even in the face of teachers' objections, he still attempted to introduce new supervision policies for the school.

He instituted supervision in the cafeteria. He instituted supervision in the halls. He wanted to move the exams into individual rooms instead of having them in the gymnasium. All these were opportunities to exercise control. And the problem is that he did this, as I say, he did this unilaterally. And then after, people would object to them and then he would have to backtrack.

At the end of two years under his administration, about one-third of the thirty-five teachers left the school, but included among those who remained were people with a strong commitment to the traditions of the school and to preserving their conception of their institution. This group tried to negotiate with Gordon, but this negotiation period was shortlived.

People had tried hard as intermediaries with Gordon, going in and saying "Gordon, that doesn't seem to be working or would you try consulting people instead of decreeing that?" Many of us were finally saying, "To hell with it. It's not working."

These more vocal and active individuals conveyed their colleagues' dismay with the administrator's actions. The anger rising in the staff was such that one teacher said that they "were just so passively aggressive and they maybe fomented others who maybe had the courage to go in and deal with Gordon." When even this failed to move Gordon from his decisions, teachers subverted his policies whenever possible by not participating. As one teacher put it, "We were used to getting only one answer or else not saying anything and just doing it the way we'd always done it."

One teacher said "You got people set in their ways and the Old Guard. If the principal can't get along with them, then you try to get rid of them." But Gordon, as a new principal who believed that changes were necessary to update practices in the school, decided to face the solidarity of the Old Guard who led the staff's disengagement from future initiatives.

Stage Three — Marginalization

Matters reached an impasse with Gordon to the point where staff no longer tried to negotiate with him when he acted contrary to the school's cultural norms. They even went to the extent of working to rule by removing their services beyond what they saw as necessary to maintain the programs for students. For Gordon, however, marginalization was not the end of his problems. Being excluded from conversations about issues that staff felt were important was bad enough, but then teachers took an even more active role in isolating Gordon from the students.

> We had sort of rebelled as a staff as well as students. We've had a few incidents of strike action among students. Many of the staff felt they wanted to be out there too, perhaps, but didn't.

Teachers' levels of frustration with the principal reached such a point of tension that several teachers took subversive action by subtly encouraging students to confront the principal, a situation which culminated in a locally publicized student walkout. This had the effect of causing Gordon to become "particularly despondent about the protest because the staff, many staff knew about it and no one told him." Through this action, teachers made Gordon realize that he had been marginalized and cut off from valuable information needed to make sound decisions.

This staff had developed the ability to withstand pressures to change when they felt that change was inappropriate. When negotiation failed, teachers withdrew their services. In another instance, a principal who had been sent by the district to "clean up" the school, and deal with some problem teachers, found that "then things stopped happening and he moved out." These patterns of response among the teachers had been nurtured and reinforced through experience with successive new principals. When I asked teachers how they felt about the rotation policy, one replied, "We found it very difficult to go through a whole slew of principals very quickly," and they developed means to cope with the changes. Instead of becoming engaged with the activities upon which each principal embarked, they tried to educate them and then negotiate adaptations to each new initiative. When these actions proved to be unsuccessful, they simply waited, knowing that the principal would be soon transferred. The same rule applied to them as it did to principals they did not like — "if you can survive three years, you'll get through it."

When the principal had a short tenure, teachers viewed suggestions for change with a "wait-and-see" attitude. As one teacher said about his colleagues, the regularity and rapidity of change "cynicizes them."

> Personally, I am not going to do all that work because in a couple of years, he's going to be gone and somebody else is going to come in and say, "Here's my idea. This is what we should do."

Although they were interested in improving their practice, Brookdale teachers had to be cautious about whether to invest effort in an innovation, especially as they knew that district policy required that every principal had to have a publicly stated vision of schooling and that each successive principal's new vision might be different from the last. When they saw the merits of an initiative, they cooperated willingly and became involved but even then they still mentioned their unease about its sustainability beyond the tenure of the current principal and his or her initiating vision. For this reason, initiatives that seemed congruent with their existing school culture and that were perceived as having the potential to survive beyond the current principal's tenure were embraced, while others were tolerated or avoided.

Each succession event for the teachers at Brookdale, then, did not necessarily mean positive or even lasting influence on their school's culture, though it did herald a new cycle of training for another novice administrator. With the announcement of each new round of principal rotation, teachers prepared themselves psychologically to begin the process of education and negotiation, and, if necessary, the marginalization of the principal. The frequency of the rotation of administrators simply meant that teachers' experience and expertise of managing the cycle became more sophisticated and their culture became much less subject to a principal's influence.

Conclusions

As with other well-intentioned organizational structures (Sieber, 1971), the systematic rotation of principals that was designed to stimulate change and facilitate its implementation produced the opposite effect. In this study, principal rotation more often resulted in teachers' resistance or apathy to change. Teachers' experiences with succession actually created barriers to their principals' initiatives. While in theory the policy aimed to rejuvenate principals and enable innovations to be transferred from one school to another, it actually led teachers collectively to harden their cultural positions *vis-à-vis* the principal and to develop strategies which reduced the long-term impact of principals and other administrators on their work. Teachers provided examples of how they progressed through a gradation of actions that they used first to limit the impact of the principal's initiatives on the school and then to bring the principal's initiatives into line with their concept of what was needed.

Teachers have few alternatives other than their service to the school with which to negotiate how change initiatives in their schools are adaptated, altered or terminated. Even with the advent of advisory councils, their voices may be dismissed if the advice is not deemed to be appropriate, or may be drowned out by other constituencies. All too often, teachers' voices are the silenced ones in times of educational reform (Goodson, 1992; Hargreaves, 1996). Nevertheless, we have seen that teachers' limited means can be effective in mounting covert or overt resistance to unwanted initiatives. For them, preserving their school's culture becomes paramount in the face of change agendas because it helps to define who they are as teachers and what they believe education ought to be.

A change of principals, then, can have far-reaching effects on the work that teachers do and how they perceive their place in schools. As Ball states,

> Change of leadership is a potentially profound threat to the established patterns of advantage and disadvantage. Furthermore, such a change can constitute a threat to the established patterns of reality . . . However, it is not simply the collapse of established patterns that causes problems in organization but also the instability created by the opposition of alternative interpretations of organizational reality. (Ball, 1987: 155–6)

In districts which do not have a principal rotation policy, teachers do not usually know whether the new leader will be principal for one year, ten years or longer. For this reason, they are forced to deal with and adapt to the potential instability and realignment of their organizational reality caused by a new leader. Parts of the school culture previously taken for granted have to be examined and evaluated. In these cases, negotiation of (and perhaps also commitment to) change is likely to be more active, overt and long-running since the energy that teachers expend may have long-term results.

Change of any kind is energy consuming. When teachers have experienced several succession events, they develop cultural patterns designed to reduce the energy that would otherwise be required to adapt to each new principal. Often, they are even able to marginalize the principal's role in the overall functioning of the school. In this way, they are not forced to re-examine or question their beliefs, values or norms and they know that any effort made by the principal to have them do so will likely evaporate with the next incumbent.

Ironically, some central office administrators and district members believe that a policy of succession helps to transplant successful change initiatives from one school to another and to turn failing or faltering schools into successful ones. They see principal rotation as a way to "scale up" educational change. The evidence of this study seriously challenges the contention that such succession strategies will necessarily or even usually be successful ones. In a system of regular rotation, nothing, it seems, fails to succeed like leadership succession. Elsewhere, Hargreaves and Earl (in press) show in one case study that even where a school is in the doldrums, and a new principal is indeed able to turn it around (suggesting, perhaps, that one key to being a good new leader is to follow a bad old one!), once that principal is transferred out through the succession policy, the improvements that were achieved are likely to wither.

What policies of succession rotation actually do change is the impact principals are able to have on their new schools while also changing the nature of the principal's role itself. Instead of teachers treating their principals as advocates for their school when there is competition for resources or teachers' and students' efforts need to be publicized, they begin to view the principal as an extension of the central office. The principal's loyalty, they feel, is toward the school district and its administration, not to the school community. It is, after all, the school district which will determine the principal's next placement. Within this district agenda, successful school changes come to be treated like merit badges or tokens of effectiveness for the principals who promoted them, tokens that can be cashed in for promotion or more desirable school placements. As one teacher observed, "Usually changes by a new person are brought about in order to leave a mark." Such perceptions reduce the likelihood of extensive participation by teachers in an initiative unless they see the benefits continuing beyond the tenure of the particular principal or unless they themselves want to commence careers in administration.

It is clear that school districts which practice principal transfer as a means to introduce change are, in fact, destabilizing the change process and reducing the likelihood of its success. When working with transient leaders, teachers develop a sense of what is common among their beliefs and values and use these to create solidarity against potential incursions by ambitious administrators, especially if those incursions strike at the very heart of what teachers believe their school to be. In effect, these incursions act as catalysts for teachers to work together to build a tacit understanding of their school and to create a school that embodies beliefs about what schools ought to be (Greenfield, 1984).

In the process of building this common understanding, teachers also seem to develop a sense of which aspects of their culture they are willing to sacrifice to appease or sidetrack the administrator; which they are willing to suspend temporarily pending the arrival of the next principal; and which they will not alter even in the face of administrative sanction. In the first instance, teachers use their treasured beliefs and practices as pawns to negotiate with administration so as to delay or alter the direction of the intended

change — in the hope that these sacrifices will be sufficient or that additional education of or negotiation with the principal will result in an initiative that is more relevant and acceptable to the school and its culture. When
these sacrifices do not appear to be sufficient, more painful sacrifices are
made and negotiations undertaken — sacrifices which are not forgotten, as
we saw in the open-door policy described earlier. Here more voices are
mobilized against the intended initiative and more serious negotiations are
undertaken in the hope of abandoning or altering the initiative. If principals are especially resolute or seem deaf to teachers' expressions of concern,
and if teachers feel that the principal's change initiative strikes at the heart
of what are their school's purposes as they see them, teachers will react by
withdrawing voluntary service, by maintaining only their basic contractual
obligations and by creating disruption in the operation of the school.

Implications

What have we learned from this study of leadership succession, school
culture and educational change? What implications are there for school districts, principals and teachers in schools?

First, the evidence of this study suggests that the policy of regularly
rotating principals within a system is a flawed one, perhaps fatally so. When
leadership succession is regular and routinized, teachers are likely to build
resilient cultures which inoculate them against the effects of succession. Principals are seen as being loyal to the system, more than to the school. Change
efforts are regarded as ephemeral and opportunistic, and teachers are
inclined to "wait them out." Systematic rotation of school principals seems
to be a career building strategy of school systems, rather than a strategy
that can really bring about successful and sustainable improvements in
schools. This is not to say that schools cannot benefit from new leaders,
nor that schools cannot benefit from new leadership. But trying to reinvig-
orate school leadership by bureaucratizing the rotation of principals is futile.
In this system, if teachers cannot outsmart their new principals, they at least
know that they can outlast them. As a result, many improvement efforts are
fated to fail. In the light of all this, school systems that currently have principal rotation policies might now do well to consider jettisoning them.

Second, this study, like many others, attests to the power of teacher
culture as a great promoter of or stubborn obstacle to educational change.
School leaders ignore school culture at their peril. Familiarizing oneself with
the school's culture prior to one's appointment, and taking time to understand that culture before making changes that will affect it are cardinal
principles of effective leadership (Fullan and Hargreaves, 1991). It is not
necessary for new principals to endorse all aspects of their schools' existing cultures, but it is important to understand and respect them. Moreover,
this culture of accumulated wisdom and experience is not just something

that principals can learn *about* as they try to manipulate it for their own improvement purposes, but also something they can learn *from*, in order to develop themselves as leaders. Developing an understanding of culture should, in this sense, be a top priority of all leadership training programs in education.

Third, the power of teacher culture resides in and reinforces the fact that principals are not the only leaders in their schools. They do not have a monopoly on vision and wisdom. Schools have found and informed teacher leaders as well, who help shape their schools' cultures, and will defend them to the last. Locating, respecting and collaborating effectively with such teacher leaders are strategies that will significantly enhance a principal's impact when he or she takes up a new position in another school.

Last, the data from the more detailed case study of Brookdale suggest that making particular school sites into training grounds for new principals can create monumental problems for the schools unless the teacher leadership in the schools is so strong and pervasive that it can resist the practices of novice principals, or play an active and constructive part in the leadership development of such principals.

Institutionalized leadership succession does not seem to have succeeded. Few bureaucratic mandates do. The keys to success instead lie elsewhere — in more complex, long-running processes of leadership development, school improvement and professional growth that cannot be locked up neatly in an inflexible implementation plan.

References

Aquila, F. (1988) The systematic rotation of principals: administrative panacea or musical chairs? *The Clearing House*, 61 (January): 236–8.

Bacharach, S. and Conley, S. (1989) Uncertainty and decisionmaking in teaching: implications for managing line professionals. In T. Sergiovanni and J. H. Moore (eds.), *Schooling for Tomorrow*, pp. 311–29. Boston, MA: Allyn and Bacon.

Ball, S. J. (1987) *The micro-politics of the school: towards a theory of school organization*. London: Methuen.

Beck, L. and Murphy, J. (1996) *The four imperatives of a successful school*. Thousand Oaks, CA: Corwin Press.

Boesse, B. (1991) Planning how to transfer principals: a Manitoba experience. *Education Canada*, 31(1), 16–21.

Carlson, R. (1996) *Reframing and reform*. New York: Longman.

Carlson, R. O. (1971) *School superintendents: careers and performance*. Columbus, OH: Charles E. Merrill.

Conley, S., Bacharach, S. and Bauer, S. (1989) The school work environment and teacher career dissatisfaction. *Educational Administration Quarterly*, 25(1), 58–81.

Creemers, B. (1996) The school effectiveness knowledge base. In D. Reynolds, R. Bollen, B. Creemers, D. Hopkins, L. Stoll and N. Lagerweij (eds.), *Making good schools*, pp. 36–58. London: Routledge.

Dalin, P. (1993) *Changing the school culture.* London: Cassell.

Darling-Hammond, L. (1995) Policy for restructuring. In A. Lieberman, (ed.), *The work of restructuring schools,* pp. 157–66. New York: Teachers College Press.

Day, C. and Baioğlu, A. (1996) Development and disenchantment in the professional lives of head teachers. In I. Goodson and A. Hargreaves (eds.), *Teachers' professional lives,* pp. 205–27. London: Falmer Press.

Elmore, R. F. (1987) Reform and the culture of authority in schools. *Educational Administration Quarterly,* 23(4): 60–78.

Finn, C. and Vanourek, G. (1998) *Selected readings on school reform,* 2(1). Washington, DC: The Thomas B. Fordham Foundation.

Fullan, M. (1993) *Change forces.* London: Falmer Press.

Fullan, M. and Hargreaves, A. (1991) *What's worth fighting for in your school?* Toronto: Ontario School Teachers' Federation.

Ganz, H. J. and Hoy, W. K. (1977) Patterns of succession in elementary principals and organizational change. *Planning and Changing,* 8(2–3), 185–90.

Giddens, A. (1991) *Modernity and self-identity.* Stanford, CA: Stanford University Press.

Greenfield, T. B. (1984) Leaders and schools: willfulness and nonnatural order in organizations. In T. Sergiovanni and J. Corbally (eds.), *Leadership and organizational culture: new perspectives on administrative theory and practice.* Urbana and Chicago: University of Chicago Press.

Goodson, I. (1992) Studying the teacher's life and work. In J. Smyth (ed.), *Critical discourses on teacher development.* Toronto: OISE Press.

Hargreaves, A. (1994) *Changing teachers, changing times: teachers' work and culture in the postmodern age.* Toronto: University of Toronto Press; New York: Teachers College Press, London: Cassell.

Hargreaves, A. (1996) Revisiting voice. *Educational Researcher,* January/February, 1–8.

Hargreaves, A. (1998) The emotions of teaching and educational change. In A. Hargreaves, A. Lieberman, M. Fullan and D. Hopkins (eds.), *International Handbook of Educational Change.* Dordrecht: Kluwer.

Hargreaves, A. and Earl, L. (with Moore, S. and Manning, S.) (in press) *Learning to change.* San Francisco: Jossey-Bass.

Hargreaves, A. and Fullan, M. (1998) *What's worth fighting for in education?* Buckingham: Open University Press.

Hargreaves, A. and Macmillan, R. (1995) Balkanized secondary schools and the malaise of modernity. In L. Siskin and J. W. Little (eds.), *The subjects in question: departmental organization and the high school,* pp. 141–71. New York: Teachers College Press.

Hart, A. (1993) *Principal succession: establishing leadership in schools.* Albany, NY: SUNY Press.

Leithwood, K., Begley, P. and Cousins, J. B. (1994) *Developing expert leadership for future schools.* London: Falmer Press.

Leithwood, K. and Menzies, T. (1996) Forms and effects of school-based management. Paper presented at the annual meeting of the University Council of Educational Administration, Louisville, KY.

Leithwood, K., Steinbach, R. and Ryan, S. (1997) Leadership and team learning in secondary schools. *School Leadership and Management,* 17(3), 303–25.

Little, J. W. (1982) Norms of collegiality and experimentation: workplace conditions of school success. *American Educational Research Journal*, 19, 325–440.

Macmillan, R. (1991) The relationships between the succession of the principal and school culture. Paper presented at the annual meeting of the Canadian Society for the Study of Education held at Kingston, Ontario.

Macmillan, R. (1996) The relationship between school culture and principal's practices during succession. Unpublished doctoral dissertation, University of Toronto (OISE), Toronto, Ontario.

Macmillan, R. (1998) Approaches to leadership: what comes with experience? *Educational Management and Administration*, 26(2), 173–84.

Miskel, C. and Cosgrove, D. (1985) Leader succession in school settings. *Review of Educational Research*, 55(1), 87–105.

Parkay, F. and Hall, G. E. (1992) *Becoming a school principal: the challenges of beginning leadership*. Needham Heights, MA: Allyn and Bacon.

Reynolds, D., Bollen, R., Creemers, B., Hopkins, D., Stoll, L. and Lagerweij, N. (eds.) (1996) *Making good schools*. London: Routledge.

Rosenholtz, S. (1989) *Teachers' workplace*. New York: Longman.

Schön, D. (1971) *Beyond the stable state*. New York: W. W. Norton and Company.

Senge, P. (1990) *The fifth discipline*. New York: Doubleday.

Sergiovanni, T. (1984) Leadership as cultural expression. In T. Sergiovanni and J. Corbally (eds.), *Leadership and organizational culture: new perspectives on administrative theory and practice*, pp. 105–14. Urbana and Chicago: University of Chicago Press.

Sergiovanni, T. (1995) *The principalship: a reflective practice perspective* (3rd edn). Boston: Allyn and Bacon.

Sieber, S. (1971) *Fatal remedies: the ironies of social intervention*. New York: Plenum Press.

Storr, A. (1994) *Solitude*. London: Harper Collins.

Weindling, D. (1992) New heads for old: beginning principals in the United Kingdom. In F. Parkay and G. E. Hall (eds.), *Becoming a school principal: the challenges of beginning leadership*, pp. 329–48. Needham Heights, MA: Allyn and Bacon.

4 Change Agentry and the Quest for Equity: Lessons from Detracking Schools

Jeannie Oakes, Amy Stuart Wells, Susan Yonezawa and Karen Ray

Many educators choose to teach because they believe in the power of equal educational opportunity, and they commit their professional lives to providing better life chances to disadvantaged children. Even so, the cultural gap between the rhetoric of equal opportunity and the reality of how society constructs it may be most visible in public schools, whose mission it is to realize equal educational opportunity. Currently, educators are under enormous pressure to make systemic reforms and restructure schools so that all students will reach high academic standards. This pressure resonates with the culture's ideals that schools serve all children well. Yet this policy pressure exists side-by-side with salient and persistent inequalities along race and social class lines, as low-income students of color experience fewer resources and less powerful learning environments — conditions about which current policy says little.

This chapter presents findings from ten racially mixed schools where change agents took the call to restructure their schools as a mandate to equalize schooling. These findings suggest strongly that equity-minded school reforms — those that are fundamentally redistributional across race and social class lines — face normative and political obstacles. These arise as educators and parents bent on reform confront the persistent American "dilemma" of inequality as it rears its head under the contemporary rubric of school restructuring (Myrdal *et al.*, 1944).[1] Even the most reform-minded educators are ill-prepared to deal with what ensues. As Hochschild (1984) explains, most educational reform literature is grounded in the premise that discriminatory beliefs and practices are at odds with basic American values, and (therefore) Americans will, if given the opportunity, naturally move away from past racist practices. However, the history of equity-minded reformers since the 1970s and the struggles faced by the change agents in the ten schools we studied suggest that this rarely happens.

Social Justice and Detracking in Ten Schools

In the last decade, growing numbers of educators across the nation have come face-to-face with the pedagogical, moral and ethical problems associated with tracking or ability grouping. They have been influenced by research showing the harmful effects of tracking on the achievement of low-track students as well as by studies demonstrating that race and class play a major role in students' track placements. Schools far more often judge African-American and Latino students as having learning deficits and limited potential (sometimes regardless of their prior achievement) and place these students disproportionately in low-track, remedial programs. Once placed, these students do not learn as much as comparably skilled students in heterogeneous classes; and they have less access than other students to knowledge, powerful learning environments and resources. Thus, school tracking practices create racially separate programs that provide minority children with restricted educational opportunities and outcomes (Oakes, 1985, 1995; Oakes and Guiton, 1995; Oakes and Lipton, 1990; Welner and Oakes, 1996).

Beyond Sorting and Stratification, a three-year longitudinal case study research project, followed the progress of ten racially and socioeconomically mixed secondary schools that have been undertaking "detracking" reforms, largely as a part of educators' efforts to close the gap between the rhetoric of equal opportunity and social inequality at the school. Our interdisciplinary research team used qualitative methods to examine changes in school organization, grouping practices and classroom pedagogy — what we call the technical aspects of these reforms. We also investigated how the schools tackle well-established school and community norms and political practices that legitimize and support tracking as a "common-sense" approach to educating students.

The ten schools vary in size from more than 3000 to less than 500 students. The schools are widely dispersed geographically, with one school in the Northeast, three in the Midwest, one in the South, two in the Northwest and three in various regions of California. The schools enrolled quite different mixes of white, African-American, Latino, Native American/Alaska Native and/or Asian students. We visited each of these ten schools three times over a two-year period. Data collection during our site visits consisted of in-depth, semi-structured, tape-recorded interviews with administrators, teachers, students, parents and community leaders, including school board members. We also observed classrooms and meetings of faculties, parent groups and school boards. We have reviewed documents and written field notes about our observations within the schools and the communities. Data have been compiled in extensive single case studies that form the basis of our cross-case analyses.[2]

Here we portray patterns across the schools. However, the stories we uncovered were unique to each place. The course that change agents took and the way they were responded to were deeply affected by the local community culture and politics, as well as national patterns around race, social class and gender. In the sections that follow, we describe these patterns and also suggest the rich variation among the schools' experiences.

A Commitment to Social Justice

In each of the ten schools, educators (and, in some places, community members) engaged in a critical scrutiny of school regularities and the part schooling plays in social inequality. These change agents were so bothered by the gap they found between the ideals and reality of schooling that they could no longer continue with the status quo.

For example, at Union High a former school board member expressed the district's equity intentions when it initiated plans for the new, consolidated school:

> I guess we just had a feeling that all kids could learn given the right opportunities, that really there weren't great differences in intellect between rich kids and poor kids, or it was just a matter of exposure.

Similarly, educators at highly regarded Liberty High chafed at the realization that, for all its national merit scholars and graduates at elite universities, the school's record of failure with low-income students of color was equally impressive. As Liberty High Principal Evan Payne put it, "If you're in the 'haves' group, it's one of the best places in America to go to high school. If you're in the 'have nots,' it's like a lot of places — it's full of failure" (Cooper, 1995).

Grant's reform was also driven by a concern for equity:

> The teachers I most connect with are the ones who really sense that we can't afford to waste anybody. We just can't afford to say that we have this group of kids [the high achievers] that will carry us. You know, they'll be our leaders . . . I'm convinced we don't live in a world like that anymore. We can't afford to lose those kids.

Tracking as a Structural Barrier to Equity

At each of these schools, change agents came to see tracking as a major impediment to their equity goals. At Rollinghills Middle School, for example, Assistant Principal Jane Griffen counseled the most alienated youngsters, and her work often took her to the South Side homes of bussed-in African-American students (Williams, 1995). Because Griffen believed that these students' inferior opportunities at school were at the root of most discipline problems, she chafed at white parents' efforts to exclude black students from the higher-level classes:

Part of my responsibility is to be respectful, but I have a hard time dealing with a racist . . . Sometimes I want to say [to white parents] ". . . you dare to sit there and put down children who may not have all the advantages that your child has but who are here working despite their disadvantages. You're sitting here telling me that they are not worthy to be in class with your child." This is a real personal issue with me.

Bearfield's principal made clear his awareness that tracking limits students' access to knowledge:

You know when you don't teach a kid anything but two plus two is four, then you give him a test and he has no idea why the one train doesn't catch the other train, we think that he's stupid. He's not stupid. Who the hell are we to decide who gets access to what learning?

And that tracking has long-term social effects:

Detracking issues are really the salvation of America. I mean, we can't build a high, medium and low America . . . I mean we really can't say to a kid in second grade, "You've been elected to low America. You're just — we're not going to give you access to learning, like we do to everybody else."

A Bearfield teacher we spoke to explained that white parents' resistance to eliminating honors is grounded in norms about race. "Quite frankly, I think the reason we have honors is parental pressure. It's a racial issue. An honors group is a White group."

In the wake of the 1992 Rodney King verdict and civil disturbance, Grant's students (several states away) targeted segregated classes as one of the major problems at the school. Reform-minded teachers and student leaders used this very public discussion about the racial composition of honors and regular classes as a mandate to detrack the school.

While we have only used examples from a few schools to illustrate the point, we found that a commitment to social justice lay behind change agents' detracking efforts at all ten.

The Easiest Part: Inventing New Structures

Within three years of Principal Evan Payne's arrival at Liberty High School, he and a cadre of strong teacher leaders had made considerable progress toward detracking. The school's entire ninth grade class was enrolled in heterogeneous two-hour English/history "cores" taught by partnered teachers, and many ninth grade college prep math classes were heterogeneous. Each of the cores was attached to one of the seven Liberty High School "families" composed of an administrator, a counselor, and a secretary. This arrangement — spurred in part by Liberty's involvement with the Coalition of Essential Schools — provided a greater degree of connectedness for the students and teachers. Students who would have traditionally been placed in a low-track English class because of low scores on the state's reading and writing proficiency exam were assigned to an English "Back-up" class designed to support learning in the core English classes.

Four tangible changes in the allocation of school resources, the schedule and registration practices made Liberty's ninth grade detracking possible: "buying down" class sizes to twenty students; providing "back up" classes with tutoring as a way to provide lower-achieving students with a double-dose of instruction; arranging common planning time for teacher-teams who shared "core" classes; and shifting from students' "self-scheduling" to their counselors deliberately composing balanced sections of the core. Professional development promised to boost teachers' knowledge and skills around thematic curriculum that provided the English and social studies departments with opportunities to collaborate. These changes were to support Liberty's goal of providing all of its ninth graders with access to high-quality, high-status, heterogeneous courses.

Like these educators at Liberty High, change agents in each of the ten schools seized opportunities provided by a wide range of current "reforms" to help them change their schools in ways that would better serve low-income, non-white kids. Two joined the Coalition of Essential Schools, two affiliated with networks of middle schools implementing Carnegie's *Turning Points* reforms, and two became part of their state's project providing funding for "restructuring" schools. Two others had been charged by their districts to develop special magnet programs, and two had reorganized as a consequence of district consolidation. Change agents used these more comprehensive reform contexts as a framework for altering tracking.

The ultimate goal at each of the schools was to provide greater access and academic achievement for low-track (disproportionately minority) students, while maintaining quality for traditionally high-achieving (mostly white) students. Each of the schools approached this ambitious goal by making changes in basic school structures, believing that such changes would lead to fundamental changes in curriculum, instruction and learning in heterogeneous classes. In addition to reducing or eliminating the number of track levels in academic subjects at various grade levels, the schools did such things as create new schedules; reorganize teachers into teams; balance class enrollments; permit students to double-up classes in particular subjects or take summer classes that allowed them to "jump" to a higher track; provide all students access to honors programs; and create opportunities for students to get extra help to master the standard curriculum, for example in "back up" classes.

In addition to these organizational changes, some teachers at each of the schools adopted new classroom strategies they believed would permit students to show their ability in previously unrecognized ways — e.g., Socratic Seminars, experiential curriculum — such as project-based science and interactive math, reduced use of textbooks and cooperative small group learning. Other teachers developed assignments that would challenge students of varying ability levels. Some invented new assessment techniques to even out the playing field in heterogeneous classes. Many developed more multicultural curricula, in an effort to make knowledge more accessible to all students.

Challenging Normative Regularities

The strongest force behind Bearfield Middle School's detracking efforts is its charismatic principal, Ben McCall, who had formerly been the principal at the community's all-white junior high. McCall worked diligently and skilfully to convince his faculty that detracking (and the team structures and multicultural curriculum that he thought necessary to support it) was key to pursuing his commitment to equality in their newly consolidated, racially mixed community. But even for McCall, the idea that detracking was a "sensible" reform did not come easily. As McCall described his conversion from a "tracker" to a "detracker," it became clear that adopting this reform challenged deeply felt convictions about how schooling should proceed:

> I really liked [a former district administrator], but she and I were at totally different ends of the spectrum. She was anti-grouping and tracking and I was a tracker and a grouper. I was just finishing my degree so I was at [the university] all the time. She just laid all this research on me that was anti-tracking and I said "Well, where's the research on my side of the fence?" She said, "Ben, there isn't any" . . . I looked one whole weekend at [the university library] and I couldn't find anything to support it and then [the administrator] and I went out to lunch that lasted till about six o'clock at night. She was right and I was wrong. When the light finally went on it was like holy shit! I was wrong.

None of the ten schools found its organizational and instructional changes easy to implement. The major difficulty, however, did not stem from the technical challenges these changes presented. Of course, there were some technical glitches along the way. But far more difficult than these were the challenges these reforms presented to educators' and communities' conventional wisdom about what secondary students are like and what good schools should be like. Moreover, because these changes were redistributive — i.e., they fundamentally altered how the schools allocated their most precious resources including time, teachers, materials and high-achieving students — they challenged traditional ways of thinking about "merit" and which students "deserve" the best that schools have to offer.

At each of the ten schools, change agents grappled with conventional norms that prevented them and others from having high expectations for all students, and from creating structures that press all students toward high levels of academic competence. Each school's reform effort was jeopardized, not only by those who actively resisted reform, but also by well-intentioned educators whose everyday "common-sense" actions unwittingly reinforced and reconstructed the logic behind traditional grouping practices (Wells and Serna, 1996). In the process of implementing structural and technical changes, they confronted (mostly) taken-for-granted conceptions of intelligence and ability, racial differences and merit, and deeply entrenched traditions of what is valued curriculum and appropriate practice at the schools.

Educators attempting to build commitment for detracking struggled with increasingly outmoded conceptions of intelligence, some of which reflect deep-seated racist and classist attitudes and prejudices. These conceptions played out in school as educators interpreted the skills and knowledge that educationally and economically privileged parents pass on to their children as innate intelligence — interpretations that guide decisions about track placements and the learning opportunities afforded to students in different tracks. Once these differences in "innate intelligence" were identified, bureaucratic efficiency dictated that the best way to accommodate these differences is to sort students into separate classes and provide them with differentiated curricula. Detracking challenged all of these norms.

Laura Miller — a veteran teacher at Rollinghills Middle School — was the parent of children in Mansford City's Enriched Program and the teacher of Regular students. Miller was unhappy with the elite cliquishness and an uninspired academic curriculum that her own Enriched children experienced at school, and she was enormously saddened by the disheartened and self-deprecating attitudes of her Regular students, whom she saw as far more capable than they saw themselves. In her search for better pedagogy, Miller regularly attended summer workshops on Gifted Education at the University of Connecticut. There, she learned through interaction with other gifted education specialists that Mansford's rigidly exclusionary grouping practices and stodgy Enriched curriculum didn't conform to the "best thinking" in gifted education. A gifted educator from another state first suggested to her that gifted youngsters might be better served in heterogeneous classrooms — a message she brought back to Rollinghills.

Multiple Ways to Be Smart

As agents in each of our ten schools worked to change structures and instructional techniques, they simultaneously challenged themselves and their colleagues to adopt the view that all students could achieve at very high levels, and to communicate through the schools' structures and practices that they expected them to do so.

"Challenge" projects at Green Valley often provide students with several options as to what they might do to complete the requirement. During a *Romeo and Juliet* lesson, for example, a student may earn challenge credit by reciting part of the play, writing a contemporary script for the play, or researching the fashion of the time and submitting a portfolio of drawings and text. According to one teacher, these opportunities have enabled some of Green Valley's "non-gifted" students and its lower achieving Latino students, who traditionally have not been exposed to Shakespeare, to prepare elaborate responses to their experiences with the play.

> Oftentimes they're really quite adept at drama. They like it a lot. So they enjoy going in front of their peers, performing. And that's generally the one they will choose — something that's a performance. They also like memorizing. The kids who can't do well on tests for example — I find it quite odd, and I'd like to do some research on this sometime — have wonderful memories. They will take a speech and do a dramatic interpretation of a speech.

Educators at a number of schools used new theories about the multi-dimensional nature of intelligence to explain and dignify racial differences in students' academic performance and school behavior. This new understanding led teachers to see diverse instructional strategies as legitimate ways to press all students to achieve. At some schools, educators gave greater emphasis to hard work and persistence, as opposed to conventional conceptions of ability. One Plainview teacher, for example, told us she doesn't believe in the traditional concept of intelligence. Rather, her view is that high achievement stems from a *different motivational level. A student who has more faith in his or her ability, or more confidence, that student is going to be a higher achiever.* A team of Bearfield teachers decided that low ability shouldn't preclude students from an award for being outstanding. They agreed to nominate a student who *is not perfect, but works industriously.* At the same time, this group bypassed a high-achieving student, *because he's not working hard for his ability.*

Creating structures and school cultures that redefine who is smart and that make "honors" possible for every student challenges powerful school norms. Educators at the schools were far from unanimity on these matters. Despite some teachers' efforts to reconceptualize intelligence as multi-dimensional, developmental, and manifest equally across racial groups, traditional conceptions retained a firm hold.

Grant's experience was quite typical. Many teachers held fast to a traditional view of students' abilities, and stubbornly resisted changes on that basis. But even Grant's reform-minded language arts teachers struggled with ways to judge the work of students who may be very intelligent, but who have not learned how to *jump through the hoops* traditionally expected of top students. As one teacher told us,

> Some people give me real fine indications of their intelligence, but they're not getting the grade, because the grade is the reward for the hoops. As a teacher, it would be nice to just say, "God, you're a really smart person. I'd like to give you an 'A.'" But that would then degenerate into "I like you, so I'm gonna give you an 'A'" . . . I'm not sure, when the grading comes out, I'm not sure how I'm gonna handle this, really.

Teachers at several of the schools reveal vestiges of a nativist view of intelligence. For instance at King Middle School, one administrator commented that the school's open structure and climate works best for "those kids in the upper quartile who have the work ethic, and are not just *innately bright and lazy.*" A Bearfield teacher also revealed this conception in describing high-achieving students at the school: "Most honors kids are just academically talented. Few of them have a lot of *native intelligence.* Most of them are quote, unquote 'good kids' — ones who will study without you telling them to."[3]

Teachers who are entertaining newer developmental and multidimensional conceptions of intelligence must withstand the scrutiny of skeptical parents who fear they have much to lose if traditional conceptions are altered. For instance, a Plainview High English teacher created a heterogeneous American Studies class after reading research persuaded her that neither society nor schools really understand intelligence or know how to measure it. When she presented her research to parents — at the principal's request — her message was not well received, particularly by those parents whose children were in Advanced Placement classes. According to the teacher, "if you were raised under the system that said you were very intelligent and high achieving, you don't want anyone questioning that system, OK? That's just the way it is." She said that what parents were most threatened by was how this research was going to be used by the school, and whether it would undermine advanced classes.

Confronting Racial Stereotypes

Stereotypical views of minority students ability and motivation for academic work also remained salient in schools and communities. In all schools, some educators drew connections quite openly between students' abilities and race and social class. For example, one educator lamented, "We're getting fewer honors kids, and that's just demographics." Another told us, "the percentage of academically capable . . . African-American students versus the percentage of white students is very disproportionate." In a third school we heard, "They [Native American students] don't have the support at home, and they don't have the ability."

In many cases, these racial differences in ability are attributed to differences in background and culture. For example, Central High's Latino population has traditionally been stereotyped as unmotivated. In the words of one social studies teacher:

> It's hard though! 'Cause there's only so much you can do with the kids. We don't get really well-motivated, well-educated kids. Most come from, not ideal family situations. They're not very well-motivated . . . and it's really hard to do anything in that situation. No matter what you do as teachers, there's just some kids, nothing is going to help them, or nothing is going to solve your problems.

Similarly, Green Valley has what some teachers term a *pear-shaped* academic population — light on high and middle achievers and heavy on low achievers. This, according to one teacher, "is a function of where we live." This teacher believes that demographic shifts make the college prep track inappropriate for everyone.

One Plainview AP teacher analyzed the gap between black and white student achievement, with this statement:

> You know, every time we do something, I think, how will we deliver to Afro-American students. I don't think that a lot of teachers here really know where these kids come from, and I don't think they've seen the houses that they live in. I mean, maybe they have, but . . . I guess it's really hard to realize that somebody's mother might have been 15 when they were born, and they live with granny, and there's no books in the house. You can't give . . . that kid doesn't have an equal chance against the kid whose mother and father are both working and have a nice home with a stereo . . .

Another explained:

> You know, groups of African-Americans go through the normal solid high school program, but it's rare to find one that . . . has an ambition to start off with the Freshman Biology, and wants to get that extra science in. Again, I'm not sure why. Part of it, I think, is skills. Part of it, I think . . . has to do with attitude towards excelling or ambitions for the future. I think most of the African-Americans I talk to have much more limited ambitions.

At Explorer, many Native students have been identified as "communication disordered," an official school classification which is not a learning disability, but refers to Native students' verbal discomfort. It is a classification that seems to ignore a number of facts about Native students, such as the different use of language, and learning not to speak out, compete for attention, or upstage their peers. Some in the Union community maintained classist and racist stereotypes of the low-income white and African-American students at the school; Union staff regularly heard comments like, "Why'd they build such a nice school for those students?"

These culturally and racially specific views of intelligence were echoed in the voices of some educators, parents and community members we interviewed at each of the ten schools. Thus, both educators' and community resistance to detracking reforms reflected larger social conflicts over whether the culture and style of life of middle-class whites shape schools' definition of valued knowledge, and thus lead educators and parents to equate middle-class thinking with "intelligence."

Confronting Political Pressures around Race and Class

Reformers also battled resistance and opposition from those in the communities and on their own faculties who feared that detracking would jeopardize the benefits they received from the status quo. The pressure placed on most schools by savvy parents who want their children enrolled in the "best" classes may be the most salient of all of the responses to detracking. Parents of high-track students have been clearly advantaged both in educational opportunities and status. And because nearly all the schools previously operated competitive systems, permitting only a small percentage of student slots in "high"-track classes, these parents have had few options but to push to have their children better educated than others. Because schools need political support — not only for funding and physical resources, but also for credibility — tracking policies that provide advantages to more privileged children have been exchanged for the political credit that more advantaged and involved parents bring to a school.[4] Schools and districts respond to parental resistance by reigning in the reform; and change agents sometimes suspend their efforts out of frustration.

Protecting Privilege as "Deserving"

Parental resistance is particularly contentious among parents who feel their school is neglecting "gifted" students, or using resources "meant" for one group of students on other, "less deserving" students. This belief is especially salient among a group of white parents at Liberty High, nicknamed the "Mothers of Excellence." According to one:

> Liberty overlooks how very important it is to academically orient kids to get an academically stimulating education. Sometimes in Liberty it gets treated as a luxury. Oh, these kids are bright, they're going to do fine anyway. Well in reality, that's not true. A lot of these kids, if they're not stimulated, are going to fall back . . . losing these kids, losing any kids is a tragedy. And it bothers me when, somehow, the district acts like losing a bright kid is not as tragic as losing the kids at the bottom.

Similarly, some white parents in the Bearfield community feel that their tax dollars are wrongly used to supplement the education of the African-American community's children:

> People from Allison Park, there's whites in there and there's blacks in there. It's mostly black . . . First of all, they don't pay taxes like we pay taxes out in Dalton. And I don't think that's right that I have to pay those kind of taxes when they don't but they still go to our school . . . it has brought down our school system and I don't feel that it should . . . I'm not a racist, but I am — I don't want my school being brought down because of a lower caliber.

Central High's faculty proposed a new "custom calendar" so that students could earn course credit at a more individualized pace. The school year would be divided into nine-week quarters, followed by two-week intercessions. During the intercessions, students could make up lost credits or repeat classes. The custom calendar was touted as complementing detracking because it would allow lower-achieving students to make up work or get ahead during the intercession. Central's principal reasoned,

> The paradigm here is that it takes every student . . . 180 days to learn Algebra 1, and my question is, how valid could that be? Aren't there some students who might need a couple more days to do that? Now is it better to tell that student that they're a failure and can't learn because they can't learn it in 180 days, or is it better to give them a few extra days to do it?

The custom calendar had features created with the special needs of migrant students and other at-risk students in mind. Migrant students often are away from the school for long periods of time; if the custom calendar had been adopted, migrants would be able to complete classes within a nine-week quarter. The parents who spearheaded the move to defeat the custom calendar initiative did so on the grounds that the majority of students were well-served by the existing calendar and the custom calendar was designed to benefit only a few. While most Central faculty favored the custom calendar, the proposal was denounced by powerful parents in the community and more conventional teachers. An assistant principal realized only later that, although the calendar was not framed as a redistributive policy, it was seen as a symbol of policymaking aimed at helping students traditionally disadvantaged by the system (at this school low-income, limited-English-speaking Latino students) and taking from those who benefit from the status quo. He felt the custom calendar was used as a symbol of a liberal ideological effort to take away from the haves and give to the have-nots.

Even in Green Valley, where parent opposition to detracking is mild, one district administrator claims that the high school actually loses a fair amount of disillusioned white, middle-class students to private schools:

> If they [white parents] don't feel that there's a program here that is giving their child every opportunity, they pull their kids out and put them in private school . . . I keep saying, "The educational opportunities are there if your child chooses to take advantage of them." I think parents . . . are saying, "All of the emphasis is on giving kids a second chance, a third chance, a fourth chance" . . . The teachers are draining themselves trying to nurture kids who come to school with nothing. The other [parents] are saying, "What's in it for my child?"

One important lesson we learned from the schools in our detracking study is that many parents of students in high-track classes exude a strong sense of entitlement. According to these parents, their children are entitled to "more" — i.e. resources, teacher time, challenging curriculum and better instructional strategies — because they are more intelligent and talented than other students. Strongly related to this sense of entitlement is the social construction of intelligence and the white, middle- and upper-middle-class cultural capital inherent in such a construction (see Oakes *et al.*, 1995b).

A counselor at one high school in our study noted that parents of honors students will not take time to listen to teachers or administrators about pedagogical reasons for doing away with the honors track. She said they are simply "not as concerned with the whole [school] as much as they should be" (Datnow, 1995: 63). Another school's coordinator of "gifted" programs lamented that parents were not interested in the substance of what she offered students in heterogeneous settings, only in maintaining the status that a separate and different program brought their children. An assistant principal in one of the high schools noted that "many upper-class, professional parents hold occupational positions in which they work toward equity and democracy, but expect their children to be given special treatment" (Ray, 1995: 2).

In part these fears are reasonable, given the higher education system in the US and how it forces high schools to differentiate between various courses and, ultimately, the students in those courses. We have seen in the schools that the demands of competitive, high-status universities and politically powerful parents who want their children to attend these institutions drive K–12 educators to use differentiated credentials as exchange value for students in separate and distinct tracks.[5] Given that the parents most likely to influence curriculum policymaking at the school level are generally those who are college educated themselves, the symbiotic relationship between tracking and stratification at the secondary level and the college admissions process again perpetuates the inter-generation transmission of advantage. Parents who have attended universities, particularly high-status ones, have a clear understanding of what their children's high school transcripts should look like to assure them a seat in the college of their choice.

For example, in several of the senior high schools we are studying, parents consider the College Board's Advanced Placement courses, with strict entrance requirements and an academically rigorous, test-driven curriculum as critical to making their children competitive for slots in the best colleges. This parent pressure overrides the concerns of educators at these schools who complain that the Advanced Placement curriculum neither provides students with access to engaging subject matter nor involves them in inquiry-based learning experiences that teachers often see as consistent with high standards.

Fear of Bright, White Flight

Parental opposition understandably leads to a fear that white and wealthy parents will abandon the schools, taking the schools' political credibility with them. This fear compels even reform-minded individuals to proceed with caution, and sometimes retain programs they find problematic.

Rollinghills Middle School's current tracking practices grew out of its county-wide, court-ordered school desegregation plan. Many educators and parents told us that the district created its four-track structure expressly to appease fearful white parents, who, according to one Rollinghills teacher, *wield a big stick.* Consequently, Rollinghills proceeded slowly and strategically with detracking, knowing, as Assistant Principal Jane Griffen put it, that for white parents only "part of their agenda is 'I want a challenging academic program for my child,' and part of their agenda is that it can't be that way if there are twelve black children in the classroom with them."

At Plainview, Principal St. John is convinced that the AP course offerings are essential to maintaining the white student population in Plainview. His allegiance to the AP program is grounded in his prior experiences as an administrator at Hamilton, a nearby suburban high school. The student population at Hamilton shifted from all-white and upper-middle-class to all-black lower-middle to poor in a matter of ten years. Mere mention of Hamilton and "what happened there" serves as a not-so-subtle reminder of the need to appease white parents. Consequently, Plainview's principal and many faculty feel they must encourage minority achievement within the present tracked system, rather than attempt to disassemble tracking. Bearfield's superintendent is also deeply concerned about the potential "white flight" that might ensue if the white community perceives that schools are catering to the African-American community. As he put it:

> If we're going to start talking about all kinds of other things like equity in schools, how are we going to train the parents to understand what we're even talking about? Because what's going to be perceived is "You're just trying to give me a bunch of mumbo-jumbo so you can take care of those black kids" . . . We're going to upset people and spend a lot of money . . . and what'll happen is the white people will leave the system.

Silence of the Less Powerful

The political influence of uncomfortable high-track parents was balanced by other voices only rarely. At most schools, parents of lower-achieving and minority students have relatively little political clout, and have, for the most part, been silent.

For example, Native American parents were mostly uninvolved at Explorer Middle School. Some felt that the school has not approached the Native community in an appropriate manner. Others blamed an ugly racial history in the community. Adults in the community remember Natives being beaten in school for speaking their language, and many were sent away to boarding schools. Native parents and community members told us that, when they were young, stores and businesses in the town posted signs that read "No Natives or dogs." Only two Natives work at Explorer, and many community members cite racist hiring practices. The last superintendent discontinued a process begun by his predecessor of working with the Native community to address student problems, angering and further alienating the community.

At Rollinghills, African-American parent voices were also much quieter than those of whites, and Rollinghills Vice Principal Jane Griffen told us, "They do not have the same powerful network as the white parents do." Only one African-American sat on the School Board, largely because of the gerrymandered downtown subdistrict, and one Rollinghills teacher told us, "The African-Americans who are principals and superintendents . . . are afraid to speak out because their jobs may be in jeopardy."

We heard various reasons from educators for this silence. Some Grant teachers said that they have trouble contacting parents of failing students. Teachers at Grant and Bearfield told us that they don't have time for all their students, so they concentrate on those students who seem to have concerned parents. One Bearfield teacher stated that he focuses on students who have two parents, because he fears his efforts might be wasted on single-parent children.

Many minority parents told us that the school makes little effort to reach out to them, and that they feel uncomfortable at the school. This problem may be exacerbated at schools that draw their minority populations from outlying areas. For example, a major problem at Rollinghills is the school's uneven dissemination of information about the heterogeneous program. Although the teachers meet yearly with parents of prospective sixth graders at all *neighboring* feeder schools, many parents from the city are uninformed about the programs available at Rollinghills, especially the heterogeneous program. Efforts to reach out to city parents have enjoyed minimal success. Central and Green Valley, which both have large numbers of Spanish-speaking parents among their student populations, find that this language barrier also inhibits efforts to generate support for their reform efforts (see Yonezawa and Williams, 1995).

Going It Alone

At many schools, parental dissatisfaction causes nervous district office personnel to "pull in the reigns" on school reform efforts. Reformers at Liberty, Union, Explorer and Central all confront strong skepticism or opposition from their district offices. And although the Bearfield district has a written policy denouncing tracking, district officials make no attempt to enforce it. Some are clearly uncomfortable with Bearfield's detracking efforts. In the Spring of 1993, Bearfield found that their Comprehensive Tests of Basic Skills (CTBS) scores had dropped slightly in some areas, although they remained steady or even improved in others. This slight decline was used by district-level officials as "proof" that heterogeneity was negatively impacting achievement. Due to pressure from the district office, Bearfield focused during the 1993–94 school year on raising test scores — a focus that most of the faculty felt was misguided:

> Our CTBS did not [go up] . . . And so [district officials] were riding Ben [the principal] last year. We could feel it when we came back to school this year. That the stress was there, we need to get these scores up. And it was not like Ben. And we spent so much of this year worrying about tests, standardized tests. And . . . uh, it's unfortunate. It's unfortunate because that's not what we're about and that's not what we should be about.

Union also is hampered by equivocation by its district administration. According to the vice principal:

> What little support that we have for the program is being eroded. Then our program will be gutted, and they'll come in here and build walls in those centers upstairs, and the chairs in their rows, and it will be business as usual . . . It will be some external force that causes us . . . not to be able to do what it is we're trying to do here . . . We've seen some of that already. Chinking away at the armor here and there.

As a consequence of such reform ambivalence at the district office, few change agents believe they have support or buffering, and most feel they face enormous community pressures alone.

What Have These Change Agents Achieved?

Surprisingly enough, at a structural level, these ten efforts must be judged to have been successful. All of the schools reduced some, and many eliminated all, of their basic or remedial courses. Most provided all students with access to the schools' most challenging or "honors" curriculum, and several developed a common curriculum in key academic subjects at some grade levels. All became far more attentive to providing greater curricular access and richer learning opportunities to low-income students of color.

In fact, in several instances we found detracking actually convinced educators that low-track students are far more capable of engaging with higher-level curriculum and instruction in heterogeneous groups than they had previously thought. As one middle school counselor put it, "Heterogeneous grouping has made teachers think differently about all kids. They see more potential in kids; they will work harder with them and their needs." Other educators' comments affirm that this has indeed been the case. For example, one told us, "The program has done amazing things for standard-track kids."

Moreover, a number of teachers across the ten schools suggested the mechanisms through which detracking enabled them to improve the quality of student work in their classrooms. One attributed the change to an atmosphere of higher expectations in heterogeneous classes. All of sudden somebody says, "You can do this!" Another credited the greater access to knowledge in saying, "Heterogeneous grouping helps to stimulate, motivate students because of just the exposure that the students have." Others suggested that heterogeneous grouping makes more salient to teachers the need to employ a broader array of teaching strategies, and the greater opportunities that result enable former low-track students to achieve. A senior high school English teacher suggested how this greater exposure might take place when she told us:

> [the student] who normally wouldn't succeed does succeed because the teacher is using strategies that appeal to various learning modes. Roles change, reverse. More time is spent on concepts, themes, thinking about things, projecting, making predictions, connections between the works read.

At Plainview Senior High, several states away, another teacher echoed this view as she told us how she set up her heterogeneous class to permit a lot of independent student learning, as well as dynamic class discussions that engage students of different backgrounds and academic strengths. Doing so, this teacher believes she has created a learning environment in which she sees more students looking for what she *calls the genius within them.* Her multidimensional classroom, she explains, allows students to develop insight into their own ways of knowing and learning, and when they do that, they become highly motivated students in the broader sense of the word, thirsty for a greater understanding of the world around them. Several teachers told us that a more individualized, yet interdependent approach to teaching and learning may be particularly helpful in racially and socioeconomically mixed schools, in which students bring different ways of knowing to school.

Some of the schools have even made headway in ameliorating racial tensions in their schools. For example, by emphasizing themes such as "Building a community of friends" and "Different is not deficient," Bearfield Middle School has defused the racial disharmony rampant in its surrounding community and has harmoniously brought the African-American and white communities together under their school's roof.

However, none of the change agents has achieved nearly the extent of detracking originally sought, and several worry that old patterns of inequality are being replicated within their schools' new, "detracked" structure. Most feel battered and bruised by their efforts to reform, and some have not survived as school leaders. They know now that they missed important lessons not taught by the change literature: a literature that generally neglects the unique problems encountered by schools implementing reforms designed to give more to our least powerful citizens — low-income and non-white students — in a societal culture that usually demands that they receive less. Most of the change agents that we observed were caught unprepared when the process and the shape of their equity-minded reforms were profoundly affected by norms and politics concerning race, gender, sexual orientation, language and socioeconomic status.

In response to normative and political pressures, all the schools have — intentionally or unintentionally — left some classes "out" of the reform, ensuring that the highest-achieving students can still get some sort of "special" treatment: separate honors, advanced, AP or Regents classes exist at all ten schools. These elite classes aid several of the schools in maintaining the delicate balance between satisfying the demands of an important parental power base and providing equitable opportunities for all students. Most of the students and families who "benefit" from these compromises are white.

For instance, the relatively small number of "gifted" parents in the Green Valley community are dissatisfied with the ninth and tenth grade heterogeneous English curriculum, but they tolerate the classes because honors classes are available in eleventh and twelfth grade. And, despite the fact that parents of gifted students are generally satisfied with the "standard" rich curriculum offered at King, no doubt they are further reassured that their children will be well served by the existence of the Regent's classes in the eighth grade. Grant High's effort to eliminate separate language arts honors classes has been particularly difficult because of the district-wide tradition of offering self-contained gifted classes at the elementary and middle school level. Some parents who are accustomed to this special treatment argue that their children cannot be well served in an integrated system. Thus, while Grant's principal initially condoned the changes being made by the language arts department, he has been influenced recently by a small but vocal group of parents of "gifted" children. On the basis of their complaints, the principal refused the department's request to eliminate separate honors classes for ninth graders in the 1994–95 school year. Consequently, the department will once again offer both honors classes with open enrolment, and regular classes with honors option at the ninth grade level. Green Valley's "gifted" parents are also used to special programs in the elementary and middle schools. They, too, express considerable discomfort about the absence of special treatment at the high school. Many Explorer parents are pushing for the resumption of pull-out programs; some even advocate separate all-day classes for gifted and talented and special education students.

Plainview also has an active parent group that works to preserve and expand the school's AP offerings: The PTO Executive Board, a fairly tight-knit group of almost all white parents, meets monthly with the principal to serve as his sounding board. One teacher noted that there is "such great community support for tracking . . . there's absolutely no way, and the administration would never want to do this anyway, that they would ever get rid of AP."

Because of these pressures, educators who are committed to change often try "to straddle the fence" between pleasing powerful parents and giving low-achieving students more access by reducing the number of tracks rather than dismantling the track structure. For example, Rollinghills Middle School offers parents a "choice" between tracked and detracked classes for their children, However, the shortage of African-American families choosing Rollinghills combined teams has been striking. Most teachers are not clear about whether African-American parents do not have good information about the combined teams, or whether they actively choose not to participate. Some — particularly the small number of African-American teachers — believe that the bussed-in African-American children have been deliberately excluded in order to keep the combined teams whiter than the rest of the school. Most years, the principal has assigned a handful of African-American students to the detracked teams to balance the large number of white choosers.

The problem with such strategies is that they reproduce a hierarchical structure supported by a culture that values the knowledge and life experiences of some students more than others. This allows white and wealthy parents to maintain very separate classrooms for their children and any lower-income or non-white students who "act white and wealthy," which means buying into the dominant culture view of the educational system as fair and meritocratic. This persistent tracking structure, albeit with fewer and ostensibly "higher" tracks, drives on-going curriculum differentiation which leads to unequal expectations and inevitably unequal standards for students of different racial, social class and cultural backgrounds. As Bearfield's principal put it bluntly:

> as our business manager, superintendent once told me, the power is neither black nor white; it's green — as in money. And that's where the power is. Rich people have clout. Poor people don't have clout.

Lessons from the Schools — Theories of School Change

Recent scholarship in educational change makes clear that the job of leading school reform goes far beyond bringing a generic set of technical and managerial skills to bear on a fairly predictable change process (e.g., Fullan, 1991; Hargreaves, 1994). The task of marshaling commitment and capacity for any particular school reform is complicated by the fact that those who are expected to change (teachers and students) and those who are expected to accept the changes (parents and other community members) assign their own meanings to changes and respond to them in ways that are consistent with their existing knowledge, beliefs and practices. Consequently, even when change agents are "successful," reforms are transformed as they make their may into the cultures and political milieu of particular schools.

Many of the reform leaders at these schools were reasonably well versed in the change literature and, understandably, fairly optimistic about their reforms' prospects for success. Depending on their fluency with the literature, these educators knew that change would likely not go forward precisely as planned (Elmore and McLaughlin, 1988; Sarason, 1990); that school reform is a process, not an event (Fullan, 1991); that change involves mutual adaptation (McLaughlin, 1976; Tyack and Cuban, 1995); that reforms will differ depending on the unique culture of each school (Sarason, 1982); that the change process is non-rational and non-linear (Louis and Miles, 1990; Wise, 1977); that successful policymakers set the conditions for effective administration but refrain from predetermining how those decisions will be made and, instead, charge local practitioners with the development of solutions (Elmore and McLaughlin, 1988; Firestone and Corbett, 1989); that schools are "bottom heavy" and "loosely coupled" (Elmore, 1983; Weick, 1976); and, of course, that we cannot mandate what matters (Elmore and McLaughlin, 1988; McLaughlin, 1976).

These school leaders saw themselves as change agents spearheading an ongoing process of improvement. Moreover, in accordance with the change literature, the detracking reforms had a healthy "bottom-up" beginning in all ten schools. Initially, at least, this "bottom" comprised only a fraction of each school's faculty and community; however, all of the schools' reform leaders understood the importance of establishing a culture of change (see Sarason, 1990). Thus, they need not plan merely to tinker with the technical but, rather, to create enabling structures which would help them to eliminate tracking and support their schools' ongoing quest for inquiry and improvement.

However, the difficulties these change agents faced connected in quite profound ways with racial and cultural politics in local communities and the larger society. By tackling detracking reform, each of the schools became entangled in larger cultural struggle (and ambivalence) over the meaning of equality and opportunity in racially mixed settings. As such, detracking, like other equity-minded reforms, differs from other school change efforts because it creates a struggle between individuals over scarce resources, and because it entails an ideological struggle over the meaning of culture as it is enacted in schools. These struggles created enormous tensions between schools and resistant community members, and they also fostered considerable friction within schools.[6]

The reformers we studied found little in the change literature to help them with these contentious aspects of their reform. Most of this literature, useful as it is to schools generally, is silent on matters of race and social class, and the politics of altering the distribution of access and achievement. Perhaps, this is because nearly all of this work assumes a relative neutral "change process," and, largely by omission, fails to consider how the race and social class make-up of faculty and students and/or the extent to which particular reforms attend to race and/or social class equity may impact the course of change.

Our findings suggest that our search for *basic* principles of change agentry and strategies for dealing with *typical* change barriers may blind us to how reform leadership must be contextualized in light of powerful and particular race- and class-linked meanings that particular reforms and their implementation engender in schools and communities (see Oakes *et al.*, 1996). In both the process and outcomes of their work, educators tackling reforms that expand access to status and opportunity also struggled to construct new meanings of equal educational opportunity in their schools while they struck new political arrangements necessary to democratize the school experience.

Lessons from the Schools — the Practice of School Change

This chapter has focused on change agents in racially mixed schools whose detracking efforts were driven by their concern for equity. There is much to be learned about reform from these schools in which social justice and diversity were central to the impetus, plans and processes of change. Their experiences suggest a cornerstone principle of school change: race and social class systematically affect the course of reform. The stories of these schools reveal that the major issue around tracking and detracking reforms is not which grouping strategy "works" best in the conventional sense. Educators grapple far more with normative and political issues around race, ethnicity and poverty than they do with developing the more technical features of a reformed, diversity-oriented school. Their experiences raise fundamental questions about whether or not society wants schools to push beyond the conventional meaning of equal educational opportunity, and whether and how policymakers and other decision-makers can enable educators to make the necessary structural and cultural changes.

The struggles of these ten schools deserve policymakers' and educators' attention because they can learn practical and political lessons from them. Their stories provide insight into the depth and complexity of detracking's connections with larger normative and political struggle. Through their experiences, we can broaden our understanding of the uniquely political nature of educational reform when social justice is its goal.

Effective and obvious strategies for dealing with these normative and political challenges do not emerge from these stories. However, these schools' experiences offer considerable insight into how educators might proceed thoughtfully — knowing, of course, that the profound dilemmas that schools will encounter as they detrack reflect deep cultural conflicts that are unlikely to be "settled" in the course of school reform. In that spirit we offer the following suggestions to equity-minded school reformers.

• Aim for the "ideal" of completely detracked schools, and eschew labeling and ranking of students on global categories. While you will probably need to proceed incrementally and slowly, keep clear on these ideals. Promise worried parents that, as you change the grouping structure, you will accommodate any child whose intellectual "gifts" are so extreme or whose disabilities are so severe that they require different schooling arrangements on a case-by-case basis, but not with new ways of differentiated grouping for particular classifications of students.

- Affirm the democratic values that detracking efforts embody and openly acknowledge that this is a reform with a moral as well as an empirical grounding. At the same time, however, share the empirical evidence about the problems of tracking and the promise of detracking in order to re-assure anxious parents and skeptical colleagues that your principled actions also have firm grounding in educational research. Bearfield's principal, Ben McCall, is only one of many who have found the research compelling as they struggle with decisions about what is both right and effective at their schools.

- Emphasize the educational high ground on which detracking rests, at the same time as being vocal about the social justice basis for reform. You can argue with legitimacy and conviction that detracking can leverage higher-quality teaching and learning for all students. Such an argument has considerable validity, since those teaching strategies and learning experiences that seem to work best for heterogeneous groups — those that actively engage students in rich and complex concepts and problems — are also those recommended for meeting the needs of gifted and talented students and raising academic standards generally. As such, detracking can be positioned as reform aimed at benefiting all students. This argument may not allay white, middle-class parents' anxieties about increased racial and social class mixing at school, but it rightfully moves the argument away from the contention that detracking reforms sacrifice the needs and interests of high-achieving children in the interest of equity. Of course this argument will only have political salience if it is backed by real changes in teaching practices in detracked classrooms.

- Cultivate a climate of continuous learning and inquiry among faculty and parents, acknowledging that it takes serious investigation about all of these issues for educators and parents to take risks with practices that society has taught us "work" to our children's advantage. Challenge explicitly the existing norms of intelligence, student ability and what is valued knowledge. Promise to treat the reform itself as part of the inquiry process, and then investigate the impact of any changes. Have faculty use at least some of their professional development time around detracking to examine the relationship between common-sense conceptions of intelligence, student ability, and valued knowledge and social factors — e.g., race, class and gender. The growing bodies of literature on the developmental and multidimensional nature of intelligence and learning and about the relationship between culture, social context, and cognition can help ground these discussions of values, beliefs and "common sense."

- Finally, make sure that all voices are represented and heard as you deliberate about detracking. This will probably require a deliberate and tenacious effort to bring parents and community members from different racial groups and socioeconomic positions to the same table to talk. For example, Grant High's language arts department created and met with a detracking advisory group comprised of a highly heterogeneous group of parents who visited classrooms and helped shepherd reform. However, simply bringing diverse groups together isn't enough. Genuinely democratic deliberation among such groups will likely require that change agents develop strategies for helping parents of lower-track students speak with as much confidence and sense of entitlement about what they want for their children as the parents of high-achieving children usually do. White middle-class parents must be allowed to struggle openly and in the presence of those who are not white or middle class with the contradictions between their very understandable hopes for their individual children and an educational system that is manifestly politically and academically skewed in their favor. While this is enormously difficult, it is ultimately neither respectful nor effective for educators to pit themselves as advocates for children who are disadvantaged by the status quo against the parents of children who benefit from it. Only with the full participation of all segments of the community can educational change agents hope to engage schools in grappling seriously and effectively with the gap between equal educational opportunity as it is expressed in the American Creed and the reality of educational failure of so many students.

Notes

1 While Myrdal focused on racial discrimination and inequality in the US, we extend this idea to include social class, gender and sexual preference.
2 For a full description of this study and its methodology, see Oakes *et al.*, 1995b.
3 For an elaborated discussion of how conceptions of intelligence were struggled over at the schools, see Oakes *et al.*, 1995a.
4 For a more complete discussion of this issue, see Wells and Serna, 1996.
5 K–12 is the grade span of US primary and secondary education.
6 We argue elsewhere that if we conceive of schools as "mediating institutions," themselves situated within locally constructed "zones" of normative and political mediation that embody larger cultural patterns, we can better understand the profound differences between equity-minded reforms and other change efforts. See Oakes *et al.*, 1996.

References

Cooper, R. (1995) *Liberty High School*. Los Angeles: Research for Democratic School Communities, UCLA Graduate School of Education and Information Studies.

Datnow, A. (1995) *Central High School.* Los Angeles: Research for Democratic School Communities, UCLA Graduate School of Education and Information Studies.

Elmore, R. F. (1983) School decentralization: who gains? who loses? In J. Hannaway and M. Carnoy (eds.), *Decentralization and school improvement: can we fulfill the promise?* pp. 33–54. San Francisco: Jossey-Bass.

Elmore, R. F. and McLaughlin, M. W. (1988) *Steady work: policy, practice, and the reform of American education.* Santa Monica, CA: RAND.

Firestone, W. and Corbett, H. D. (1989) Planned organizational change. In N. Boyan (ed.), *Handbook of research on educational administration,* pp. 321–40. New York: Macmillan.

Fullan, M. G. (1991) *The new meaning of educational change.* New York: Teachers College Press.

Hargreaves, A. (1994) *Changing teachers, changing times: teachers' work and culture in the postmodern age.* New York: Teachers College Press.

Hochschild, J. L. (1984) *The new American dilemma: liberal democracy and school desegregation.* New Haven, CT: Yale University Press.

Louis, K. S. and Miles, M. B. (1990) *Improving the urban high school.* New York: Teachers College Press.

McLaughlin, M. W. (1976) Implementing a mutual adaptation: change in classroom organization. *Teachers College Record,* 77(3), 339–51.

Myrdal, G. and colleagues (1944) *An American dilemma: the negro problem and modern democracy.* New York/London: Harper and Brothers.

Oakes, J. (1985) *Keeping track: how schools structure inequality.* New Haven, CT: Yale University Press.

Oakes, J. (1995) Two cities: tracking and within-school segregation. *Teachers College Record,* 96(4), 681–90.

Oakes, J. and Guiton, G. (1995) Matchmaking: the dynamics of high school tracking decisions. *American Educational Research Journal,* 32(1), 3–33.

Oakes, J. and Lipton, M. (1990) Tracking and ability grouping: a structural barrier to access to knowledge. In J. I. Goodlad (ed.), *Access to knowledge,* pp. 187–204. New York: College Entrance Examination Board.

Oakes, J., Lipton, M. and Jones, M. (1995a) *Changing minds: deconstructing intelligence in detracking schools.* Paper presented at the annual meeting of the American Educational Research Association, San Francisco.

Oakes, J., Wells, A., Datnow, A. and Jones, M. (1995b) Detracking: the social construction of ability, cultural politics and resistance to reform. Paper presented at the Annual Meeting of the American Sociological Association, Washington, DC.

Oakes, J., Welner, K., Yonezawa, S. and Allen, R. (1996) Norms and politics of equity-minded change: researching the "zone of mediation." Paper presented at the Annual Meeting of the American Educational Research Association, New York, 1996.

Ray, K. (1995) *Grant high school case report.* Los Angeles: University of California at Los Angeles Center for Democratic School Communities.

Sarason, S. (1990) *The predictable failure of educational reform.* San Francisco: Jossey-Bass.

Tyack, D. and Cuban, L. (1995) *Tinkering toward Utopia.* Cambridge, MA: Harvard University Press.

Weick, K. E. (1976) Educational organizations as loosely coupled systems. *Administrative Science Quarterly*, 21, 1–19.

Wells, A. and Oakes, J. (1998) Tracking, detracking and the politics of educational reform: a sociological perspective. In Calos Torres and Ted Mitchell (eds.), *Emerging issues in the sociology of education: comparative prespectives*, pp. 155–80. Albany, NY: SUNY Press

Wells, A. S. and Serna, I. (1996) The politics of culture: understanding local political resistance to detracking in racially mixed schools. *Harvard Educational Review*, 66(1), 93–118.

Welner, K. and Oakes, J. (1996) (Li)Ability grouping: the new susceptibility of school tracking systems to legal challenges. *Harvard Educational Review*, 66(3), 451–70.

Williams, E. (1995) *Rollinghills Middle School.* Los Angeles: Research for Democratic School Communities, UCLA Graduate School of Education and Information Studies.

Wise, A. (1977) Why educational policies often fail: the hyperrationalization hypothesis. *Curriculum Studies*, 9, 43–57.

Yonezawa, S. (1995) *Bearfield Middle School.* Los Angeles: Research for Democratic School Communities, UCLA Graduate School of Education and Information Studies.

Yonezawa, S. and Williams, R. (1995) *Seeking a new standard: minority parent and community involvement in detracking.* Paper presented at the Annual Meeting of the American Educational Research Association, San Francisco.

5 Changing Classroom Assessment: Teachers' Struggles

Lorna Earl and Steven Katz

There is no shortage of evidence that educational change is a difficult process, or of ways that change can be undermined. Changes may be poorly conceptualized, poorly researched, too ambitious, too fast or too slow; the changes may be pursued in isolation; commitment may not be sustained over time; parents may be opposed; and leaders may be too controlling or ineffectual. "Even with this impressive knowledge base and expertise about the factors that can enhance or undermine educational change, too many changes remain disappointing and ineffective" (Hargreaves, 1997: viii). While this has always been true, the complexity and pace of the current educational reform agenda make it even more difficult now: not only are current reforms themselves far-reaching, but there are many new factors that mitigate against easy transitions.

This chapter explores teachers' interpretations of recent major policy changes. While organizational and sociological explanations have characterized much of the educational change literature, our contribution is psychological in focus. It is based on the notion that while learning may be an intensely social activity and the sociocultural milieu is an important determinant of learning (Vygotsky, 1978), each person ultimately comes to his or her own unique understanding (Clay, 1996). We have been exploring this terrain through a longitudinal study designed to help us understand what change really looks and feels like to teachers, how they make sense of it, what reserves of imagination and effort they draw on to translate paper reforms into worthwhile practice, what kinds of support sustain them and what sorts of obstacles get in their way (Hargreaves *et al.*, 1997). Our interviews and discussions have provided a rich information base of teachers' stories, struggles, insights and resolutions.

During the years from 1994 to 1998, we traced the experiences and responses of twenty-nine grade 7 and 8 teachers in four large school districts in Ontario, Canada, through successive waves of provincial, district and school-level reform. The teachers in our sample were initially identified by district administrators as being actively engaged in and committed to implementing a set of provincial curriculum policies current at that time, including curriculum integration, common learning outcomes and alternative forms of classroom assessments. We interviewed them on three occasions, first in 1995 and again in 1997 and 1998, over the span of a rapidly changing political climate and reform agenda. The interviews lasted from one to two hours and addressed the teachers' interpretations of the key features of the reforms of the day (curriculum integration, common learning outcomes and assessment reform); how and where they had acquired this understanding; how they were integrating the changes into their practices; what these practices looked like; successes and difficulties they had encountered during their process of implementation; what professional development they had sought or been offered to support implementation; and the nature of their schools and their roles in them. We also asked the teachers about their longer-term record of investment in change, about their sense of efficacy or control over the changes, and about the relationship between their professional commitments and personal lives. (For a more complete account of the parent study, see Hargreaves *et al.*, 1997.)

Recent policy documents have provided teachers with little conceptual guidance or specific direction for change. Further, there has been a steady stream of new initiatives, each containing complex constellations of requirements for change in almost every aspect of education, with new directives often contradicting earlier ones. For example, during the time of this study, Ontario's Ministry of Education released two different curriculum documents for elementary schools, under the direction of two different political parties. The documents are similar in some ways and radically different in others. Teachers have had to translate the various policies into practical ideas and find ways to make them fit in their classrooms and schools.

It seemed useful to look closely at one pattern in this chaotic tapestry. We chose to focus our attention on teachers' response to the changes to classroom assessment and evaluation that are embedded in the current wave of school reform. Studies of classroom assessment, as well as our own research, suggest that it is one of the hardest and most consequential areas of teachers' work that carries a high emotional charge because it is where teachers' relative success becomes visible to parents and to the public at large (Gipps, 1994; Hargreaves *et al.*, 1997; Stiggins, 1994). We believed that understanding how teachers see the possibilities and work through the complexities of new assessment requirements would be an enlightening avenue for understanding how teachers process and respond to educational change more generally.

While assessment reform has been a cornerstone of recent policy in Ontario, this has not been the case historically. At the time of the study, teachers were encountering large-scale district and provincial assessments for the first time. As they described their strategies for assessment, they shared their struggles, confusion, worries and hopes. They tried to come to grips with the relationships among outcomes, proficiencies, indicators, criteria and standards. This proved to be a formidable task.

Assessment — the Hardest Part

We were struck by the scope and the complexity of the questions that teachers asked themselves and their colleagues about assessment. One of them put it this way:

> How do we measure the indicators for the outcomes? We say this is the beginning and middle for this particular outcome and you know at grade 9, you're talking about 3, 4, 5 dimensional matrices to really be able to understand it . . . There are too many twists and turns . . . If there's too much there to start with, how do you assess the "too much"?

The daunting profusion of assessment indicators was matched by the equally challenging problem of how to communicate with parents:

> There are specific outcomes for the end of grade 3, 6 and 9. But, they're still meant to be general and you're going to have kids at the end of grade 3 that aren't there yet. How are we going to rationalize the evaluation to parents?

Reporting to parents was especially difficult because the reporting format was often discrepant with the new approaches to assessment that teachers were using.

> We had a lot of trouble this year because the marks don't mesh with the [new outcomes-based] report card. I can certainly see if a kid is exceeding or meeting [the outcomes], but then when you have to match that with a mark, that's where we're having trouble.

Teachers genuinely tried to be clear about what they were doing, but they felt ill at ease and had difficulty reconciling the contradictions they were experiencing. They found it difficult to square the requirements of outcomes-based reporting with pressures for accountability and common standards that seemed to call for more traditional grading and reporting on their students' progress and achievements. They found this contradiction infuriating:

> [It includes] integrating all the subjects and looking for the outcomes of skills, not necessarily content-driven but they want them to do common testing . . . We're supposed to be teaching for those outcomes of learned skills and how to learn. What has that got to do with common testing?

> I worry, when they go to high school, will they be able to write a test in the amount of time that they need in order to produce what they know because, in the end, we're testing knowledge, not testing, "Okay — you have 30 seconds to answer this." This is not testing knowledge.

The contradictions were particularly problematic when the curriculum had to be modified to meet the needs of students with learning disabilities or other special needs. The teachers tried to accommodate individual differences and maintain consistent standards at the same time.

> I modified the program so they can be successful. Well, what is success-
> ful? Is successful 50%, 60%, 80%? When you modify for those children so
> that they are successful, if you have a watered down program to the extent
> that these children are, on paper, a success, and they go off to high school
> and those modifications aren't met, you've watered it down to the extent
> that it's not a true outcome.

For many of the teachers, assessment felt like a hidden land-mine. They
felt vulnerable and exposed, like assessment impostors masquerading as
experts and being expected to make judgements they weren't sure about
and might not be able to defend.

> I think for too long we've kind of evaluated on a more subjective basis.
> And OK it feels like an "A" to me when I'm reading this language, but
> what are the exact things . . . ? And I don't think we've been very scientific
> about that.

> I have a hard time with subjective evaluation. It's very difficult for me. I
> don't know. Especially now, teaching language for the first time, I don't
> know what is an "A" paper, what is a "B" paper. I have to sort these things
> out and so do my colleagues.

> Because I really stopped and thought, "Why am I evaluating everything?"
> and I started thinking about my kids, where we are going and what I was
> really doing in assessment and what was I really evaluating, and that made
> a big jump.

Making Sense of Teachers' Making Sense

Some of the teachers were genuinely confused and frustrated. Others found
ways to rationalize and integrate at least some of the changes in assessment
into their practice. We searched for insights about how they had come to
this state. How were they thinking about the assessment demands? Why did
some fit and others not? What were the differences in how teachers characterized the changes in assessment practice? Our search took us to the
literature on learning theory and about teachers' conceptions about how
learning occurs. Perhaps if we understood the teachers' own views about
learning and assessment, it would help us interpret their confusion.

How teachers teach and how they assess are inevitably based on their
visions of competence and beliefs about how to help students learn.
Although teachers may become acquainted with theories of learning during
their pre-service training, these typically are not a high priority for practic-
ing teachers. Teachers are more likely to hold intuitive views about how
students learn that guide how they teach. Olson and his colleagues have
described two quite different models of teaching and learning that they call
"folk pedagogies" that characterize intuitive views about learning in school
(Olson and Bruner, 1996; Olson and Katz, in press). We refer to the folk

pedagogies as "mind as container" and "mind as constructor," building on the work of Bereiter and Scardamalia (1996). Our hypothesis was that teachers' responses to the assessment reforms would differ depending on which view they held.

Mind as Container

The assumption underlying "mind as container" is that learners' minds are *tabula rasa*, initially devoid of facts, rules and principles. Important knowledge must be transferred from the instructor, text or other resource to the learner. Astington (in press) reports a wonderful characterization of the "mind as container" folk pedagogy, a cartoon in a local newspaper that reads: "Sign on school door: Free knowledge. Bring your own container." If the mind is a receptacle, teaching is telling and learning is remembering. What is told and remembered is propositional knowledge; it is a transferable commodity and exists independent of the individual. Considered in this light, knowledge is certain and permanent; there are only right and wrong answers. This folk pedagogy assumes a working distinction between opinions and facts. As the gospel of journalism states, "Comment is free, but facts are sacred." Disagreements between people are attributed to the lack of sufficient knowledge. As Chandler *et al.* (1990) describe it, knowledge is a

> free-standing attribute of the world that only secondarily comes into the passive possession of those who, because they happen to be in the right place at the right time, automatically end up with some portion of the unmitigated truth directly embossed upon the recording equipment of their minds. (p. 377)

In this model, the teacher's role is to ensure that students acquire as much knowledge or truth as possible; teachers are the authorities (Kitchener *et al.*, 1989; Kuhn, 1992). Students are expected to listen and remember what is taught. Belenky *et al.* (1986) call this "silent knowing": the individual accepts the authority's proclamation about what is true.

In the "mind as container" folk pedagogy, assessment involves ways of making the learning visible and determining how successful the transfer of knowledge has been. How much knowledge has been retained? Teachers use assessment and evaluation to determine how well the student can return the words or ideas of the authority, be it person or text. How well can the student reproduce the knowledge? Assessment, in this framework, is judging.

Mind as Constructor

The "mind as constructor" folk pedagogy is well captured in the writings of psychologist Howard Gardner and philosopher John Dewey. Gardner (1985) describes it this way:

> Human subjects do not come to tasks as empty slates; they have expectations and well-structured schemata within which they approach diverse materials. The organism, with its structures already prepared for stimulation, itself manipulates and otherwise reorders the information it freshly encounters. (p. 126)

As Phillips and Soltis write in their commentary on Dewey, "thinking and learning are 'practical' capacities, in the exercise of which we actively interact with our surroundings" (1991: 38).

The "mind as constructor" model emphasizes the child's interaction with the physical environment. Learning occurs when previously acquired ideas are combined or modified to form new superordinate ideas. Initially, understanding develops from, and thinking focuses on, concrete experiences and examples; as children develop, abstract thought emerges from the coordination of these superordinate structures. Rooted in Vygotskian theory, this model views cognitive development as a socially mediated process. Perhaps the best metaphor is one of "conversation." As students and the teacher engage in a dialogue, the children (and the teacher) construct meaning.

In considering the child's point of view, the "mind as constructor" folk pedagogy acknowledges the mind as a place of privately held beliefs and ideas (Olson and Bruner, 1996). It assumes that individuals are capable of making sense both on their own and through interaction with others. Teaching involves creating opportunities for interchanges of ideas, for sharing beliefs, and for investigating ideas that are stored as the collective wisdom of the culture (in textbooks, narratives, theories, models and so on). When teaching is directed by a belief in "mind as constructor," the learning environment is active and dynamic.

Knowledge, for the "mind as constructor" model, is neither God-given truth nor an indisputable fact of nature. It is fundamentally uncertain, always developing, open to challenge and varies from person to person as they interpret the world around them. Belenky and her colleagues (1986) describe this as "subjective knowing." Personal belief counts as evidence for knowing and beliefs are justified by sharing and validating them with others. Teaching requires investigation, debate, collaboration and clarification, and learning is subjective interpretation.

In the "mind as constructor" view, assessment provides an opportunity for students and teachers to reflect, question, plan, teach, study and learn (Earl and LeMahieu, 1997). It is a mechanism for making what students believe to be true visible to themselves and others in order to build or adjust their learning. Students can self-assess and regulate their own learning, to "activate and sustain cognitions, feelings, and behaviours oriented toward attainment of academic goals" (Gettinger, 1995: 671; see also Zimmerman and Martinez-Pons, 1992). Students reflect on their own successes and failures as learners and alter their future directions as a result. In this framework, then, assessment is an integral part of the learning process.

Teachers' Folk Pedagogies

Our analysis of the interview data focused on how teachers viewed assessment and how this conception of assessment was connected to their beliefs about knowledge, teaching and learning. We began our investigation with the expectation that teachers' prevailing beliefs would reflect one folk pedagogy or the other.

Our analysis revealed that many of the teachers had very decided beliefs that were consistent with "mind as container" about what their students were expected to know; about how they and their students should behave to establish this expected knowing; and about how the acquisition of this knowledge would be assessed.

For example, some teachers described what students are expected to know in terms of an absence of knowledge:

> The kids are coming up with gaps in their learning.

> The kids were just so far behind with so many gaps in their learning that it was quite shocking.

Often, the identification of missing knowledge content was illustrated in concrete terms:

> I gave them a page of different word uses. Instead of reading the word minute (small), the kids would automatically read it as minute (time).

> The idea of possessive. "The boys' arrows," s', many told me that it was incorrect, that the apostrophe had to come before the s even though it was correct. They didn't know the idea of possessive.

Other teachers talked explicitly in terms of "what students need to know."

> They need to know what the differences and similarities are between plant and animal cells. How those make up organ systems in mammals and reptiles. How they come together to make up a system.

These teachers felt responsible for communicating their expectations to the pupils themselves: if "the known" is thought to exist independently of the subjective, then the teacher's role is sensitizing the naive to the portions of "the known" that they must learn:

> I show the kids what is expected.

> There is a model for them to look at on the sheet that I give them and they follow that model.

> I give each child a large draft-board with all of the outcomes right across the curriculum on it.

> I tell the students beforehand, "This is what I'm expecting from you."

The role of students in this kind of learning was clear to the teachers. For "the known" to be successfully received, students have to pay attention in order to receive the instructional messages:

It has been sit down, get quiet, learn to focus, learn to concentrate.

They are able to listen to lessons now. They know how to listen with their eyes as well as their ears. They know how to put pencils, toys, and rulers down.

I find I have to repeat myself incredibly when it comes to instructions and then wait time and again. I keep telling them that there is no point in me talking unless they can hear me.

The teachers saw the task of determining the success of student learning as the teacher's, not the student's. Assessment was focused on recall, reconstruction and repetition of learned material (Earl and LeMahieu, 1997). Decisions about the success of learning were an authority-determined judgement based on the degree of correspondence between the taught material and its reproduction in the testing situation. The teachers used traditional testing practices to see how much the children have retained:

We've got a lot to cover and the quickest way I'm going to do it is to teach those lessons and then test them.

I had five classes all day yesterday and three of the periods were taken up with quizzes.

If they can do well on a test then I've done my job.

Success in learning was quantified:

In order to be successful they need to have at least eighty percent.

I'm looking at around 750 marks for them.

But many of the same teachers also made comments consistent with "mind as constructor." For example, they exhibited a concern for the subjective features of their students' knowing and talked about the need to consider student individuality and diversity:

If I've got a lot of children that love to research then I need to meet their needs. I also have kids that need activities, so I'll structure the unit towards that as well.

The whole thing centers on the child. A lot of us here have the same view of the child in mind. Some people don't really take a look at these kids and say, "Hey, where are these kids coming from?"

A successful activity or lesson was often defined as one which offered something for everyone:

It's good because all of the students can do it at one level or another. It integrates all of the different levels in the class.

In acknowledging the subjective dimension of knowing, the teacher's role shifted from expositor to that of facilitator:

I did a lot of facilitating in the unit. I tend to not like to talk very much.

I try to move them along in their own learning rather than me just spouting information.

Learning was described as a partnership process, with the teacher as a fellow learner:

If we're trying to teach kids to be lifelong learners then we need to be as well.

You cannot go through this day to day business without learning something yourself.

I learned something new from *Scientific American* the other day and used it in class with the grade sevens. They were as amazed as I was.

The students' role often was described as collaborative or communal, suggesting teachers' beliefs that sharing ideas is part of the learning process and can help justify a subjective position:

I encourage peer tutoring a great deal.

We were doing a jig-saw [cooperative learning strategy]. Everybody had become an expert on one of the five kingdoms.

They do research projects on World War II in a small group situation.

The teachers in our study endorsed Stiggins' (1994) view that the promotion of self-assessment is part of learning:

I have students involved in the generation of learning criteria on an ongoing basis, doing things like self-assessment.

I want them to have confidence in their abilities as learners and I want them to be able to communicate and reflect on that.

They write down what the activity was, what they did, what they learned from it, how they felt about it, and what they'd like to do next.

Some of the teachers explicitly encouraged their students to use assessment to assume responsibility for the direction of their future learning:

I tell them they're my little scientists. They have to go out there and do it on their own. I'm trying to teach them to be inquirers.

I've given them the chance to go and investigate for themselves. They decide, "What can I go and learn from here and not have Mrs. [name] tell me that I have to learn this?"

To our surprise, we found that most of the teachers demonstrated beliefs in both folk pedagogies. Even the teacher who demonstrated a solid belief in a view of learning of "mind as constructor" held some "mind as container" views and struggled with the dissonance between the two:

> Normally I would give them the rubric beforehand so they know what is expected. The problem is that, if you want them to discover things instead of being creative they will follow the rubric to get a high mark, and that's all they do.

By the same token, the teacher whose orientation was most consistent with "mind as container" showed glimpses of the "mind as constructor" viewpoint in comments like:

> I got them to think about their own learning and what they had been doing, what they did in the past, how they felt about it, what they are doing now and how they feel about it.

Most of the other teachers were eclectic, moving from one folk pedagogy to the other throughout their work.

Living with Ambiguity: Blending Conceptions

The teachers in this study were simultaneously considering both transmission of the "known" and the subjective mental life of their students. While folk pedagogy as a construct holds a certain utility in characterizing different epistemologies, it is less useful when applied to individual teachers. Perhaps this is not surprising, because teachers do have responsibility for both ensuring the understanding of predetermined knowledge and the subjective dimension of individual student thought. In an attempt to understand, we turned to the details of their responses to assessment reform. In practice, the teachers' decisions seemed more pragmatic and situational than theoretical. They selected elements from the policy directives that worked for them and tried to reconcile different expectations with their existing practices. The way that these teachers tried to create a coherent and defensible flow to the daily routines of their classes seemed to us rather like producers blending sounds for complex recordings: some added new tracks to the existing tape, others went completely digital, and many used a blend of techniques.

Adding Tracks

For some teachers, the process of incorporating new assessment strategies was like laying new sound tracks onto an existing audio-tape. Their original approach to teaching remained intact, but some additional material was superimposed upon it. For example:

> I like doing anecdotal reporting, just to make note of behavior, question-
> ing kids, conferencing. But traditional quizzes and tests are the backbone
> of my evaluation. One to one would be better but I don't have the time
> ... I haven't used peer and self-evaluation much but when I do they are
> pretty accurate. The kid that did the most work ends up giving himself the
> highest mark and the other one gets a lower mark and the partner is honest
> ... It's hard to keep up though. I've got a stack of marking at home and
> I still haven't gotten to it.

This teacher was trying to add new assessment practices, but he seemed
to have no indication of any deeper purpose for the changes in his
practice.

Digitized Recording

At the other end of the spectrum was an approach to assessment that was
like working with a sophisticated digitized recording system. Only one of
the teachers fully exemplifies this approach. The teacher who followed this
strategy had a sense of the components of the work and the mood he
wanted to create but operated using an open and changeable approach,
skipping to anywhere in the work, adding little flourishes and maneuver-
ing all the bits to keep the whole production flowing:

> I see our role changing from imparting knowledge to teaching kids, or
> showing kids how to use the knowledge that is available ... [The project]
> just branched out from a little tour of the neighborhood, but all of it fits
> with the outcomes of the common curriculum ... I use a lot of rubrics, a
> lot of peer evaluation, parental evaluation ... with the sheets I sent home,
> the kids were evaluating themselves everyday, they had to explain what
> they were doing everyday in literacy analyses and they had to take it home
> and explain it to their parents and so the parents are doing some of the
> evaluation too ... We do a lot of peer evaluation ... We talk about the
> outcome, how to present the material in different ways to different audi-
> ences, we look at different ways in which it should be evaluated and the
> kids and I make it up together and then they assess using each criteria.
> They evaluate their own and make a comment, then they evaluate each
> other's ... They had to have at least five other people evaluate it ... Then
> I evaluate it and their parents will also put a comment on it. I do lot of
> this with almost everything they do ... There are really no surprises for the
> parents.

The teacher who used a digital approach was able not only to use a
variety of techniques every day but to move beyond them to circumnavi-
gate what other teachers had experienced as obstacles. Queries and curiosity may come from parents and the community but this teacher understood
why he was doing what he did and was comfortable describing and sharing
his practice.

Mixed Production Style

The third and most prevalent production style was really a mixed one, some of it audio-tape, some digitized, and the transitions weren't always smooth. Such teachers played with the digitized approach but kept coming back to the original tape. These teachers frequently expressed uncertainty about their practice.

> [My assessment] has changed. In the past, I gave marks for classroom participation, I gave marks for homework completion, and there'd be tests and quizzes so it would be very hard evidence in the back of my binder for how 87.5 was established. With ABCD it's so easy to assess someone who is outstanding, someone who is very good, someone who is having difficulties . . . translate that nowadays into a rubric and change the titles to awareness, mechanical and refined so really that is ABCD . . . Sometimes, I reflect and maybe I do something a little more, hard facts for my marks book.

> How do we measure them, that's the hardest part of introducing [the new elementary curriculum] is how do you assess these outcomes . . . For all of them I have a second page of self-evaluation to attach to the report card but I doubt if parents even look at it."

> Because we modify, we have to modify expectations and we took a fair bit of time convincing parents why I had to have four different levels of math tests and why my special needs kids get the easiest task and why that A should be as good as the A another one gets. Both are As. The parent is saying, "You're fooling this kid into thinking he's an A math student because the parents still think traditionally" . . . The kids also do a fair bit of self-evaluation. I have a weekly homework sheet to help them smarten up and get their homework done . . . there's a sheet for each day of the week and they record what I have improved at and what do I need to improve at . . . they still don't use it properly . . . they don't really buy into it enough and again don't give me enough information.

The teachers using a mixed production style saw assessment as the most difficult dimension of their practice to understand and change. As the comments suggest, they were confused and frustrated, and in some cases they did things that confused and frustrated their students and their parents. And just explaining it again only louder and slower didn't seem to help.

And the Struggles Go On

Our study provides a vivid picture of the struggles that teachers experience in times of educational reform. They are in the throes of trying to understand what has to change, why it should change and how they can respond to the forces for change without compromising their personal and professional integrity.

The conjecture that teachers have consistent "folk pedagogies" about learning and teaching that guide their practice proved to be too simplistic, not because they do not hold such beliefs but because they work in a context that requires them to reconcile and negotiate their personal views with many other competing demands. Assessment provided a good opportunity to "see" teachers' thinking. It caused stress and confusion, largely because assessment is the public statement of what education is all about. The teachers juggled their personal discomfort with concerns about their students, all within an uncertain policy context. On a personal level, they questioned themselves and their role in facilitating and judging student learning. In the broader context, assessment reform has become the battlefield for defining what counts in education, as well as who gets to judge.

On reflection, perhaps we should have anticipated that the teachers would not (even could not) hold a single or consistent "folk pedagogy." Educational reform is a product of the current uncertainties about how best to approach teaching and learning for the future. The teachers were caught in a transition that is personal, institutional and political, trying to reconcile a range of competing ideologies, organizational constraints and personal beliefs, and establish practices that weave incompatible ideas together into something workable.

- It is a time of enormous change. Inherent in the change is a major paradigm shift about how learning occurs and how assessments should be constructed and used. Assessment theorists are using a "mind as constructor" view of learning to suggest a move away from a notion of assessment as judging and categorizing students to a notion of assessment as feedback to support learning (Gipps, 1994; Earl and LeMahieu, 1997). Many current teachers had been successful students themselves in an earlier time where "mind as container" was the dominant view. Some of them are struggling to recast their own views to include the "mind as constructor" in their beliefs and practice.
- The teachers in our study do not operate in a vacuum. Curriculum guidelines and province-wide reporting requirements put clear constraints on what teachers can do. Teachers are accountable for the implementation of the curriculum and for conforming to system expectations, while at the same time teaching the particular students in their classes. They are often caught between requirements for "meeting standards" and their convictions about the learning needs of individual students.
- The curriculum and assessment reforms themselves contain contradictions. In 1991, content based guidelines that had existed for over a decade were abandoned in favor of broad learning outcomes and more integrated curriculum. More recent curriculum documents have softened these directions and reverted to more subject-specific content. Provincial and district assessments have escalated, accompanied by accountability demands, at the same time as guidelines instruct teachers

to use more performance assessment and ongoing, fluid assessment schemes.

Although the psychological lenses of theories of mind provided a somewhat narrow picture, they nevertheless offer a fascinating view of how teachers are trying to make sense out of and conform to policy reforms and the extent of the struggle required to integrate personal beliefs with policy expectations. These teachers did not have the luxury of establishing and maintaining consistent views of learning and assessment. A few were more closely aligned with a "mind as container" theory and one was clearly operating from a theory of "mind as constructor." But this is only part of the puzzle that each of them is piecing together. It is no wonder that most of the teachers vacillated back and forth from the familiar to the new, either adding bits to their practice (like a new track on an audio-tape) or switching to new practices for special units or assignments but reverting to the traditional when it really counted (mixed production). A multitude of conditions beyond their personal beliefs governs their decisions and they routinely face additional dilemmas arising from the incompatibilities inherent in assessment decisions.

References

Astington, J. W. (in press) Reflective teaching and learning: children's and teachers' theories of mind. *Teaching Education.*

Belenky, M., Clinchy, B., Goldberger, N. and Tarule, J. (1986) *Women's ways of knowing: the development of self, voice, and mind.* New York: Basic Books.

Bereiter, C. and Scardamalia, M. (1996) Rethinking learning. In D. R. Olson and N. Torrance (eds.), *The handbook of education and human development,* pp. 485–513. Cambridge, MA: Blackwell.

Chandler, M., Boyes, M. and Ball, L. (1990) Relativism and stations of epistemic doubt. *Journal of Experimental Child Psychology,* 50, 370–95.

Clay, M. (1996) Accommodating diversity in early literacy learning. In D. R. Olson and N. Torrance (eds.), *The handbook of education and human development,* pp. 202–24. Cambridge, MA: Blackwell.

Earl, L. and LeMahieu, P. (1997) Rethinking assessment and accountability. In A. Hargreaves (ed.), *Rethinking educational change with heart and mind,* pp. 149–68. Alexandria, VA: ASCD.

Gardner, H. (1985) *The mind's new science: a history of the cognitive revolution.* New York: Basic Books.

Gettinger, M. (1995) Book review of *Toward an integrated theory of self-regulation* by D. Schunk and B. Zimmerman (eds.). *Contemporary Psychology,* 40, 670–73.

Gipps, C. (1994) Beyond testing: towards a theory of educational assessment. London: Falmer Press.

Hargreaves, A. (1997) Rethinking educational change. In A. Hargreaves (ed.), *Rethinking educational change with heart and mind,* pp. 1–26. Alexandria, VA: Association for Supervision and Curriculum Development.

Hargreaves, A., Earl, L., Moore, S. and Manning, S. (1997) *Learning to change: a study of teachers committed to innovation in grades 7 and 8.* Toronto: Ontario Institute for Studies in Education at the University of Toronto.

Kitchener, K. S., King, P. A., Wood, P. A. and Davidson, M. L. (1989) Sequentiality and consistency in development of reflective judgment: a six-year longitudinal study. *Journal of Applied Developmental Psychology,* 10, 73–95.

Kuhn, D. (1992) Thinking as argument. *Harvard Educational Review,* 62, 155–78.

Olson, D. R. and Bruner, J. S. (1996) Folk psychology and folk pedagogy. In D. R. Olson and N. Torrance (eds.), *The handbook of education and human development,* pp. 9–27. Cambridge, MA: Blackwell.

Olson, D. R. and Katz, S. (in press) The fourth folk pedagogy. In B. Torff and R. J. Sternberg (eds.), *Understanding and teaching the intuitive mind.* Hillsdale, NJ: Erlbaum.

Phillips, D. and Soltis, J. (1991) *Perspectives on learning* (2nd edn) New York: Teachers College Press.

Stiggins, R. (1994) *Student centred classroom assessment.* New York: Merrill.

Vygotsky, L. (1978) *Mind in society: the development of higher mental processes.* Cambridge, MA: Harvard University Press.

Whitty, G., Powers, S. and Halpin, D. (1998) *Devolution and choice in education.* Buckingham: Open University Press.

Zimmerman, B. and Martinez-Pons, M. (1992) Perceptions of efficacy and strategy use in the self-regulation of learning. In D. Schunk and J. Meece (eds.), *Student perceptions in the classroom,* pp. 185–207. Hillsdale, NJ: Erlbaum.

6 The Impact of Mandated Change on Teachers

Beverley Bailey

There have been efforts to restructure schools from the time Horace Mann first introduced the notion of universal, graded education in 1848. The most notable early proponent of school reform, John Dewey, began his work in the late 1800s. Apple, Ball, Cuban, Fullan, Hargreaves, Huberman, Louis, McLaughlin, Miles, Nias, Rudduck and Sarason are but a few of the contemporary writers on the subject of school restructuring. These researchers suggest that, in spite of repeated efforts to create significant change, schools today look much like schools of yesterday (Cuban, 1989). The reasons given for the repeated failure of educational change are varied, though they are all compelling. Another explanation for the failure of school change, the focus of this chapter, is that the context and process of mandated change often marginalizes teachers.

Teachers' perspectives have been a missing factor in the development of innovations (Barrow, 1984; Barth, 1990; Cohn and Kottkamp, 1993; Cuban, 1988; Fullan and Hargreaves, 1991; Hargreaves and Fullan, 1998; Hunsaker, 1992). Teachers — as the rank and file implementers of change, and bureaucrats — as the designers and advocates of change, may have very different views on the exigencies of any particular reform. As Silberman (1970) points out, the content and process of change are typically not in the hands of practitioners; change is assumed to be possible without their expertise, and their perspectives on change are frequently ignored. We neglect the possibility that teachers, assessing past experiences as well as current realities, may have something important to tell us. As Hargreaves and Fullan (1998) suggest, resistant teachers may have especially revealing stories to tell:

> [W]e advised leaders in education to take a less stigmatising and dismissive approach to teacher resistance to change. We urged more empathy with "resistant" teachers because their cautiousness about investing in change was often a rational response to bad changes or bad experiences with change in the past . . . Resisters may be right. They have "good sense" in seeing through the change as faddish, misdirected, ideological or unworkable (Gitlin and Margonis, 1995). At the very least their perspective on change will be different and divergent from yours. Quell resistance and you remove the opportunities for learning. (p. 120)

Through my own experience as a school teacher and counselor as well as through my research, I have come to believe that substantive curricular change only occurs when it begins with the teacher (Huberman, 1993; Schlechty, 1988), and is fundamentally concerned with the immediate needs of children (Ball, 1987; Cooper, 1988), in a school climate open to problem solving (Clune, 1990) rather than stifled by a hierarchically organized structure (Timar, 1989). Mandated change directs teachers rather than engaging them. Rather than supporting teachers in their classrooms, bureaucratic change processes tend to simply recreate themselves (Cuban, 1989; Deal, 1986). Much more could be done if researchers, policymakers and administrators worked *with* teachers rather than *on* them.

This chapter reports on a study conducted between 1991 and 1994 on teachers' experiences of mandated change. They were an eclectic group: elementary, secondary, novice, veteran, male, female, old and young, from eleven jurisdictions in three Canadian provinces. Despite this diversity, the teachers all characterized themselves as marginalized to some degree by mandated change processes. The study took place at a time of significant and ambitious policy activity intended to encourage "student-centered" learning; the teachers' marginalization is all the more compelling because so many of them identified themselves as "student-centered" teachers — for these teachers, the content of the reform doesn't matter so much as the deprofessionalizating process of change, the decontextualized, top-down "being told what to do."

The teachers I studied most intensively — Emma, David and Robert — were interviewed an average of ten times throughout a full school year and observed in their schools and classrooms. All three described themselves as unafraid of change, having made many changes in their own teaching, but as concerned about being asked to make changes that would not be beneficial to their students and which might actually harm them. Emma was a veteran elementary teacher who had worked for some years in an inner city school and had a history of creative classroom teaching. Robert, who worked with older elementary students in a school in a privileged neighborhood, was from the "old school," educated in Britain and appreciated by parents as a "straight shooter" who would make their children "toe the line and learn the three Rs." David, an elementary teacher in a school with a 95 percent immigrant population, developed caring relationships with his students and was an active supporter for many families.

All three teachers found ways to continue teaching as they saw fit in spite of provincially mandated change initiatives, but their resistance was costly. Emma became politically active, working with a parent group that had formed out of concern about the mandated changes, conducting workshops, and continually expressing her view of the long-term impact of the mandated changes to fellow teachers, administrators, trustees, reporters and university professors. She spent one third of the year sick with an ongoing string of illnesses that puzzled her doctors. Robert relied on his students' parents to support his claim that his teaching was consistent with their desires, but he was also planning an early retirement and counting down the days. David waged a quiet counteroffensive, asked to teach in a portable away from the eyes of administrators and colleagues, hid the textbooks he liked to use when "old stuff" was being cleared out of the school, put his energies into coaching school sports, and tried to affect an appearance of compliance while "doing his own thing." He suffered a nervous breakdown a year after the research and has not yet gone back to teaching.

The perspectives of ten other teachers also inform this chapter. Each of these teachers was interviewed only once. Each came to me when s/he heard about my study. Each had a story about mandated change that s/he believed no one else wanted to hear. None started out resistant; some were even enthusiastic supporters; but their stories reveal how even enthusiastic teachers can be marginalized as the result of their participation in mandated change.

Many teachers are marginalized by the context and process of mandated change. Such marginalization contributes to the failure of school restructuring initiatives. This chapter first discusses the many faces of marginalization, making a case that marginalizing teachers has costs in terms of expertise and experience. Next I discuss the context of change, pointing out the disjunctures between mandated change and the already dense and difficult working lives of teachers. Third, I outline how the process of change can alienate teachers and limit the possibilities of change. Last, I offer some suggestions for how school reform might be more productively accomplished.

Marginalization

Marginalization is an ambiguous and at times vague term. Its meaning depends upon the context and occasion in which it is used. The terms derived from the root "margin" (e.g., marginal, marginalized, to be marginalized) are relational rather than categorical. To be marginal, or to be marginalized, always occurs in a social context: one is always marginalized with respect to a particular group and a specific set of circumstances. The impact of marginalization is more severe for some people than for others. A sense of powerlessness is common to those in marginal positions; yet there can be considerable variation from situation to situation. While the three teachers in the core of the study are marginalized to a great degree, the other ten teachers most often saw themselves as marginalized with respect to particular issues or circumstances.

"Being marginalized" lies on a continuum and one's place on the continuum can shift over time and with varying circumstances. Two teachers might be marginalized with respect to their administrators, but one might

simply be ignored while the other may be the subject of private administrative discussions about "transfer" or "early retirement." On a continuum of
marginalization, the former teacher would be considered less marginalized
than the latter. Further, marginalization can be issue-specific. For example,
a teacher could be marginalized in an administrator's view with respect to
her teaching style but not marginalized, in the view of that same administrator, with respect to her rapport with colleagues or students.

The study was not designed to discover how many or what proportion
of the teaching population are marginalized, though my own experience
leads me to believe that more teachers than not are marginalized through
mandated change processes. The study does shed some light on the nature
of the phenomenon: some of the participants had experienced mandated
change at earlier stages in their careers and wanted nothing to do with the
current versions of what they saw as "the same old, same old." Other teachers were more committed to the ideas embedded in current policies but
found living through implementation so problematic that they insisted they
would never again become wholeheartedly involved in mandated change.

People placed (or who place themselves) in marginal positions are both
stigmatized and ignored. When people do not agree with the dominant political agenda, their resistance may lead others to construct a "stigma-theory,"
an ideology that explains the inferiority and possibly even danger represented by the different person (Goffman, 1963). Teachers who reject the
ideas of the dominant culture can become labeled as problems in their
school, resistant, intransigent, and too old to change (Fullan and Miles,
1992). Marginalized teachers pay a price. Resistance is hard work. Teachers
also suffer as a profession in terms of the marginalization of teacher expertise and knowledge. The stigmatization of teachers has powerful consequences for schools: marginalized teachers may retreat to their classrooms
where their own ideas can be put in place and may form professional
liaisons only with people who share their values and concerns (Goffman,
1963; Woods, 1990). When this occurs, teachers will be less willing to work
collaboratively thus essentially reducing the potential for positive educational change.

The negative impact of stigmatization on teachers has been the focus
of other research. For example, Riseborough (1981) studied how British high
school teachers became marginalized as the result of the amalgamation of
two very different secondary schools. In the long run the teachers who had
come from the lower-status school came to define themselves in terms of
their opposition to the head teacher (principal); this was a new identity for
them. Mandated change sharply diminished their own sense of classroom
competence and value to their students. In Huberman's (1989, 1993) four-
year study, mandated change drove Swiss high school teachers to a cynical
awareness of the unreliability of administrators, and anger toward those they
believed had failed them. These after-effects can have lasting and negative

results that may overshadow any of the innovation's more immediate benefits: teachers' levels of commitment, engagement and investment fell progressively over their careers. (Huberman also found, in contrast, that teachers who had been allowed to "tinker" in their classrooms ended their careers with a sense of satisfaction.)

Marginalization is a double-sided phenomenon; it also has a positive face. The marginal position is ambiguous, not fully institutionalized, and removed from what most people would see as society's central institutions and values. Because marginal people stand outside the taken-for-grantedness of everyday life, some have an ability to take a clearer look at the marginalizing event and to ask tough questions. A marginal position brings into question basic ingredients of reality and calls typicality and preconstituted knowledge into question (Berger, 1981; Hargreaves and Fullan, 1998; Musgrove, 1977; Woods, 1991, 1993). Willis goes so far as to suggest that those in power may in fact be working out of a place of stultification, reification and pretence, while those on the margins may be "best placed to exploit the revolutionary double edge of unexpected things around us" (1978: 6).

It is important to note that teacher resistance may have several different causes (Huberman, 1993) and may result in negative as well as positive consequences for students: for example, resistant teachers may protect their own interests against those of students or parents whom they believe have no right to comment on what happens in schools (Zeichner, 1991); resistant teachers may work to undermine educational equity for students and gender equity for teachers (Datnow in this volume). But because marginal people live at the intersection of two cultures (Lortie, 1975), with a foot in both camps, their view can be multidimensional. Such a position can provide important understanding for teachers themselves and for others who are concerned about the quality of educational programs.

Marginalization is both a process of stigmatizing teachers and a process which can open the possibility for a clearer view of the marginalizing event. There are good reasons for attending to teachers who have been marginalized by change processes. First, however, we need to understand in some detail the ways in which the context and process of change contribute to marginalization.

The Context of Change

The disjunctures between the assumptions embedded in mandated reform and teachers' realities can marginalize teachers. It is impossible for change mandated by someone other than those who are to effect the change, change not rooted in classroom realities, to take into consideration either teachers' working conditions or their core values.

Teaching has become an almost impossible task. Connell (1985) describes some of the expectations placed on teachers:

Time spent preparing the lesson, time spent getting the class settled and willing to listen, time spent supervising exercises and correcting them. Beyond this, running a class involves keeping order, dealing with conflicts between kids; having a joke with them from time to time and building up some personal contact; discussing work with them individually; planning sequences of lessons; preparing handouts and physical materials; collecting, using and storing books and audiovisual aids; organizing and marking tests and major exams; keeping records; liaison with other teachers in the same subject . . . That is for conventional classroom work. Beyond it there is a very wide range of jobs to be done to keep a school humming along or even bumping along. Supervising the kids in playgrounds, at the canteen, at sporting events, onto transport, on excursions. Planning, arranging, swimming carnivals, athletic days, football and netball matches, geography excursions, biology excursions and so on outside the school: drama workshops, concerts, gymnastic displays, fetes, speech days, bingo nights and so forth inside it. Going to parent/teacher nights, Parents' and Citizens' Association meetings, union meetings, staff meetings. Departmental meetings. Organising, getting facilities for, and supervising the school magazine, the chess club, the drama club, the debating teams, the students' council, the end-of-term disco, the farewell to grade 12; making school rules, policing them, administering punishments . . . (pp. 71–2)

Hargreaves (1990) wonders if the nature of teachers' work situations is such that they sometimes feel as though they cannot find the time to teach. The work lives of teachers are so complicated that the act of teaching actually appears to get lost in the mix. Apple (1993) worries that the pedagogical concerns of teachers are increasingly undervalued and may no longer be seen as concerns at all. McNeil (1988) suggests that teachers feel that to "really" teach may be going against the expectations of the school. This busyness and denseness is compounded when change is mandated: teachers must devote increased attention to more classroom details as well as to more time spent outside the classroom learning, planning and, as Earl suggests in this volume, justifying their actions to others.

Teachers' work is further complicated when we consider their values. Many researchers have pointed out that ensuring the success and well-being of children is of vital importance to teachers (Fullan, 1991; Huberman, 1993; Jackson, 1968, 1990) and a major source of reward (Lieberman and Miller, 1984). This concern with students has been characterized as the moral purpose of teaching: "The moral purpose is to make a difference in the lives of students regardless of background, and to help produce citizens who can live and work productively in increasingly dynamically complex societies" (Fullan, 1993: 5; see also Cuban, 1988). Indeed, the teachers in the study were not opposed to change *per se*; they had been changing their teaching, as one teacher said, "all the time," most commonly because they believed each year's class required different approaches and strategies.

If I want something new to work in my classroom then I have to build on my strengths. I will size up the class, figure out how they learn, and then decide which way to teach. My teaching strategies change from year to year, from week to week, even from day to day. (Isabell)

Pat saw her fellow teachers constantly working to change and improve their practice, needing

to put a new twist on things all the time . . . I think that if teachers were given more permission to do what they think best, then they would go for it. I think that most teachers see how things go and find their own ways of making sure that the kids are getting what they need.

But teachers may be placed in the position of violating their own deeply felt beliefs about what children in their care need when they are told how and what to teach. The study participants believed mandated changes required them to abandon methods and materials that had been successful with their students. With mandated change, their impulse to evaluate new methods before adopting them was disallowed: they were essentially denied their right to professional expertise. As a result they often felt like they were teaching "blindly," and not "doing right by (the) kids:"

It is hard to do a good job of something when you are doing it because you have been told to do it. (Jenny)

When they want me to to do all that stuff I can't do it good enough so that I know that the kids are learning what they need to know. Children should not be treated like guinea pigs. That is what happens when I am asked to teach programs and I don't know anything about them. It is not fair to the kids. (David)

These concerns and the disjuncture between teachers' realities and mandated changes made them deeply skeptical. While documents that accompany mandated change initiatives typically argue that change is needed to better prepare children for the future, some of the teachers believed that these rationales were merely "smokescreens" to provide an appearance of governmental action and to redirect public attention away from intractable problems (see also Alberta Teachers' Association, 1993; Cuban, 1988; Johnston, 1993). They had no evidence that the mandates were developed as the result of studies of the sorts of conditions they experienced in their own classrooms. They saw administrators using change to "earn brownie points" with their superiors. They saw government bureaucrats as too far removed from schools to be able to understand current classroom needs:

They are ambitious and I have no time for that. They sit on the fence, push paper and have nothing to do with the kids. (Robert)

It is the same with anyone on a career path. They are made nervous by the people above them. It is hard when you want to go up the ladder and you have to do all the right things and keep a lot of people happy. It is too bad that they can't just be themselves. Sometimes it meant that they don't feel that they can do the things that have to be done because those things are not "politically correct." (Emma)

They were not reassured by assertions that mandated changes were based on research:

> You see it written up in journals and they had all kinds of extra people running around and anyway how writers say it happened and what actually happened are two different things. (Pat)

Teachers questioned the quality of research, concerned that published studies tended to be based on work with selected teachers, focused only on what was going well, served to promote certain schools, and failed to give the whole story. Because many of these teachers lived in university cities, they, or other teachers they knew, had been in schools where evaluation research was carried out. Teachers whose classrooms were studied and analyzed were those who "loved" the latest innovation; they themselves, as marginalized, resistant "dinosaurs," had not been part of the research base. Wolcott (1977) had reported the same phenomenon some years earlier from his perspective as a researcher. When invited into a school to evaluate the success of a particular innovation, he was directed to speak only to teachers who were enthusiastic about the new curriculum; only by talking to all the teachers did he get a picture of the mandated scheme that allowed him to discover what was working well, what needed changing and what should be discontinued.

The Process of Change

Teachers have a pivotal role in schools and they are essential to the success of any school restructuring plan (Barrow, 1984; Barth, 1990; Cohn and Kottkamp, 1993; Cuban, 1988; Fullan with Stiegelbauer, 1991; Fullan and Hargreaves, 1991; Lortie, 1975; Sarason, 1990). McLaughlin (1990) stresses the importance of "teachers' perspectives as informants and guides to policy" (p. 15); change is a problem of the smallest unit. But the processes needed to ensure teacher involvement in and ownership of change are rarely in place. Sources of change tend to be scholars, not practitioners (Cuban, 1988). Implicit in the process is a view of teachers as technicians whose job is to implement the carefully designed plans using teacher-proof materials prepared by "experts" (DeYoung, 1980). Wolcott (1977) fears that too often teacher autonomy has been sacrificed to managerial efficiency. While teachers should be asked, and be asking, the questions that drive educational reform (Cohn and Kottkamp, 1993), the process of mandating change is not in their hands.

Even when a new curriculum is presumably teacher and student centered (Henley, 1987), teachers are seldom given the opportunity to help conceptualize the program that they are expected to teach. There is neither time nor support for the building of personal philosophies or communal reflection that might give teachers the basis to work more effectively

(Rudduck, 1991). As a result, teachers become passive consumers in their own educational structure (Gitlin, 1990; House, 1974). One consequence of treating teachers as technicians is what Apple (1982) calls *deskilling*.

A top-down process of mandating change discourages teachers' abilities to set goals, develop skills, respond to feedback, and become engaged in improving their practice; instead, it encourages teachers to become dependent on the latest innovation, driving them further from a sense of their own expertise and professionalism (Fullan, 1993). Inservice training to help teachers learn new processes and skills is typically based on an assumption that there is a deficiency in the teacher (Thiessen, 1992), and that researchers and curriculum developers know what is best (Clark, 1992). When mandated change implies a criticism of what they are currently doing, the stage is set for teacher resistance (Connell, 1955).

Teachers' efforts to comply with mandated change are usually inadequately supported (Fullan and Hargreaves, 1991; Kemmis, 1987; Louis and Miles, 1990). Change is typically introduced and instituted through a system of principals, consultants, and other "change agents," workshops and inservice activities. But study participants found these strategies problematic. They did not view their principals as knowledgeable about the mandates, aware of the range of needs that existed in their schools, or having the necessary skills to help teachers improve their practice. Jenny, who taught first grade, enrolled in a university class at her own expense to help her teach reading properly, but found her principal quite unsupportive:

> Here I am using my own time and my own money to figure this out. My classes are on Thursdays. All the school functions are on Thursdays and the principal won't change because he thinks that it is a good night for meeting. He won't even compromise. Just ask me if I feel supported! (Jenny)

Several teachers found the training provided by their school systems inadequate: short, sporadic, non-specific and even patronizing:

> They organised a Mickey-Mouse-let's-all-get-to-know-each-other activity when they knew that we almost all knew each other. Then they had us do all this stuff that went out of date years ago. Didn't they know who they were talking to? We all had real issues about teaming and changing the timetable that we needed to talk about with each other and this would have been a great time to do that. (Jerry)

Professional development activities were usually organized by consultants, people with particular expertise to work with teachers as they developed or improved their curriculum. When they found the professional development activities inadequate and wanted more specific help, some teachers wanted the consultants to come and work with them in their classrooms:

> If they want to help me change then they have to come into my classroom for at least a week and work with the forty kids and the ones with learn-

ing problems and behavioral problems and disabilities. Then tell me how to do things. Don't haul me off to a workshop and give me all these wonderful ideas that work so well on paper. Come and show me with the real, live kids. (Isabell)

Several participants reported that consultants were hard to get hold of and even harder to get into schools. Emma had asked for a consultant to come and work in her classroom, but despite frequent phone calls she had received only written material and notices for workshops. At the same time class size was increasing, budgets were decreasing and classes for children with specialised needs were being closed. She saw class size as a major problem and felt that a better use of resources would be to put the consultants "back into the classroom," thereby creating the smaller classes which would enable her to do a better job of teaching.

If you want to cut back, the best place to start is with that pack up there with their nine hundred muffins a day and their wonderful outfits and their endless cups of tea. Telling everyone how busy they are and their needs have to be catered to and they haven't got time to come into the schools because they are just too busy, "right off my feet," but just phone their offices and see where they are, most likely in the cafeteria . . . Let other people watch them teach for a while. They are consultants, they should know just what to do. So put 'em back in there and find out how long they will last. They are terrified that they will have to put their money where their mouth is. (Emma)

Nearly all the teachers in the study had attempted to work with mandated changes. They had taken extra classes, gone to workshops, worked with consultants, pored over binders of materials sent out by the Ministry of Education. But just as they began to feel that they were achieving some degree of understanding and mastery the mandated change "sort of fell from favor," to be replaced by some new enthusiasm. As Nancy expressed it:

When if a teacher sticks their neck out to do something new there is so often not good support for them to follow through . . . They put a big push on at the beginning of some new approach and then that is it. It only lasts for about a year or two.

Mandated changes may occur at the same time educational funding is cut. At the time of the study, school boards began getting less money for professional development activities shortly after teachers began working on several simultaneous and complex curriculum reforms. The teachers recognised the problems caused by budgetary restraints:

If others are going to want me to change what I am doing in my classroom then I need to know that they are really serious and are ready to put their money where their mouths are. But that isn't happening. They won't make me good at something, they won't train me. I do not want to do a half-assed job. I am too good for that. There may be a lot of good stuff but unless we get the bucks to back it up then it won't happen. Like we are trying to do new things and classes are getting into the high thirties. (Patrick)

The "orphaning" of mandated programs elicited different responses, depending on teachers' past experiences. Some had "been there before" and were resignedly accepting that teachers had been once again "hung out to dry." For others, betrayal and desertion were new experiences. The over-arching consequence of orphaning programs may be teachers' increasing reluctance to try anything new.

Some of the teachers had enthusiastically supported particular man-dated changes, pleased that some of their own cherished ideas might finally be manifested, but discovered that, as they worked with the innovation, they could only go so far before they ran into roadblocks created by a system which was not also changing:

> One of the things that drives me silly is the language of the paradigm shift (that is one of the pet words this year). But when you actually look at the way in which the command structure works, it is still under the old para-digm. The administration hasn't shifted, just the talk has shifted. So that meant that we were running up against these obstacles that were within the traditional model. (Gordon)

For example, while teachers were being required to work with holis-tic forms of assessing student progress, provincial expectations for paper and pencil tests for young children were still in place. While teachers were being required to integrate curriculum or include special needs students in their mainstream classrooms, the very structure of schools discouraged any-thing but traditional practice:

> There have to be some fundamental changes in the way that a school is set up and I don't believe for one minute that those changes will be made, like taking the timetable and saying "Okay, all the old rules are out and how would you like to revise it?" (Gordon).

> The structure of the system affects the thinking of those who work in it. Like for instance I saw all kinds of ways of arranging a room but they all looked like they were in a box, because they were. So our thinking is affected by that. Our architecture means that we are not moving away from one teacher and thirty-odd kids. If we move to become facilitators and have self-directed kids they are still really only able to refer to very few people in that process of self-direction, because they are more or less con-fined to one room. The very physical structure of the school determines how we work with children . . . Individuals can make changes but I am not sure if the system can make changes. The system tells us that change has to happen and yet the individuals who change do not affect the system. The *system* does not really support that change or even allow that change to take place. (Anne)

While teachers were making paradigmatic shifts in their teaching, they did not have the authority to bring about the kinds of structural changes necessary to realize the promise of those shifts. For such teachers, the process of change was frustrating and highly problematic. Neither supported in their efforts to comply with mandates, nor able to go all the way with the changes they worked on, they were left wondering what it was all about.

Conclusion

I have attempted to demonstrate how the context and process of mandated change leads to the marginalization of teachers. I have suggested that marginalization occurs because such changes are not rooted in teachers' realities and expertise and that as a consequence teachers have serious doubts about their efficacy and cannot be morally committed to their implementation of mandated programs. I have suggested that failing to deal with the concerns of marginalized teachers is a key cause of failed educational change, both because of teachers' demoralization and because there are serious practical implications to ignoring what teachers know about bringing about real and sustained change. I conclude by considering what it would take for reforms to become more relevant and logistically compatible with what is occurring in real classrooms and schools.

The connection between teaching and the bureaucratic structure in which teachers work is convoluted and contradictory. On the one hand the study participants believe change is necessary and report that they have voluntarily changed their own practice. On the other hand, such changes are not supported by a system that is conservative and intractable by nature:

> The way that teachers are trained, the way that schools are organised, the way that the educational hierarchy operates, and the way that education is treated by political decision-makers results in a system that is more likely to retain the *status quo* than to change. When change is attempted under such circumstances it results in defensiveness, superficiality or, at best, short-lived pockets of success. (Fullan, 1993: 3)

> Instead of stimulating discussion in which no assumption is sacred, no alternative automatically off limits, and arguments for practicality and the status quo are not inhibitors of envisioning alternatives; intractability has reinforced the repetitive compulsion. (Sarason, 1990: 148)

Teachers who want to change their teaching strategies more than superficially challenge that conservative and intractable system. Pat recounted how difficult it had been for her to obtain official approval to do a novel study. Yet within a few years using basal readers became unacceptable practice and teachers were expected to do novel studies. The system only accepts change in pre-approved ways.

How might the educational system support teachers' desires for change rather than thwarting them? David Hunt (1992) suggests that bureaucracy is problematic:

> [a] renewing organisation is horizontal rather then hierarchical to reflect an
> acknowledgment of the expertise of each individual member. In the renew-
> ing organisation, persons with greater responsibility are not traditional
> experts but are responsible for the free flow of resources and expertise
> among members. (1992: 104)

Hunt suggests that if we want ongoing change and renewal then all parts
of an organization have to change. The expertise of *each* member is recognized, and the experts are supportive, encouraged to share what they
know. Gitlin and Margonis (1995) identify some preconditions of reform:

> [One precondition for reform is] giving teachers the authority and time they
> need to teach in ways they find educationally defensible. The educational
> hierarchy ought to be transformed so that school administrators and dis-
> trict personnel support the efforts of teachers, and teachers' workloads
> should be decreased to allow time for planning, curriculum development
> and innovative pedagogy. (p. 404)

Nancy had a similar suggestion:

> What they should be doing is finding the master teachers and facilitating
> them to work with other teachers, to give workshops or whatever. Teach-
> ers really want to hear from other teachers and we do not get much chance
> to do that.

Another component of this new framework for change, then, is the
teachers themselves. There are many precedents for teacher initiated change.
For example, Gordon's high school changed its program significantly in
response to student need and parent request. Emma worked with parents
as they built organizations that represented their views to the community at
large. In my own career I have experienced two episodes of successful educational change, one in England and one in Canada. In the first example,
the English infant schools, teachers began to work on integrated program
and child-based learning. Concepts developed by teachers were spread by
visiting inspectors who saw their role as facilitative rather than directive.
The second experience was in British Columbia, where whole language concepts began to manifest themselves in many classrooms as the result of the
work of a few teachers, supported through local professional development
activities, teacher organizations, and much hard work on the part of individuals — long before such programs were mandated.

Getting teachers deeply involved in envisioning and managing change
means giving up the idea of a "preconceived outcome" (Gitlin and Margonis, 1995), and abandoning the notion that there is one best way to teach.
As researchers, administrators and policymakers, we cannot assume that we
understand enough about particular school cultures or the needs of individual classrooms. We lack the knowledge to design a one-size-fits-all
program which will fix all the ills of school and society. Teachers who resist
our cherished notions, research results or policy content are not necessarily wrong. As Edward Pauley points out:

While schooling clearly contributes to students' achievement — children who go to school learn more than those who don't — there is no known school policy or program that consistently and predictably helps students learn more than any other school policy or program. (1991: 109)

At the same time, we cannot assume that teachers have all the answers or that local problems cannot be informed by a broader perspective and more comprehensive knowledge base. As Pauley suggests, we need to form partnerships that create

policies whose effectiveness grows out of classroom reciprocal power. Obviously, such policies must take different forms in each classroom, which is one reason why they don't fit the conventional mould of prescriptive education policies. The goal of classroom-oriented policies is to discover ways to support people in each classroom as they pursue what ever method of teaching and learning are effective for them, while pressing them to do less of whatever prevents them from teaching and learning. The goal of these classroom-support policies is to improve student achievement, while taking advantage of the central role of reciprocal power in tailoring each classroom's activities to its members. (Pauley, p. 158)

We need to work with teachers to bring our knowledge and expertise to meet and mix with the knowledge and expertise of local practitioners in real school settings. This is admittedly an idealistic belief. Teacher resistance is not always rooted in unadulterated altruism. But researchers, administrators and policymakers must also confront their own biases, listen more respectfully to teachers, take the issue of supporting teachers seriously, familiarize themselves with the realities of classrooms and schools, and acknowledge that teachers must be involved as an intimate part of the process if positive educational change is to take place.

The participants in this study are committed to doing their best for the children in their care. They are on the margins of their profession not by virtue of incompetence or weakness but rather because they cannot in all conscience support mandated policies and programs. They are on the margins because they work in a system that does not recognize their expertise. Their perspective is seen as problematic. *They* are seen as problematic. Such teachers become tired, physically and psychically. Policymakers, administrators, researchers and teachers can do better by working to form relationships with teachers that are firmly grounded in the actual needs of children in real schools. It is time to take that leap of faith.

References

Alberta Teachers' Association (1993) *Trying to teach*. Interim report of the Committee on Public Education and Professional Practice as approved by Provincial Executive Council for discussion at the 1993 Annual Representative Assembly.

Apple, M. (1982) *Education and power.* Boston: ARK Paperbacks.

Apple, M. (1993) *Official knowledge.* New York: Routledge.

Ball, S. (1987) *The micro-politics of the school: towards a theory of school organisation.* London: Methuen.

Barrow, R. (1984) *Giving teaching back to teachers: a critical introduction to curriculum theory.* New York: Althouse Press.

Barth, R. (1990) *Improving schools from within.* San Francisco: Jossey-Bass.

Berger, P. (1971) *A rumour of angels.* London: Penguin Books.

Clark, C. (1992) Teachers as designers in self-directed professional development. In A. Hargreaves and M. Fullan (eds.), *Understanding teacher development*, pp. 74–84. New York: Teachers College Press.

Clune, W. (1990) Three views of curriculum policy in the school context: the school as policy mediator, policy critic, and policy constructor. In A. McLaughlin, J. Talbert and N. Bascia (eds.), *The context of teaching in secondary schools: teachers' realities*, pp. 256–70. New York: Teachers College Press.

Cohn, M. and Kottkamp, R. (1993) *Teachers: the missing voice in education.* New York: SUNY.

Connell, R. (1985) *Teachers' work.* Sydney: George Allen and Unwin.

Cooper, M. (1988) Whose culture is it anyway? In A. Lieberman (ed.), *Building a professional culture in schools*, pp. 45–54. New York: Teachers College Press.

Cuban, L. (1988) *The managerial imperative and the practice of leadership in schools.* New York: SUNY.

Cuban, L. (1989) The persistence of reform in American schools. In D. Warren (ed.), *American teachers: history of a profession at work*, pp. 370–92. New York: Macmillan.

Deal, D. (1986) Educational change: revival tent and tinkertoys, jungle or carnival. In A. Lieberman (ed.), *Rethinking school improvement*, pp. 115–28. New York: Teachers College Press.

DeYoung, A. J. (1980) Professional and politics: toward a more realistic assessment of the issue. *The Clearing House*, 53(6), 268–70.

Fullan, M. (1993) *Change forces.* London: Falmer Press.

Fullan, M. and Hargreaves, A. (1991) *What's worth fighting for? Working together for your school.* Toronto: OPSTF.

Fullan, M. and Miles, M. (1992) Getting reform right: what works and what doesn't. *Phi Delta Kappan*, 73(10), 745–52.

Fullan, M. with Stiegelbauer, S. (1991) *The new meaning of educational change.* New York: Teachers College Press.

Gitlin, A. (1990) Understanding teaching dialogically. *Teachers College Record*, 91(4), 537–64.

Gitlin, A. and Margonis, F. (1995) The political aspect of reform: teacher resistance as good sense. *American Journal of Education*, 103, 377–405.

Goffman, E. (1963) *Stigma: notes on the management of spoiled identity.* New York: Prentice Hall.

Hargreaves, A. (1990) Teachers' work and politics of time and space. *Qualitative Studies in Education*, 1(4), 303–20.

Hargreaves, A. and Fullan, M. (1998) *What's worth fighting for in education.* London: Open University Press.

Henley, M. (1987) Something is missing from the educational reform movement. *Phi Delta Kappan*, 69(4), 284–5.

House, E. (1974) *The politics of educational innovation*. Berkeley, CA: McCutcheon.

Huberman, A. M. (1989) Teacher development and instructional mastery. Manuscript submitted for publication.

Huberman, A. M. (1993) *The lives of teachers*. New York: Teachers College Press.

Hunsaker, L. (1992) Teachers under construction: a collaborative case study of teacher change. *American Educational Research Journal*, 29(2), 350–72.

Hunt, D. (1992) *The renewal of personal energy*. Toronto: OISE.

Jackson, P. (1968) *The practice of teaching*. New York: Teachers College Press.

Jackson. P. (1990) *Life in classrooms*. New York: Teachers College Press.

Johnston, B. (1993) The transformation of work and educational reform practice. *American Educational Research Journal*, 30(1), 39–65.

Kemmis, S. (1987) Critical reflection. In M. Wideen and I. Andrews (eds.), *Staff development for school improvement: a focus on the teacher*, pp. 73–90. London: Falmer Press.

Lieberman, A. and Miller, L. (1984) *Teachers, their world and their work: implications for school improvement*. Virginia: ASCD.

Lortie, D. (1975) *Schoolteacher: a sociological study*. Chicago: University of Chicago Press.

Louis, K. S. and Miles, M. (1990) *Improving the urban high school: what works and why?* New York: Teachers College Press.

McLaughlin, M. (1990) The Rand change agent study revisited: Marco perspectives and micro realities. *Educational Researcher*, 19(9), 11–16.

McNeil, L. (1988) *Contradictions of control: school structure and school knowledge*. New York: Routledge.

Musgrove, F. (1977) *Margins of the mind*. London: Methuen.

Pauley, E. (1991) *The classroom crucible: what really works, what doesn't, and why*. New York: Basic Books.

Riseborough, G. F. (1981) Teacher careers and comprehensive schooling: an empirical study. *Sociology*, 15(3), 355–81.

Rudduck, J. (1991) *Innovation and change: developing involvement and understanding*. Philadelphia: Open University Press.

Sarason, S. (1990) *The predictable failure of educational reform*. San Francisco: Jossey-Bass.

Schlechty, P. (1988) Leading cultural change: the CMS case. In A. Lieberman (ed.), *Building a professional culture in schools*, pp. 185–221. New York: Teachers College Press.

Silberman, C. E. (1970) *Crisis in the classroom*. New York: Random House.

Thiessen, D. (1992) Classroom based teacher development. In A. Hargeaves and M. Fullan (eds.), *Understanding teacher development*, pp. 95–109. New York: Teachers College Press.

Timar, T. (1989) The politics of school restructuring. *Phi Delta Kappan*, 71(4), 265–75.

Willis, P. (1978) *Profane cultures*. London: Routledge and Kegan Paul.

Wolcott, H. (1977) *Teachers versus technocrats*. Eugene, OR: Related Centre Publication.

Woods, P. (1990) *Teacher skills and strategies*. London: Falmer Press.

Woods, P. (1991) The struggle for self: teacher development through grounded life history. Paper presented at a meeting of the International Study Association on Teacher Thinking, Surrey, UK.

Woods, P. (1993) Managing marginality: teacher development through grounded life history. *British Education Research Journal*, 19(5), 447–65.

Zeichner, K. (1991) Contradictions and tensions in the professionalization of teaching and the democratization of schools. *Teachers College Record*, 92(3), 364–379.

III CONTEXTS OF CHANGE

7 Gender Politics in School Reform

Amanda Datnow

School change experts proffer several explanations for derailed reform. Some argue that reforms often fail to address the core processes of teaching and learning (Elmore, 1996). Others argue that reform fails when teachers do not make meaning of the change (Fullan, 1991) or when the change effort does not address the context in which the school is located (Sarason, 1990). It could also be that the system and its goals are not stable enough to sustain locally developed reform (Stringfield *et al.*, 1997). Using qualitative data collected in two secondary schools undertaking detracking reforms, this chapter shows how school change efforts can be derailed for a very different reason: *gender politics.*[1]

Competing Ideologies, Micropolitics, and Gender in School Change

Assumptions about Teacher Agency

Teachers are considered by most policymakers and school change experts to be the centerpiece of educational change. Therefore, not surprisingly, most reform efforts are directed at teachers, and the involvement of teachers in the school reform process is seen as critical. Policies aimed at decentralization, including grant maintained schools in the UK, charter schools in the US, and self-managing schools in New Zealand, to name a few, all rely on teachers to "reinvent" schools. School change experts also echo the belief that schools are best changed from the bottom up (Fullan, 1991; Heckman and Peterman, 1997; Sarason, 1996; Wideen, 1994). Teachers need to own the process of change, and reform efforts need to be grounded in an understanding of teachers' professional lives and development (Fullan and Hargreaves, 1996; Hopkins and Wideen, 1984; McNeil, 1988; Sikes, 1992; Sirotnik and Oakes, 1986).

While a teacher-centered approach may be fundamental to successful school change, it has some limitations. Most notably, it does not recognize the dynamic nature of the school reform process and the complex realities of locally developed school reform. In fact, teachers act in a variety of ways in response to reforms: some teachers push or sustain reform efforts; others resist or actively subvert these efforts. Common assumptions about the role of teacher agency in school change also do not take into account the micropolitics that occur among teachers at the local level as they struggle to redefine what "school" means for students.

School change is much messier than many policy analysts think. Ideological differences, micropolitics and gender dynamics among teachers are all part of a school's culture and, accordingly, all play into the school reform process. The school culture itself may be the subject or site of a struggle over competing ideologies, as teachers from various subcultures often have differing opinions on what to change and how to change it. As research on teacher development has pointed out, teachers' responses to change are always impacted by the differing values, beliefs and assumptions that teachers hold (Nias, 1998).

Conflicting ideologies can be the source of teacher resistance to change. That is, teachers who find that their ideologies are inconsistent with the proposed reform may actively or passively resist the change. Muncey and McQuillan (1996) found that teacher resistance to change resulted when teachers felt that their vested interests or taken-for-granted beliefs and values were threatened by the reform agenda. Bailey (this volume) and Sikes (1992) documented how teachers resisted top-down mandates when the rhetoric of the changes did not match with the realities of teachers' experiences.

Ideology and resistance to reform also can correlate with teachers' personal characteristics. Huberman (1989) has shown that veteran teachers are more likely to resist change than younger teachers because such efforts are "out of phase" with their age and career stage. Similarly, Riseborough (1981) documented the how the "old staff" at a secondary school resisted changes proposed by a new headteacher, whose values and methods were at odds with their own. Acker (1996) and Apple (1986) show that teachers (who were mostly women) actively and subtly resisted reforms aimed at deskilling and increasing control over their work. In a similar vein, Casey (1993) and Foster (1993) found that black and politically progressive women teachers resisted the status quo (e.g., racism and sexism) and the dominant ideology that supported it. Black teachers also resisted school reforms that they believe are grounded in white, middle class perspectives, rather than in the experiences and values of the black community (Foster, 1994). Indeed, as Gitlin and Margonis (1995) argue, researchers need to pay attention to the "good sense" or insight that may be embodied in teachers' resistance to change.

Gender and School Change

As the research cited above suggests, teachers come to the school reform process from different social locations (e.g., age, gender, race, ethnicity), and this positionality impacts their role in the politics of school change. Gender is a particularly important feature of social differentiation among teachers. Yet, only recently has the school change literature begun to recognize the impact of gender (Acker, 1996; Blackmore, 1998; Blackmore and Kenway, 1995; Robertson, 1992). The lack of attention to gender (and race and ethnicity, for that matter) is interesting, given the fact that gender operates on the societal level as a system of unequal power relations. In most societies, men simply have more power, controlling government, law and public discourse. These social relations of power are played out on the terrain of everyday public discourse in societal institutions, including schools. Therefore, it would follow that gender would impact the process and politics of change in most, if not all, social institutions.

While there is a dearth of literature on the intersection of gender and school reform, there is a plethora of literature on gender and teaching more generally. This research focuses on three major areas: the gendered nature of teaching as a profession (particularly at the elementary school level) (Acker, 1994; Apple, 1994; Biklen, 1995; Weiler, 1988), the divergence of career opportunities among men and women teachers (Acker, 1989; Grant, 1989; Riddell, 1989; Shakeshaft, 1989; Sikes *et al.*, 1985), and the counter-hegemonic, anti-sexist efforts of feminist teachers (Blackmore and Kenway, 1995; Casey, 1993; Weiler, 1988). A number of these works also discuss women teachers' lives in terms of the structural forces of patriarchy that have shaped them. This research has been very important in establishing the role of gender in structuring the professional lives of teachers, and, in the case of feminist scholarship, making women's voices and understandings the central focus of research.

The Micropolitics of School Change

Part of understanding the role of gender in school change is making sense of the relations of power among teachers. What I am referring to here is school micropolitics, which is seldom dealt with in school change research (see Blase, 1998; Hargreaves *et al.*,1996 for this critique). Muncey and McQuillan's (1996) study of the Coalition of Essential Schools is a notable exception, as it highlights the "shifts in power, prestige, and responsibility" that result when reform is introduced (p. 159). Ball's (1987) study of the introduction of mixed ability classrooms in schools in the UK also addressed how micropolitics shaped reform efforts and relations among teachers, as did Noblit, Berry, and Demsey's (1991) study of a reform effort aimed at increasing teacher professionalism.

Micropolitical analysis emphasizes power, ideological diversity, and political action (Ball, 1987; Iannacone, 1991; Malen, 1995). Hoyle (1986) describes micropolitics as the "organizational underworld" that we know very little about because it is "almost a taboo subject in 'serious' discussion, yet informally it is a favorite theme of organizational gossip as people talk about 'playing politics', 'hidden agendas', 'organizational mafias',

'Machiavellianism' and so forth" (p. 125). By studying micropolitics, we can gain an understanding of how and why certain individuals and groups shape what happens in schools through their power and dominance over others.

What are common to definitions of micropolitics are the elements of subversiveness and seediness. It is therefore not surprising that most studies of school change do not address micropolitics, particularly because of the research relationships and ethics that might be placed at risk by it. In addition, teachers often shy away from using political language to describe their actions in schools, and thus data on micropolitics are difficult to gather (Siskin, 1994). Yet the micropolitical perspective reminds us that school reform is rarely politically neutral; some even argue that reforms enter schools already politically organized (Noblit *et al.*, 1991). The micropolitical perspective also reminds us that schools are as much a venue for adult–adult relationships as they are for teaching and learning (Nias, 1988). Reform not only creates the opportunity for new arenas of micropolitics, it also often awakens latent hostilities (Blase, 1998; Muncey and McQuillan, 1996; Noblit *et al.*, 1991).

Thus far, few studies of micropolitics have looked at the ways in which gender or, more generally, social relations of power impact the micropolitics of schools. In fact, Ball (1987) states that one of the risks in micropolitical analysis is to downplay the role of structural features in organizing everyday life and overemphasize internal factors. Further work needs to be done in relating the external elements of the school environment to the internal political behaviors (Blase, 1998; Iannacone, 1991). This chapter offers insight into how social relations of gender impact the micropolitics of school change.

The Politics of Representation

The aforementioned literature on micropolitics leaves us wanting for a way of making sense of how hostilities between opposing groups, with different ideologies and goals, might be expressed in the context of school reform. Just how might we expect the struggle over reform to play itself out among teachers? How do we make sure to attend to gender and other wider social relations of power? The *politics of representation* serves as a helpful organizing framework for understanding these issues.

The politics of representation is the competition that takes place among individuals or factions over the meaning of ambiguous events, people and objects in the world. The way in which events, objects or people are represented in discourse gives them a particular meaning (Mehan, 1993). Representations do not mimic reality, but rather are the practices by which things take on meaning and value (Shapiro, 1987). Modes of representing events differ according to a person's social location: speech is constituted by the history of a person's place in gender, class, race and institutional arrangements. Groups or individuals can have profoundly different meanings for the same situation, depending on their ideologies, belief systems or experiences. This is true of teachers in schools who may view a reform either as an opportunity or as a major hindrance. However, not all definitions are equally valid. In an unequal power situation, more powerful groups or individuals can impose their definition of a situation on others (Mehan, 1990). This has striking consequences for teachers in schools as not all teachers have equal power. Sometimes these power differences overlap with gender.

What is key to the politics of representation is the inextricable connection between language and power. The overarching point here is "the more powerful the people, the larger their verbal possibilities in discourse" (Wodak, 1995: 33). Power is often expressed through the use of language and symbols in the micropolitics of the school. The strategic use of discourse is among the most influential micropolitical processes. More powerful groups can use language to define what questions and issues are seen as important in the setting (such as whether or not reform is necessary), rendering the definitions held by less powerful groups seemingly irrational (Berger and Luckmann, 1967; Corson, 1995; Marshall and Scribner, 1991). The connection between language and power is also evident in gender studies, and it is here that we can see the influence of social location on the politics of representation. Feminist researchers, both in education and more broadly, see gender relations as constructed through the discourse of organizations (Biklen, 1995; Blackmore and Kenway, 1995; Casey, 1993; Gherardi, 1995; Mann, 1994; Uchida, 1992). Arguably then, how gender is constructed between men and women in schools is a key micropolitical issue in school change.

What I have attempted to show in this review of the literature is that the relationship between gender politics and educational change can best be understood in the context of a framework that regards language as constitutive of political phenomena, rather than simply about political phenomena. Bringing perspectives from the literature on school change, gender and micropolitics to bear upon qualitative data from schools in which gender politics emerged as a shaping force in the reform is a powerful way to investigate how teachers struggle to redefine what "school" means.

Examples of Gender Politics in Two Restructuring Schools

In the subsequent section, I investigate the gender politics among factions of teachers at two schools — Central High School and Explorer Middle School.[2] Specifically, I focus on the conventions and discourse strategies that are revealed in the contest over meaning among these gender-based factions.

Case Study Methodology

The data for this chapter were collected as part of a larger comparative case study of racially mixed detracking secondary schools, the Beyond Sorting and Stratification study (Oakes and Wells, 1995, 1996).[3] The main purpose of the overall study was to understand what happens when schools undertake alternatives to tracking, or the grouping of students according to their perceived ability. In order to answer this question, we used a longitudinal, qualitative case study approach to studying secondary schools across the country. There were six high schools and four middle schools in the study, including Central High School and Explorer Middle School, both discussed in this chapter. All schools were racially mixed and they were located in various regions of the country, situated in urban, suburban and rural areas.

Case study methodology enables educational researchers to examine the process and consequences of changes in the real-life context in which they occur, when there is no control over events (Yin, 1989). The schools in the detracking study were at various stages in the process of implementing alternatives to tracking, and we were able to document reform efforts as they were taking place. Each school was assigned one researcher who took primary responsibility for that school throughout the study. For example, as the primary researcher for Central High School, I made three visits to the school between 1992 and 1994, lasting three to five full days each, as part of the detracking study. During each visit, I was accompanied by one or more researchers on our team. In August 1995, I circulated a lengthy case report to five people at the school for feedback. In addition, in June 1996, I returned to the school and conducted further interviews with teachers and administrators in order to further validate findings and to get a sense of what had changed in the school over the past two years. The data collection efforts at Explorer Middle School were similar and were led by another research associate on the study.[4]

During each regularly scheduled visit to the schools, our research team conducted an average of thirty-five to forty interviews. We used semi-structured interview protocols, asking open-ended questions of respondents. All of these interviews were taped and transcribed at the completion of each school site visit. The interviewed teachers represented a diversity of departments, ages, racial backgrounds, length of time at the school and involvement level in the reform. We also conducted numerous interviews with the principal, assistant principals, district administrators, school board members, counselors, students and parents. We made formal observations of classes and school meetings, and collected many school and district documents relevant to both the school context and the reform efforts taking place. Using multiple sources of evidence allowed for triangulation of the data (Yin, 1989). In the process of analysis, these data were brought into an ongoing conversation with a theoretical framework that brought together literature in education, sociology, political science, and anthropology (Strauss and Corbin, 1990).

Central High School

Central High School is typical of a southwestern United States urban high school. During the period of the study, Central served approximately 2200 students of mixed ethnicity and race in grades 9 through 12. Almost half of the students, mostly recent immigrants from Mexico, were classified as Limited English Proficient. The Latino and non-native English speaking population was increasing, while the white population was decreasing. The school had a bi-modal socioeconomic distribution; most of the low-income students were Latino.

Historically, Central High School had a reputation in the community as a "tough school" fraught with violence and gang problems. Some community members called this an "undeserved negative reputation" due mostly to bad press by local papers, but by most measures, and by comparison to other schools in the district, Central did not boast a stellar academic record. When data collection began in 1992, Central was sending only 10–12% of its graduates on to four-year colleges, the majority of whom were white. Tracking was extensive and minority students were disproportionately placed in non-college preparatory tracks. Central's history was also distinguished by the considerable turnover in the administrative staff; the school had had seven principals over the last twenty years.

When the study began, several teachers and administrators told us that a small faction of male teachers known as the "Good Old Boys" had long held the power in this school characterized by weak leadership and low academic standards. An educator at Central described the Good Old Boys as "male, very veteran, very able to be very outspoken, and not at all unwilling to be abrasive to the point of abusive in order to get their way." The "Good Old Boys," a sobriquet widely used among faculty and administration at the school, described a group of at least nine male teachers from a variety of departments who were in their late forties, had been at the school for over twenty years, and were described by administrators and other teachers as "entrenched staff" who were strong union supporters. In addition to their union and district office ties, the Good Old Boys also derived power from their status as coaches in this community in which athletics took precedence over academics.[5]

The seeds for reform at Central High School were planted in 1989, when the American Federation of Teachers Union President, Albert Shanker, spoke at a staff development workshop for district teachers. After hearing his speech, a small group of teachers at Central High School brainstormed about possible changes that they could make at their school. After much deliberation, the teachers drew up plans for a pilot "school-within-a-school" program: Central Lifetime Achievers, or "CLA." The underlying goal of CLA was to improve the achievement of non-college prep track students, in particular minority students, by offering them a challenging program of study that would allow them to meet the college entrance requirements. The CLA teachers created an interdisciplinary, integrated curriculum across the core academic subjects in which teachers would follow students through their four years of high school. Over time, the CLA program was able to raise students' standardized test scores and their college enrollment rates.

In the Spring of 1992, buoyed by the success of the CLA program, several CLA teachers approached the site administration about the possibility of implementing something similar to CLA school-wide. The administration embraced the idea of school-wide reform and made the strategic decision to engage a broad-based group of support. They made an open invitation to the entire staff and community to meet on a Saturday to establish their ideal vision of Central High School graduates and to generate ideas for how the school could be restructured to achieve that goal. While the CLA program laid the groundwork for school-wide restructuring, the CLA teachers agreed that it would not have been possible without the school's new, forward-thinking principal, Bob Foster.

Over fifty people, including educators, parents and community members, met to develop a vision for Central High School. From the original group who met that day, a core group of sixteen people emerged, turning the vision into a plan for restructuring. This group called themselves the "Idea Team." Nine of them, who were certainly the most active members of the Idea Team, were white women in their late forties. Most of them had been teaching for over twenty years. Four members of the Idea Team wrote the restructuring proposal, and these women, including the assistant principal, were the ones most associated with restructuring from that point onward. They had assistance during the writing process from a restructuring coach, a private consultant who had significant experience working with schools.

In the Fall of 1992, the state granted Central $1.3 million of funding over five years under a law which provided funds for comprehensive school restructuring efforts. The proposal for restructuring included the plan to detrack the school by "offering all students access to and assistance in a rich and challenging curriculum." Along with detracking, the school had plans to move toward a house structure, homerooms, interdisciplinary thematic instruction, alternative assessment, a customized calendar and a new governance structure. The Idea Team also hoped to start a health and social services center at the school and to institute a peer coaching professional development model. The restructuring proposal included statements of support from the district office, the school board and the teachers' union.

After the grant was funded, the restructuring process began with the establishment of numerous restructuring work groups centered around such issues as heterogeneous grouping, curriculum, and professional development. The Idea Team members served as the leaders and facilitators of these discussion groups, though members of the Good Old Boys and the teaching faculty at large were also represented. Still, the Idea Team had a forum in which their voices could now be heard, and slowly they began to move toward implementing change with the strong support of the principal.

Gender politics and ideological diversity at Central High School. When restructuring at Central first began, the discourse centered around ideologies of education. The Idea Team and the Good Old Boys clearly had very different ideologies. The Good Old Boys shared a common ideological perspective regarding student ability, the role of the teacher, and the purposes of schooling and the need (or lack thereof) for reform. The Good Old Boys viewed ability as fixed: high intelligence only exists in some students, not in all students. Veteran science teacher Walter Brown, explained his perspective, which many of the Good Old Boys shared: "Some of that may just be simple intellectual ability. Some kids are just born with, I mean, I don't know if I want to get into this controversial thing. Some kids have got it and some kids don't."

The Good Old Boys shared the belief that schools are not the problem, but rather that students have changed and certain family arrangements make educating kids difficult. One of them illustrated this belief in an interview: "I don't care what anybody tells you, it's the family structure that's causing the schools to fail. I can teach a kid and give him the material, but I can't make the kid learn." In general, the Good Old Boys believed that the role of a teacher is simply to cope with, but not improve, a student's individual situation.

Good Old Boys' ideology about education was inconsistent with the Idea Team's reform plan. Their ideology served to maintain the power relations inherent in the school's structure and culture. It is important to note how the Good Old Boys talked about the reform. The discourse the Good Old Boys used to discuss the restructuring, and in particular detracking, centered around what the changes would mean for them as teachers. They focused on how detracking would change their role or force them into the unfamiliar territory of new teaching strategies or different groups of students. However, this discourse shifted as the restructuring progressed, as we will see later.

In contrast to the Good Old Boys, the school's restructuring coach described the Idea Team as "very interested in kids and changing things to make them work for kids and being innovative and taking risks . . . And those people are normally very polite, very nice, and frankly, female." Members of the Idea Team shared common conceptions of ability, about their role as teachers, and about schooling and the need for reform. This statement from a math teacher on the Idea Team is illustrative of their conceptions of student ability: "The CLA program has done amazing things for [standard track] kids. Because all of a sudden somebody says 'you can do this.'" In general, these teachers agreed that all students can learn and the role of the teacher is to provide opportunities in the classroom for all students to excel.

Members of the Idea Team argued that the problems of education lay within the traditional school structure and culture, not within the students. This statement by an Idea Team teacher illustrates this viewpoint: "I would like to change a lot of things, and my argument tends to be that in the last few years everything around us has changed, except the schools and that can't be right!" The Idea Team teachers recognized the entrenchment of tracking and the structure and culture that reinforce it. The Idea Team sought to fundamentally transform what "school" means by moving toward an innovative structure that included detracking and a nurturing, supportive school culture in which people share the belief that all kids can learn.

It is important to note how the Idea Team teachers, particularly the most active group of women, talked about the reform. The discourse of the women teachers on the Idea Team was on the terrain of "what's best for kids" or children's interests — an arena where their ideologically constructed gender gives them equal, if not superior expertise. However, even though the ideologies and plans of the Idea Team were likely to produce better outcomes for students, we must be aware that a subtext to their argument for reform may have been a desire for more power in the school.

The largest group in the school, the "middle group" teachers who took a more passive role in the reform, did not have a name. This ideologically diverse group of teachers described themselves as "on the fence" about reform and "resistant to the pressure to take sides" with either of the two factions. Most of these teachers signed up to participate in various restructuring work groups. Even if they did not take a very active role, the participation of these teachers was symbolic of the heightened interest in broader based discussions of reform. Nevertheless, in general, these teachers shared a common bond of avoiding the politics of the reform.

Putting ideological differences among the teachers aside, what is interesting is that, during the first year of the reform, the teachers used an educational discourse to express them. This evolved over time, as restructuring at Central began to take hold and group identities shifted. As other teachers gained the power to voice their opinions, the reform process disrupted the hegemony of the Good Old Boys. The reform also challenged the Good Old Boys' sense of efficacy as teachers, as they realized that detracking would mean that they would have to learn new teaching strategies and teach different classes.

How did the Good Old Boys respond to the challenges that were raised by the reform movement? Betty Allen, an assistant principal, explained:

> [The Good Old Boys] have lost some of that power because the movement is happening in spite of them. So as a result they are more entrenched and more vocal and have started some pretty dirty tactics. You know it gets down to malicious gossip now. Then it gets down to some real personal hurts from one staff member to another.

Because the Good Old Boys no longer had the power to control the school through their loud, boisterous behavior, they resorted to crass gender politics, making jokes about those women teachers involved in reform, undermining their authority and control. They targeted eight women who were most actively involved in the reform, referring to this group derogatively as the "Dream Team."

As a result, by the middle of the second year of reform, the factionalism at Central High School became more clearly defined along gender lines. As a male teacher, new to the school, explained: "It is divided sexually in the school. The males tend to hang out with the males and the females tend to hang out by themselves, especially certain groups of females."

This exchange between an interviewer and science teacher Norm Shiro illustrates the discourse the Good Old Boys used in taking on the group of eight Idea Team women:

> *NS*: There are several members of the [Idea Team] whose husbands are well off and sometimes other faculty members get the idea that they may be teaching as a hobby.
>
> *Interviewer*: So maybe they're not as financially vested in teaching or . . . ?
>
> *NS*: Well, as far as my family goes, this is our main source of income. This is *the* job and because of that I look at it from more of a practical standpoint. There's one faculty member who takes a year off every three or four years to revitalize herself or whatever.

That the Good Old Boys employed a sexist discourse instead of taking on the Idea Team teachers on ideological grounds suggests a defensive strategy used by this entrenched group in the politics of representation. For the Good Old Boys, the women teachers were an easy target. They could fall back on stereotypical gender roles that reinforced male power in society instead of constructing a sound educational argument against the reform efforts of the women teachers. Cunnison (1989) has argued that "the practice of assessing one another by stereotypical gender roles is so deeply embedded in our society that it pervades most social situations, including those of work, regardless of whether it is formally appropriate" (p. 152).

In order to define the women teachers as less committed to their jobs, the Good Old Boys also defined them in domestic as opposed to professional terms. According to Idea Team members, the Good Old Boys had seized the teachers' cafeteria as a forum for their highly sexist discourse and jokes about domesticity. As Idea Team teacher Marlene Winters explained, the Good Old Boys sat in the faculty room, reading the newspaper, and "as women walk by, they say 'big butt' under their breath." Teacher Lucy Berg explained the situation in more detail:

> It makes it very hard to work when [women] won't go to the faculty cafeteria unless they're with someone else. They won't go alone because [the

Good Old Boys] have set up a long table along the center [and] sort of take it over . . . It reminds you of the athletes' table. Everybody sits down and chows down on steaks before they go crash heads in the big game . . . [And, they make] remarks . . . like, "men, we're hunters and we're providers and women, they're knitters and cookers and all this" . . . saying this stuff seriously. [They also] accuse the principal of surrounding himself with too many women.

The Idea Team recognized that the Good Old Boys were using a gender discourse as a strategy to attack the reform. As Lucy Berg explained, "They use all sorts of tactics, the tactic of choice, the tactic of the moment, the one which happens to work," which in this case was sexist jokes and innuendo.

The Good Old Boys also demeaned the Idea Team by defining elements of the restructuring plan reform as "women's work." Criticizing the house model of school organization, one Good Old Boy Ralph Boskey said: "The problem that I had was that they wanted to turn education back into the little one-room schoolhouse. They wanted to have little small core groups and little bitty teachers and then the students married onto the teacher and carried on with them [throughout high school]." Likewise, another Good Old Boy referred to restructuring as "all those little group things." Norm Shiro minimized the importance of what the Idea Team was working on as something that had simply "caught their fancy."

Several of the Idea Team women teachers retaliated by filing sexual harassment suits against several of the Good Old Boys, charging them for episodes that dated back several years. The principal, Bob Foster, explained the filing of these suits: "Last week I had to deal with two sexual harassment situations . . . where the boys are trying to return things to the way they were." He later added: "We had a female teacher take a male teacher to task who was kibitzing in the back. You know, basically evaluating women as they spoke."

The principal believed that these law suits were extremely significant in the struggle for power among the two groups of teachers. He talked about the women teachers as generally non-confrontational with their peers and believed that their filing of a suit symbolized the disruption of the hegemony of the Good Old Boys, who for many years "have been confrontational and have been able to control everybody else and everything else." However, while it may have lessened the gender joking, the filing of sexual harassment suits did not end the struggle between the Good Old Boys and the Idea Team. In addition to their use of a sexist discourse, the Good Old Boys also employed a variety of political means at their disposal: they used their strong connection to the union as an instrument to stave off changes, especially with regard to reforms that altered teacher work time. They also used their alliance with a school board member, who had been the principal at Central when most of them were hired, to create negativity about the reform plans among board members. And finally, as the principal described, the superintendent allowed the Good Old Boys to "come in the back door and moan and bitch and complain, and to create doubts in his mind as to what the staff (was) doing."

The Good Old Boys succeeded in creating a climate for the principal in which he felt he could no longer help the school move forward and he resigned at the end of the second year of reform. Representatives from the state department of education visited Central and, after conversations with teachers and administrators, decided to withdraw funding for one year. The incoming principal chose not to reapply for funding. As a result, the Good Old Boys' definition of the school, which included tracking and a patriarchal culture, prevailed.

At Central, the Idea Team and Good Old Boys competed over whose values would win out — the status quo or a school dramatically recultured and restructured. One dimension of the Good Old Boys' representation of school was a patriarchal school culture, which reinforced the power relations around race and class that perpetuated tracking. The Good Old Boys recaptured their dominant position in terms of school ideology by attacking their opponents through crass gender politics, and succeeded at preserving much of the traditional structure of the school and the patriarchal culture that accompanied it.

Explorer Middle School

Explorer Middle School is located in the downtown area of a northwestern US city. During the period of our study, the school served a population of 550 students, approximately two-thirds white and one-third American Indian/Alaska Native,[6] in grades 6 through 8. The white population was overwhelmingly middle-income while the Native American population was largely low-income.[7]

A major issue within the school and the district was the low achievement of Native students. Native students failed at a much higher rate than white students and were grossly underrepresented in the gifted program and overrepresented in special education at the school. Many Native students were identified as "communication disordered," referring to their perceived lack of vocabulary and their discomfort in expressing themselves verbally. Teachers, administrators and students reported that some teachers treated Native students poorly. There was also concern about the lack of representation of curriculum relevant to Natives.

Explorer became a middle school in the early 1980s when the district adopted the Carnegie Turning Points middle school model for its two junior high schools. Before implementing the middle school model, the district encouraged teachers to explore the research on middle schools and their own philosophies about educating early adolescents. After this period of research and soul-searching, teachers were given the option to transfer to elementary or high schools if they were uncomfortable with the shift to the middle school model of organization. Teachers who chose to stay in one of the new middle schools were given extensive training on team teaching, new instructional techniques, and on how to better communicate with parents, and they were given opportunities to attend conferences and visit other middle schools.

In keeping with the Carnegie Turning Points model, the district encouraged the school to reduce ability grouping and tracking. But detracking did not become a movement at Explorer until a new principal, Renee Black, joined the school in 1989. Black initiated detracking by hand sorting students into classes in order to ensure racial and ability heterogeneity. She also initiated the mainstreaming of both special education and gifted students. Additionally, she hired a number of teachers whose visions were congruent with hers and removed several teachers whose were not. The district supported her vision, with the exception of her stance toward heterogeneously grouping gifted students. However, the lack of district support left her open to attack by the powerful constituency of parents whose children were identified as "gifted."

In 1992, in order to facilitate close communication and support among teachers, Ms. Black decided to alter the teacher team and house structure at the school. Specifically, she modified the traditional middle school model from grade level teams of four or five teachers to smaller teams of two or three teachers across grade levels. Teams of two or three teachers taught all academic subjects to a team of sixty to ninety students. The principal did not dictate how teachers taught or how they organized students within teams. Teacher teams were free to organize their time as they saw fit; some maintained heterogeneous grouping across all subjects, while others regrouped students by ability for certain subjects. In addition, some teachers taught in an interdisciplinary fashion, while others taught single subjects. All teachers in each grade level had a ninety minute shared planning period each day.

Gender Politics and Ideological Diversity at Explorer Middle School. This new organizational structure divided faculty at Explorer Middle School into two camps of teachers — those in favor of the changes initiated by the principal and those against. The split among the faculty mostly mirrored an ideological division between teachers who preferred a traditional, departmentalized, junior high structure and those who supported the child-centered, interdisciplinary middle school model. Teachers also divided along old guard/new guard lines, with the veteran teachers being the more traditional and thus more resistant to the small team structure, and the newer teachers oriented toward progressive teaching strategies and the middle school model.

The ideological differences between the two camps were most evident in their attitudes toward heterogeneous grouping: the traditional camp was more comfortable with homogeneous grouping, and the progressive camp was committed to heterogeneous grouping of students. A teacher in the more progressive camp articulated her commitment to heterogeneous grouping in this way: "I don't know what it would be like if we had four gifted kids together, or four learning disabled kids, or four Native kids, or four white. I just couldn't — I can't see that. That wouldn't be really conducive to learning anything." Similarly, another female teacher stated: "[Heterogeneous grouping] offers the low kids as well as the high kids [the chance] to be connected with the same kinds of things . . . And I think that really is the foundation of meeting the needs of all students." As these comments suggest, to the progressive teachers, heterogeneous grouping simply made sense.

Progressive teachers were more likely to see ability as socially constructed. For example, a Native studies teacher argued that the patriarchal white social structure reinforced erroneous beliefs about ability: "The way I look at it, our country is predominately Western European middle-class and above. It's run by men. It has been forever . . . To me, everybody is gifted and talented . . . It's just that we have people telling us that we're too dumb, too silly, too fat, too dark, too woman, too whatever."

By contrast, traditional teachers tended to view student ability as a fixed, innate quality. Sixth grade teacher Mark Jeffrey's reiteration of his comment to a student in his low-ability math class reveals his conception of student ability: "I certainly didn't want to say this is the 'dummy' class. [I told him,] 'you'll struggle this year, but you'll get through it.' [I] attempt to encourage [the students] along, but they are aware of [their ability level] too." Mr. Jeffrey added: "I think one of the strengths of the tracking system or homogeneous grouping is that you can target those types of situations."

Traditional teachers were much more circumspect about whether or not detracking was effective. For example, seventh grade teacher Mr. Dawson stated: "In my opinion, heterogeneous grouping does benefit the low-end kids." He added: "The high-end kids are the ones that benefit the least from heterogeneous grouping. The middle [range of kids] benefit, and the low benefit, but not the high." Sixth grade teacher Tim Walker agreed, explaining that his team dealt with this by introducing some homogeneous grouping: "On our team, the science and the geography is completely heterogeneous. The math and English end up being not quite so heterogeneous." He added: "We just need to throw a dose of reality into it."

The faculty's preference for reform divided not only along ideological lines but also along gender lines. This split became most pronounced when the school began to plan its move to a new facility. Although the faculty had input into the architectural plans, the final decision to construct the school with three wings was made by the principal, Renee Black. In keeping with the new structure of the school, she asked the teachers at Explorer Middle School to self-organize into the three houses according to teaching philosophy. Each team was to identify a team philosophy or a theme and give itself a name.

The teachers self-organized into three houses: the "Power House" and the "Ropes House," which were comprised entirely of women teachers, and the "Wolf House," which was comprised of all the men teachers in the school and two women teachers who were on sabbatical leave when the team and its philosophy were formed. At least on the surface, the houses at Explorer seemed to break down along strict gender lines.

The formations of the Power House and the Ropes House were rather different from the Wolf House. According to a male teacher, even before the faculty meeting, the women teachers had "previously aligned themselves . . . [as] . . . a nucleus . . . around a common philosophy of education." The women teachers in the Power House reinforced this belief, stating: "I think we were more aggressive in forming our team the way we wanted it to be, and other people sort of sat back and waited for the chips to fall." In fact, the women teachers in the Power House recruited other women teachers whom they had worked with before from a nearby middle school. The Ropes House also began organizing before the faculty meeting, although they were not quite as established as the Power House.

Unlike the two all-women houses, the Wolf House organized at the last minute without much pre-planning. A teacher in the Wolf House, Bill Jansen, discussed how the Wolf House evolved:

> When the idea was brought up, we were all in the faculty room and the principal asked us to group ourselves with people we thought we could work with as a house . . . So as a joke, I wrote a little note and I passed it along to the other guys saying, 'when we break up, let's have all the guys go stand together, just as a joke.' So when we broke up, all the guys went over and stood in one corner . . . And so it was done purely for humor, but then we realized that there are so few men in this building compared to a usual middle school, and the men started talking and decided it was possible to cover all of the academic areas and actually have a house of just men.

Other male teachers put a less positive spin on the decision. As Mr. Carter explained: "The men gravitated together because the women didn't invite [us]. That's why." He added that the men teachers at the school felt isolated in this female-dominated school. The gender imbalance in the faculty (i.e., the large majority of teachers who were women) was viewed by the male teachers as a product of the principal's hiring preferences. Teacher Jim Danson explained that he did not feel as though he received as much affirmation by Ms. Black as some women teachers might: "I coach wrestling and cross country and put on tournaments . . . and [that] doesn't really seem to count for much in Ms. Black's eyes as . . . Whereas what we [male teachers] call the touchy-feely stuff, like going to camp [with the students], seems to count for a lot." By unifying to form a male house, the men teachers hoped to have a stronger voice in the school.

The Wolf House represented a unified male force and described themselves as all-male, even though there were two female teachers who were part of the house as well. One of the men explained: "If there were guys [on the staff who could have joined the house] . . .we might have tried to solicit their membership, but that wasn't the case." That is, there were not enough male teachers to comprise an entire house. However, in retrospect, he added, "It's probably better that we have at least one or two [women] on our team just from the standpoint of all the things to do in a given day in a junior high. I mean, you want to have at least one woman on there if nothing else to go into a women's john and check out somebody." Clearly, the women on the team were not seen as major assets as teaching colleagues.

The name "Wolf House" evolved from the desire to name the houses for Native clans, which are often identified by animal names. A teacher explained: "I thought it would be nice for kids to identify with the animals, and we were going to have a mascot of course . . . So we just picked 'Wolf' as kind of a working title." In contrast, the two women's houses decided not to go with the animal theme. Instead, one group chose to call themselves the "Power House" because, as they described it, they were teachers who were "really strong in curriculum and academic success" and were "all workaholics." The other women's house called themselves the "Ropes House," in accordance with the curricular model to which they subscribed.

The men teachers argued that while they initially grouped together as a joke or as a move for solidarity, after they began to develop their unifying house philosophy, they realized that they had more in common than just gender. A male teacher explained: "The more we talked, the more we realized that there was indeed a lot of commonality among the men and how they saw education as opposed to the women." Summing up the ideology of the male teachers and the theme of the Wolf House, Mr. Carter, the counselor in the house, stated: "Well, it's traditional teaching methods . . . The men are going to be labeled 'traditional,' [although] that's not a cool educational jargon word nowadays. A lot of parents like it, and it just happens to be a basic core value for this group of teachers." Mr. Carter further defined "traditional" as students working with "paper and pencil" and on some "drill and response."

Like the men in the Wolf House who had a strong sense of ideological consensus and solidarity, the women in the Power House described themselves as having strong common beliefs in their unifying theme of progressive teaching methods, such as interdisciplinary units, team teaching and authentic assessment. The Ropes House had also grouped together around a common progressive theme, the Rites of Passages curricular model, which includes individual education plans for each student and integrated classrooms focused on experiential learning. In the Ropes House, students completed self-directed projects which were evaluated by a group of three community adjudicators. This progressive model, developed at a university, had initially been proposed to the entire faculty by the principal.

Both sets of women teachers saw themselves as forming their houses on the basis of common ideologies about education, not on gender grounds.

As teacher Brenda Dawes stated, unlike the Wolf House, the Power House teachers "spent a lot of time thinking about what we wanted and who we wanted to work with." Similarly, another teacher stated: "We have lots of cooperation. I think our teams function really well." The women in the Power House explained that their collaboration went beyond working together for interdisciplinary instruction, for which they were flexible about scheduling, allowing each other to have longer instructional blocks when necessary. In discussing what made their collaborative efforts work well, a teacher stated: "We give and take as people rather than resent each other." This statement appears to be significant as an attempt to privilege "women's ways."

Unlike at Central, gender politics at Explorer seemed to be a two-way street. Men made comments about the women, and women made comments about the men. For example, men in the Wolf House referred to the Ropes House as the "In House," because they perceived them to be "in" with the principal, having chosen her suggested curricular model. Similarly, the women teachers referred to the Wolf House derogatively as the "Boys' House." When referring to the "Wolf House," teacher Brenda Dawes simply commented, "What a name!" The women in the Power House joked that if the men's house was the Wolf house, the women's houses could be aptly named the "Straw House" and the "Paper House" (referring to *The Three Little Pigs*). This comment appeared reflective of the women's beliefs about unequal power relations between men and women teachers in the school.

The gender divisions and gender politics among teachers at Explorer Middle School had some damaging effects on the overall school climate and the school's propensity for further reform. For example, teacher John Davis complained that one of the unfortunate outcomes of the gender politics was that all men at the school were stereotyped as being traditional and resistant to reform, even if some (like him) thought of themselves as innovative teachers interested in change. Mr. Davis also believed that the structure perpetuated the stereotype of men as subject-oriented and women as interdisciplinary. He found himself in a double bind of not being accepted by the women's houses (because he was male) and not feeling comfortable in the men's house because he did not subscribe to traditional teaching techniques.

According to both men and women teachers, the gender politics at Explorer created a loss of a sense of community. Years after the gender-divided houses were created, the houses remained divided by gender, as did the faculty. Further, based on the men teachers' perception that the principal favored the Ropes House, resentment from the other two houses toward both the principal and that house continued. Women teachers reported that this tension had resulted in a negative change in the principal's behavior; she reportedly became less sympathetic and "caring" toward teachers than she had been in the past, and more focused about promoting her agenda.

In summary, gender politics at Explorer Middle School manifested itself in teachers organizing into theme-based instructional houses on fairly strict gender lines. The men teachers saw this as their only hope to protect their interests in a school dominated by a strong woman principal and the women teachers who represented the majority of the faculty. The women teachers, on the other hand, organized their houses along philosophical lines and in order to have stronger, more collaborative teaching arrangements. The net effect was gender-based houses with distinct ideological differences: the men's house favored traditional teaching techniques and homogeneous grouping and the women's houses favored progressive teaching strategies and heterogeneous grouping.

Comparisons between Central and Explorer

Along several dimensions, the gender politics at Explorer and Central were strikingly, even hauntingly, similar. Common to both schools was the overlap of teacher ideology and gender. The men teachers characterized themselves as more traditional subject matter specialists who favored tracking and thus fought detracking and, in some cases, the "touchy-feely" reforms that accompanied it. The women teachers, on the other hand, characterized themselves as progressive educators who were interested in making schools more nurturing, challenging environments for students.

In both schools, sexist remarks and derogatory gender-specific names were commonly used by both male and female groups as defensive strategies for their position on reform. Moreover, teachers criticized each other's behaviors along gender lines: Women teachers were attacked by men for their decisions to take time off for childbearing and for their supposed ability reliance on their husbands' income. Women at Central experienced even more blatant forms of sexual harassment. Alternately, men teachers were attacked by women for their macho and loud behavior in the faculty room, for their immaturity, and for discriminating against women. Men and women also criticized each other's motivations and philosophies, frequently by attributing a gender base to these actions and ideologies.

In both schools, proposed change, or the threat of change, brought gender politics among the faculty to the foreground. Though troubling for the future of change in secondary schools, it is not surprising that teachers coalesced on gender grounds in the face of reform, given that this is a terrain upon which teachers have unequal power relations. Although it was not the specific proposal of detracking that instigated gender politics at Explorer, detracking was a feature of the school's innovative structure, and it was a subject on which traditional (men) and progressive (women) teachers had markedly differing opinions. Detracking was also a centerpiece of the change efforts of teachers at Central. The political and divisive nature of this reform cannot be underestimated in these school settings.

The opportunity for teachers to gain or lose power is an underestimated yet threatening byproduct of whole school reform efforts, particularly those that address existing organizational arrangements. At Central, the traditional male teachers engaged in gender politics in order to preserve their powerful status in the school, and the women teachers stood to gain power if their innovative plans were implemented school-wide. At Explorer, the men teachers sought to gain power and solidarity through their formation of an all-male house. Power is a strong motivating force for both reformist and resistant teacher agency in reform. In some cases, teacher self-interest can be a subtext to struggles for reform that are also in the best interests of students (Ball, 1987).

Although gender political strategies were common to both schools, what differed was the net effect of gender politics in the ultimate fate of reform. In spite of the loss of community among the teachers at Explorer, unlike what occurred at Central, gender politics did not completely bring down reform. At Central, the Good Old Boys were so politically effective that few vestiges of reform remained. These varied outcomes of gender politics can be accounted for in the differences in community context, past history of reform, leadership and patriarchy, and in the sheer power of the gender-based factions at Central as compared to Explorer.

Conclusion and Implications

This chapter has pointed out the complicated dynamics of gender in school change processes. In struggles for power, teachers at each school organized into factions according to their social locations as men and women. The movement to gender-based factions allowed the battleground of reform to be fought on the terrain of gender as well as, and at some points instead of, ideological diversity regarding education. The shifting of the discourse from education to gender functioned as a political strategy in protecting men teachers' vested interests and served to perpetuate unequal power relations between men and women teachers.

The findings in this study suggest a strong correlation between gender and ideologies about teaching. Ideological similarities are not surprising, as men and women teachers exist in gendered social contexts (Crawford, 1995; Uchida, 1992). Gender also plays strongly into the teaching profession, where teaching has been long defined as women's work and is associated with the values of caring, mothering, serving and femininity (Acker, 1994, 1996; Apple, 1994). Women teachers in this study embodied such notions in their ideas for school change (e.g. house model of organization, smaller learning communities), and men teachers resisted them, in part because they saw them as being associated with women's attributes. The men teachers' ideologies reflected more nearly the masculine leadership styles, values (e.g. subject specialist) and language that are taken-for-granted features of secondary schools (Acker, 1996; Ball, 1987). That this forceful correlation between ideology and gender existed points to the need for further inquiry into how gender socialization and gendered relations of power impact the ideologies of men and women teachers, as well as their role as advocates or resisters of school reform.

By revealing that teacher resistance to change can be gendered, the findings presented in this chapter contribute to research showing that teachers' attitudes toward reform may be linked to personal characteristics such as age or career stage (Huberman, 1989), race and culture (Casey, 1993; Foster, 1993), or in this case, gender (Acker, 1996; Apple, 1986; Casey, 1993). Gender appears to be a highly salient characteristic, even more salient perhaps than age. In this study, men teachers resistant to change were roughly the same age (both late in their careers) as the women teachers who pushed change. Moreover, teacher resistance to reform was gendered, but in a somewhat different way than what is suggested by Casey (1993), Apple (1986) and Acker (1996). In those studies, women teachers resisted efforts aimed at further marginalizing them and the profession of teaching. Women teachers in those studies also believed that either the current condition (which they were fighting against) or the suggested reforms (e.g. increased testing) were harmful to students' learning. In this study, men teachers resisted reforms (proposed by their women colleagues) that they felt would marginalize them and upset the power of patriarchal relations. Men teachers' resistance to reforms centred less on the reforms being harmful to students' learning, and in fact, the men fought the battles mainly along gender lines. Clearly, men teachers have vested power interests that they will not give up. When the reforms themselves adopt gendered characteristics, resistance from men teachers is likely to be even greater.

The findings presented in this chapter also contribute to the literature on the political nature of teacher resistance (Gitlin and Margonis, 1995) and to research that shows that resistance is not limited to externally imposed, top-down mandates (see Bailey, this volume; Sikes, 1992), but also exists when change is led by a group of teachers (Muncey and McQuillan, 1996). In fact, the resistance and micropolitics that ensued in the change processes at the two schools in this study were perhaps more active and heated than what is typically observed when top down mandates are imposed — perhaps because the leaders of the change were in the school themselves and because the changes called existing power relations into question.

We can no longer afford to ignore micropolitics in school change research. It is not enough to say that politics got in the way of successful reform. As educators and researchers, we need to learn more about how teachers with competing interests and ideologies gain consensus on the means and the substance of school change. We need to know how school cultures are negotiated by educators representing different social locations. By studying battles for political control among teachers, researchers and educators may work toward developing critically important strategies for change in schools where ideology is contested. Studies of the micropolitics of school change must also attend to gender issues, particularly given the forceful overlap between gender and teacher ideology. The dearth of gender issues in school change research is so striking that the role of gender in and of itself in shaping school change needs to be given special attention.

Given these political complexities, transforming our schools into socially just learning environments for children can be very difficult. In order to thwart the damaging effects of micropolitics, teachers and administrators involved in school change efforts should engage in an open and honest dialogue about the following questions: (1) Whose interests are being served by the current system (Sirotnik and Oakes, 1986)? (2) Whose interests would be served by the proposed change? (3) How are professional relationships between teachers influenced by gender, race, and class relations? (4) How might these power relations be addressed by reform? By openly addressing these questions, educators can bring micropolitical issues out into the open, rather than allowing them to fester beneath the surface — only to later find that they can derail reform. When power inequities are brought to the forefront, educators can work toward dismantling them and toward creating meaningful, long-term school reform.

Notes

1 Portions of this chapter are drawn from two works: Datnow, 1997 and 1998.
2 For the purposes of confidentiality, pseudonyms are used for all place and person names.
3 The principal investigators of this study were Professors Jeannie Oakes and Amy Stuart Wells at the UCLA Graduate School of Education. The study was staffed by eight research associates, including myself, Robert Cooper, Diane Hirshberg, Martin Lipton, Karen Ray, Irene Serna, Estella Williams and Susan Yonezawa.
4 The UCLA research associate who led these visits was Diane Hirshberg.
5 Some suggested that there were a couple of younger, newer members of the Good Old Boys who were socialized into the group because they shared a common bond with the Good Old Boys: they coached sports and/or fitted into what one Good Old Boy (and science teacher) called the "traditional jock" stereotype.
6 The term "Native" is used by people at Explorer to refer to American Indian/Alaska Native students, and as such this abbreviated form is also used in this chapter.
7 This section on Explorer Middle School draws from the case report on the school (Hirshberg, 1995) and from conversations with its author, Diane Hirshberg.

References

Acker, S. (ed.) (1989) *Teachers, gender, and careers.* London: Falmer Press.

Acker, S. (1994) *Gendered education: sociological reflections on women, teaching, and feminism.* Bristol, PA: Open University Press.

Acker, S. (1996) Gender and teachers' work. In M. W. Apple (ed.), *Review of Research in Education.* Washington, DC: AERA.

Apple, M. W. (1994) Is change always good for teachers? Gender, class, and teaching in history. In K. Borman and N. Greenman (eds.), *Changing American education: recapturing the past or inventing the future?*, pp. 71–105. Albany, NY: SUNY Press.

Ball, S. J. (1987) *The micro-politics of the school: towards a theory of school organization.* New York: Routledge.

Berger, P. and Luckmann, T. (1967) *The social construction of reality.* New York: Doubleday.

Biklen, S. K. (1995) *School work: gender and the cultural construction of teaching,* New York: Teachers College Press.

Blase, J. (1998) The micropolitics of educational change. In A. Hargreaves *et al.* (eds.), *International handbook of educational change,* pp. 544–577. Dordrecht: Kluwer Academic Press.

Blackmore, J. (1998) The politics of gender and educational change: managing gender or changing gender relations? In A. Hargreaves *et al.* (eds.), *International Handbook of Educational Change,* pp. 460–481. Dordrecht: Kluwer Academic Publishers.

Blackmore, J. and Kenway, J. (1995) Changing schools, teachers, and curriculum: but what about the girls? In D. Corson (ed.), *Discourse and power in educational organizations.* Cresskill, NJ: Hampton Press.

Casey, K. (1993) *I answer with my life: life histories of women teachers working for social change.* New York: Routledge.

Corson, D. (1995) Discursive power in educational organizations: an introduction. In D. Corson (ed.), *Discourse and power in educational organizations.* Cresskill, NJ: Hampton Press.

Cunnison, S. (1989) Gender joking in the classroom. In S. Acker (ed.), *Teachers, gender, and careers,* pp. 151–67. Philadelphia, PA: Falmer Press.

Datnow, A. (1997) *Using gender to preserve teaching's status hierarchy: the defensive strategy of entrenched teachers. Anthropology and Education Quarterly,* 28(2), 1–26.

Datnow, A. (1998) *The gender politics of educational change.* London: Falmer Press.

Elmore, R. (1996) Getting to scale with good educational practice. *Harvard Educational Review,* 66(1), 1–26.

Foster, M. (1993) Resisting racism: personal testimonies of African-American teachers. In L. Weis and M. Fine (eds.), *Beyond silenced voices: class, race, and gender in United States schools,* pp. 273–288. Albany: State University of New York Press.

Foster, M. (1994) The role of community and culture in school reform efforts: examining the views of African-American teachers. *Educational Foundations,* 8(2), 5–26.

Fullan, M. (1991) *The new meaning of educational change.* New York: Teachers College Press.

Fullan, M. and Hargreaves, A. (1996) *What's worth fighting for in your school?* New York: Teachers College Press.

Gherardi, S. (1995) *Gender, symbolism, and organizational cultures.* London: Sage.

Gitlin, A. and Margonis, F. (1995) The political aspect of reform: teacher resistance as good sense. *American Journal of Education*, 103 (August), 377–405.

Grant, R. (1989) Women teachers' career pathways: towards an alternative model of career. In S. Acker (ed.), *Teachers, gender, and careers*, pp. 35–50. London: Falmer Press.

Hargreaves, A., Earl, L. and Ryan, J. (1996) *Schooling for change: reinventing education for early adolescents.* London: Falmer Press.

Heckman, P. and Peterman, F. (1997) Indigenous invention and school reform. *Teachers College Record*, 98(2), 307–27.

Hirshberg, D. B. (1995) *Explorer Middle School case report.* Los Angeles: Research for Democratic School Communities, UCLA Graduate School of Education.

Hopkins, D. and Wideen, M. F. (1984) *New perspectives on school improvement.* London: Falmer Press.

Hoyle, E. (1986) *The politics of school management.* London: Hodder and Stoughton.

Huberman, M. (1989) The professional life cycle of teachers. *Teachers College Record*, 91(2), 30–57.

Iannaconne, L. (1991) Micropolitics of education: what and why. *Education and Urban Society*, 23(4), 465–71.

McNeil, L. M. (1988) *Contradictions of control: school structure and school knowledge.* New York: Routledge.

Malen, B. (1995) The micropolitics of education: mapping multiple dimensions of power relations in school polities. In J. D. Scribner and D. H. Layton (eds.), *The study of educational politics.* London: Falmer Press.

Mann, P. (1994) *Micro politics: agency in a postfeminist era.* Minneapolis: University of Minnesota Press.

Marshall, C. and Scribner, J. (1991) It's all political: inquiry into the micropolitics of education. *Education and Urban Society*, 23(4), 347–55.

Mehan, H. (1990) Oracular reasoning in a psychiatric exam: the resolution of conflict in language. In A. Grimshaw (ed.), *Conflict talk*, pp. 160–77. Cambridge: Cambridge University Press.

Mehan, H. (1993) Beneath the skin and between the ears: a case study in the politics of representation. In S. Shaiklin and J. Lave (eds.), *Understanding practice: perspectives on activity and context*, pp. 241–68. Cambridge: Cambridge University Press.

Muncey, D. and McQuillan, P. (1996) *Reform and resistance in schools and classrooms: an ethnographic view of the Coalition of Essential Schools.* New Haven, CT: Yale University Press.

Nias, J. (1998) Why teachers need their colleagues: a developmental perspective. In A. Hargreaves, A. Lieberman, M. Fullan and D. Hopkins (eds.), *International handbook of educational change.* Dordrecht: Kluwer.

Noblit, G., Berry, B. and Demsey, V. (1991) Political responses to reform: a comparative case study. *Education and Urban Society*, 23(4), 379–95.

Oakes, J. and Wells, A. S. (1995) Beyond sorting and stratification: creating alternatives to tracking in racially mixed secondary schools. Paper presented at the annual meeting of the American Educational Research Association, San Francisco, CA.

Oakes, J. and Wells, A. (1996) *Beyond the technicalities of school reform: lessons from detracking schools*. Los Angeles: Center X, Graduate School of Education and Information Studies, UCLA.

Riddell, S. (1989) It's nothing to do with me: teachers views and gender divisions in the curriculum. In S. Acker (ed.), *Teachers, gender, and careers*. London: Falmer Press.

Riseborough, G. (1981) Teacher careers and comprehensive schooling: an empirical study, *Sociology*, 15(3), 352–81.

Roberston, H. (1992) Teacher development and gender equity. In A. Hargreaves and M. Fullan (eds.), *Understanding teacher development*, pp. 43–61: London: Cassell.

Sarason, S. (1990) *The predictable failure of educational reform*. San Francisco: Jossey-Bass.

Sarason, S. (1996) *Revisiting the culture of the school and the problem of change*. New York: Teachers College Press.

Shakeshaft, C. (1989) *Women in educational administration*. Newbury Park, CA: Sage.

Shapiro, M. (1987) *The politics of representation*. Madison: University of Wisconsin Press.

Sikes, P. J. (1992) Imposed change and the experienced teacher. In M. Fullan and A. Hargreaves (eds.), *Teacher development and educational change*, pp. 36–55. London: Falmer Press.

Sikes, P. J., Measor, L. and Woods, P. (1985) *Teacher careers: crises and continuities*. London: Falmer Press.

Sirotnik, K. and Oakes, J. (1986) Critical inquiry for school renewal: liberating theory and practice. In K. Sirotnik and J. Oakes (eds.), *Critical perspectives on the organization and improvement of schooling*, pp. 3–93. Boston: Kluwer-Nijhoff.

Siskin, L. S. (1994) *Realms of knowledge: academic departments in secondary schools*. Bristol, PA: Falmer Press.

Strauss, A. and Corbin, J. (1990) *Basics of qualitative research: grounded theory procedures and techniques*. Newbury Park, CA: Sage.

Stringfield, S., Millsap, M. and Herman, R. (1997) *Urban and suburban/rural special strategies for educating disadvantaged children: findings and implications of a longitudinal study*. Washington, DC: US Department of Education.

Uchida, A. (1992) When "difference" is "dominance": a critique of the "anti-power-based" cultural approach to sex differences. *Language in Society*, 21, 547–68.

Weiler, K. (1988) *Women teaching for change: gender, class, and power*. New York: Bergin and Garvey.

Wideen, M. F. (1994) *The struggle for change*. London: Falmer Press.

Wodak, R. (1995) Power, discourse, and styles of female leadership in school committee meetings. In D. Corson (ed.), *Discourse and power in educational organizations*, pp. 31–54. Cresskill, NJ: Hampton Press.

Yin, R. (1989) *Case study research*. Beverly Hills, CA: Sage Publications.

8   In the Margins: The Work of Racial Minority Immigrant Teachers

Nina Bascia and Dennis Thiessen

There have been many calls for North American teachers to become more committed to, and more skilled in, working with an increasingly multilingual, multicultural and multiracial student population. Recent changes in initial teacher training and curriculum policy attempt to foster more culturally and racially sensitive classroom practices and greater teaching proficiency in working with students whose native language is not English (e.g., Banks, 1993; Cummins, 1986, 1993; Irvine, 1992; Olsen and Mullen, 1990; Ontario, 1993; Sleeter and Grant, 1987). New professional development schemes attempt to encourage teachers' collaborative work to develop and deliver programs that address their particular students' academic needs (Cochran-Smith and Lytle, 1992; Little, 1993; McLaughlin, 1993) and to demonstrate teacher leadership in educational settings beyond their own clasrooms (Fullan, 1993; Little, 1990b; Smylie and Denny, 1990; Wasley, 1991). New school-level initiatives attempt better links among educators, parents and other community members to create a network of support for students, especially those from traditionally underachieving social groups (Comer, 1980; Levin, 1987). And policy researchers also emphasize the importance of recruiting and retaining linguistic, cultural and racial minority teachers, arguing that such teachers will respond particularly effectively to minority students (Dei, 1996; Ladson-Billings, 1994).

These efforts, touching on so many dimensions of the educational enterprise, suggest a sophisticated understanding of what it takes to deliver responsive educational programs to an increasingly diverse student population. Taken together, they embody a coherent approach to educational change, an approach that embodies both policy pressure *and* support at a variety of levels (Fullan, 1992; National Commission on Teaching and America's Future, 1996). But this aggregate portrait of policy strategies is misleading: it does not capture the reality of efforts to teach minority and immigrant children in any particular place. Changes in local practice are typically much more piecemeal — a teacher education course here, a professional development opportunity there, an affirmative action requirement somewhere else. Policy efforts are rarely so coherent: in fact, in many parts of North America, at the same time that teachers are being called upon to teach new types of students, technical conceptions of teaching are driving new policies that standardize curriculum and assessment as if all students are the same (Earl *et al.*, 1998). Further, as policy analysts remind us, the sheer complexity of the educational system makes it impossible to predict the impact of any particular policy or change, planned or not (Clune, 1990; Darling-Hammond and McLaughlin, 1995; Werner, 1991). Rationalist notions of change based on assumptions about the importance of skills improvement are belied by very real differences in educators' experiences, values and power — differences that challenge efforts to change teachers' relationships with students, parents and each other (Bascia, 1994; Blackmore and Kenway, 1995).

This chapter describes the work lives of four teachers who exemplify the broadened conceptions of teaching described above. Their work in real elementary and secondary school settings presents a picture of what is really required to respond effectively to the educational needs of minority students. They are immigrants to Canada and racial minority teachers who work in schools where many students are first- or second-generation Canadians. Their own status and the status of their students compels them to take on work beyond traditional classroom teaching. They do this work because they believe it is necessary and because no one else can or will do it. The absence of structural and normative support for their work hinders their efforts to construct positive learning environments for their students and productive professional identities for themselves. Rather than leading to systemic change, their work is largely individual, invisible, "time-consuming, contradictory, open-ended and uneven" (Blackmore and Kenway, 1995: 239).

The chapter emerges from a study conducted between 1992 and 1994 on the life histories of racial minority immigrant teachers. We were interested in understanding their values, intentions and talents, their capacities to affect the quality of education for majority as well as minority students, and their abilities to influence the nature of school programs and practice beyond their own classrooms (Bascia, 1996a; Thiessen *et al.*, 1996).[1] In this study, a half dozen researchers each worked with one or two teachers. We conducted extensive semi-structured interviews to elicit information about the teachers' childhood and school experiences, decisions to become teachers, training and career histories, transitions from their countries of origin to new conditions in Canada, and current personal and professional lives. As the interview process continued, it became more explicitly interactive, with questions to clarify events and interpretations within the teachers' stories in broader terms, "to position and locate that story by bringing in other data, other insights, other theories, other questions which have not been raised in the initial rendition of the story . . . maybe even other testimonies". In several cases we also observed teachers at home, in their classrooms, with students, and in other educational or community contexts. Sometimes our interactions extended beyond the interview period as the teacher read, critiqued and in some cases participated in the construction of the written life history.

Teachers were located for the study through a variety of opportunistic means — they were friends, acquaintances, colleagues, former students, or recommended by friends or colleagues. They varied with respect to gender and race (but all were non-Caucasian). They were diverse in terms of age, career stage, teaching role and life experience; some had come to Canada as children and attended Canadian schools, while others were educated and may even have first taught elsewhere before arriving in Canada as adults. Rose Chu is an ethnic Chinese woman who emigrated to Canada from Hong Kong at the age of 7, has been teaching for ten years, and teaches ESL (English as a Second Language) at the intermediate (middle school) level; Mei Lam is an ethnic Chinese woman from Taiwan, who has been in Canada since her early twenties and has been teaching grade 3 for three years; Edgar Culver is an ethnic East Indian man from Guyana, who has been in Canada since the late 1960s, has been teaching for twenty-five years, and currently teaches ESL at the junior (grades 4–6) level; and Carleton Manning is a black man from St. Thomas, who has been in Canada since his university days in the mid-1960s, began teaching in the late 1960s, and currently is a school counselor. The teachers live within the greater metropolitan areas of Toronto and London, Ontario and Vancouver, British Columbia.

The teachers in our study worked in schools with relatively typical educational programs and few or no other minority teachers. While we did not select them on the basis of this fact, all of the teachers, either by personal inclination, because of the expectations of others, or by a combination of the two, assumed various roles to support students who were recent immigrants, students whose first language was not English, and racial minority students. While some — Rose and Mei — described their professional activities almost exclusively in terms of classroom practice, the work of others — Edgar and Carleton — was characterized by a broader set of responsibilities, relationships and identities in their schools as well as in other educational and community settings.

This chapter focuses on the four extensive life histories written as the result of the study, but it draws from the entire data set. In the sections that follow, we describe the teachers' work in classrooms, schools, wider professional contexts and the community, noting the tensions and challenges they face by virtue of their roles, actions and professional identities.

In the Classroom

Mei, Rose and Edgar primarily taught racial minority students who (or whose parents) were newcomers to Canada. Their common experiences as immigrants created a particular bond between the teachers and their students, one which appreciated the complex links between their personal and school lives. This capacity to identify with the interrelated world of their students led to a range of pedagogical strategies to help students cope with their situations inside and outside school.

A Culturally Relevant Pedagogy

Because of their own recollections of immigration, the teachers understood the transitions their students faced in a new school in a new country. As a young adult entering graduate school, Mei remembered how she had to learn what many Canadian-born took for granted and immigrants of all ages confront:

> As a newcomer, I had to feel my way sensitively and consciously all the time. I started to pay attention to things I previously ignored. I carefully read the labels on the cans in the supermarket so I wouldn't end up with cat food for dinner. I noticed the differences in weather and customs. I observed the similarities and differences in people's attitudes and, generally, made comparisons between the two countries. In the process of mastering a new language, I paid attention to the true meaning of words in two languages, English and Chinese. Over and above all of this, I started to be aware of my own identity, who I was, what I was. Many people were interested in my background and expressed their concern about my well-being in the new country. As an immigrant, I had to learn to respond to such questions as where was I born, how many years have I been living in this country, how I learned the language, why I came to Canada and where my relatives were. These were questions that I was never asked or even thought about in Taiwan. Now they constantly surfaced in social situations. (M. Lam, 1996: 56)

Recounting the early days after arriving in Canada at the age of 9, Rose noted that "a lot of it is how you look and then it's how you talk and then how you behave" (C. Lam, 1996: 21). Learning the English language also involves responding to situations with an attitude and style similar to other children in the classroom. Such personal memories reminded the teachers that the past and present lives of their students outside school informed and often framed how they established themselves in school.

All three teachers described a particular empathy for those students who arrived at their doors with the desire to belong immediately yet who were unable to do so until they could express themselves in a new language. Mei and Rose recalled a number of tactics they adopted to avoid the alienation and isolation that accompanied English language gaps and lags. They feigned an understanding when they did not know the words; they opened their mouths only to have nothing come out; they acted as if they had a hearing problem when, if anything, their hearing was already too acute; they gave up ("I don't speak English") in order to gain time for translation; they caused laughter (by inappropriate use of words), though no joke was intended; and they received admonishment for inattention ("Aren't you listening?") when straining to hear every sound. They frequently were reminded of these poignant moments from the past when observing their own students.

The teachers knew from their own biographies that this linguistic rite of passage comes with greater expectations than mere proficiency. Over time, their students would need to speak without an accent; reflect in English (Edgar still thought "first in *patois* and then translated into English"); routinely contribute their points of view as part of the instructional process (an assertive style neither Mei nor Rose readily adopted initially); and display independence and creativity in their social and academic comments. Within and beyond the walls of the school, Mei, Rose and Edgar wanted their students to develop the capacity to represent themselves confidently, to navigate through whatever barriers they may face, and to negotiate an equitable place for themselves in the multicultural landscape of their new homeland.

In addition to adjustments to the social conditions of a different environment, and to the trial and error process of becoming literate, the teachers anticipated that their students would likely have to persist in these adaptations amidst comments about their difference. The teachers readily listed a number of misplaced questions, fumbling overtures or insulting remarks which made up part of their lives in Canada. Their racial, ethnic or immigrant status made them not only the objects of unwelcome curiosity but also the brunt of unfair and unjust behavior. Such incidents demonstrated that others saw them as different and set them apart from those around them. With the likelihood that their students would go through their own version of such incidents, Mei, Rose and Edgar appreciated that these experiences influenced how students made sense of and engaged in activities in the school and community. Consequently, they created classroom environments where their students could talk about situations where attention was drawn to their differences and about how to make sense of and, if necessary, to respond to any unwanted or harmful examples.

The teachers approached their work with the knowledge that what their students did at school was part of a wider story of relocation, dislocation and translocation. Previously unquestioned cultural traditions, religious norms or language preferences were now consciously held, cautiously scrutinized, or even tentatively modified as students and their families struggled to redefine their individual and shared lives in Canada. Because of their own histories, the teachers knew all too well the tensions and contradictory forces at play as their students tried to discover where they belonged and who they were. With the progress of their students deeply intertwined with their life circumstances, any strategy by the teachers to support their development in schools had to take into account and incorporate the multidimensional realities of their unfolding identities.

An orientation which considers the wider spectrum of students' lives as integral to what and how they learn in schools both challenges and recasts more conventional notions of child-centeredness. For these teachers, responding to the *whole child* involved more than attending to the cognitive, affective and physical needs of each student. Mei, Rose and Edgar had a more contextualized perspective on these qualities. The whole child they saw lived at the intersection of many communities where the dynamic interplay of language, culture and social condition framed their beliefs, ideas and actions. Their pedagogy took into account the lives and careers of their students (Fielding, 1997; Pollard *et al.*, 1997; Rudduck *et al.*, 1996) and the manner in which they critically and equitably examined and sought changes in their world where necessary or desired.

Addressing Difference

A critical dimension of the teachers' culturally relevant pedagogy (Ladson-Billings, 1990, 1995) was their approaches to addressing difference. Many of their classroom practices centered on the ways students construed and coped with a world where their ascribed, perceived and felt differences had a prominence they had not experienced before. The teachers adopted and combined at least three pedagogical stances to guide how they worked with students which we call: *bracketing difference, comparing difference*, and *asserting difference.* Though each teacher enacted these stances with different emphases and in different forms, they shared a commitment to creating learning communities which respected their students' past and present lives.

Initially, *bracketing difference* was about helping students fit into their surroundings. The focus was on those skills and knowledge that students needed to participate successfully in school and in the community: a proficiency in the English language; some awareness of local custom and routine; a capacity to make their preferences known and, where appropriate, heeded; and a general grasp of *how things are done around here*. Cultural differences were temporarily in the background; knowing how to act like everybody else was more important. The teachers wanted to make the strange familiar so that their students could make their own way without unwanted attention to their differences and with fair and equitable treatment.

Mei, for example, strove for an enlightened, inclusive classroom where students first recognized what was similar among them.

> Many people believe in celebrating the differences. I don't object to the idea. But I believe the celebration of differences can only be achieved in a harmonious social context. When two strangers meet, if they can discover their commonalities, the probability is high that a friendship will develop, leading to a sense of closeness and an attitude of acceptance. If the differences are recognized in an uncomfortable context, this will widen the gap, possibly leading to hostility. Hence, as a teacher, I try to help the

children see their commonalities, before we celebrate our differences. (M. Lam, 1996: 74–6)

Rose had even stronger reservations about any pedagogical consideration of difference. In her experiences, there had been few advantages and much resentment when the differences of her students became the primary lens through which they were approached and taught. She rarely spoke to her Chinese students in their first language. "By highlighting difference, more resistance and backlash will be created" (C. Lam, 1996: 46).

Comparing difference is a disposition to infuse the formal and informal curriculum with ideas which resonate with the histories and transitions of their students. Edgar and Carleton saw many opportunities to adapt curriculum. In reviewing a professional development session he conducted, Edgar said:

> I was talking today to secondary school teachers about meeting the needs of immigrant children, multicultural, multilingual groups, how we can use literature to bridge the gap . . . And they were talking about some of the gaps which occur for newcomers, especially when the high school has its own agenda, when the curriculum prescribed by the [school] board or the [provincial] Ministry [of Education] is out of line with experiences, their religion, their culture, their food, their knowledge, their geography, their history. So we're talking about literature, not only literature from the English-speaking world as such but literature that talks about the promoting of international understanding, literature that can humanize the classroom, literature that will pull kids together instead of separating them into different camps or different racial groups, we talked about that. (Bascia, 1996a: 88)

Similarly, Carleton described the efforts of a school committee to get beyond superficial approaches to multicultural education. He argued for a curriculum that recognized "the contributions that people from other countries have made to this civilization" (Thiessen, 1996a: 113). Such modifications respect the heritage and evolving stories of their students, provide a basis for constructive cultural comparisons and exemplify how schools could connect to the realities of an increasingly diverse society.

In conversational moments in the classroom, the teachers told stories about their own lives and invited their students to do the same. Some stories recounted events of childhood; others recalled their early days in Canada and the many changes they had to make; and others flashed back to incidents of confrontation and how they handled these challenges. These informal exchanges enhanced their formal curriculum, added further credence to the importance of their students' lives in their own learning, and established a forum where they could compare differences among the students in the classroom.

Asserting difference acknowledges the obligation the teachers have to teach their students how to recognize and to respond to situations where their right to be different is either threatened or seen to be a disadvantage. Rose taught her students to act like Canadians — "talking back instead of recoiling; insisting, instead of conceding; and not feeling diminished by others" (C. Lam, 1996: 31) — in order to assert themselves when they were not fairly treated. Rose attempted to instill in her students a sense of entitlement. She personalized and then elaborated this stance in the following excerpt:

> Well, you know how, when things like that [racist remarks] happen to you, you always think that you're the only one . . . and I think it helps them to know that it's happened to an adult and it's happened to a teacher and I always tell them, "Look I'm five foot nothing and nobody pushes me around" . . . so they really have to know that it's not size and it's not anything like that but it's really what you are willing to put up with and . . . to know that they have a right and they have the power to do something. (C. Lam, 1996: 29)

For Mei, Rose and Edgar, then, culturally relevant pedagogy manifested itself in the classroom through stances that bracket, compare and assert differences characteristic of their students' lives. This perspective of the job also extended to their work inside and outside the school.

In the Corridors

The school environment beyond the classroom was an important context for all of the teachers. Norms and procedures surrounding the treatment of children, shared expectations for appropriate teacher activities, and the possibilities for collegial relationships were all salient influences on their classroom work. While these conditions are important factors for all teachers (Hargreaves, 1994; Johnson, 1990; Little, 1982; McLaughlin *et al.*, 1990; Rosenholz, 1989), they appear particularly significant for teachers whose work, either implicitly or explicitly, involves students who are not consistently well served by conventional school programs and processes (Bascia, 1997).

Three of the four teachers believed that their own visible, cultural and linguistic differences from other teachers helped frame the parameters of their work, both in terms of career-long patterns of assignments to particular teaching positions, and in the ways individuals and institutions responded to them on a daily basis. Teaching in Canada and in the US historically has been an overwhelmingly white occupation (National Education Association, 1996; Reynolds, 1990). Edgar felt that many educators "see a black man and that's not their idea of what a teacher is." As tokens, the teachers described a sort of teacher "streaming" or "tracking," of being discouraged from certain teaching assignments (for example, Rose had little legitimacy earlier in her career as a French teacher), encouraged to assume others (Rose and Edgar both moved into teaching ESL, the most acceptable assignment for immigrant teachers), and finding administrative positions remarkably difficult to acquire. The cases corroborate other literature that suggests that minority teachers are systematically encouraged to assume teaching assignments and roles that focus their efforts on minority students and are discouraged in their attempts to assume broader administrative authority (Bascia, 1996a; see also Foster, 1991, 1992; Moses, 1989; Ortiz, 1982; Weiler, 1993).

Work with and on behalf of Students beyond the Classroom

The teachers' extra-classroom work with students was predicated sometimes on their formal job descriptions and sometimes on informal, but nonetheless powerful, collegial expectations that they take on such work by virtue of their racial and/or linguistic minority status. A teacher in the larger study, for example, was hired on the basis of her Caribbean background to manage a "literacy and life skills" program for primarily Caribbean-Canadian students, and found that "[advocacy] was supposed to be part of my job. I had to go and check and see how they were doing in their [other] classes, talk to them about it, that sort of thing." Rose found that, in addition to her own classroom work, ESL teaching carried with it other teachers' expectations that she be responsible for ESL students' adjustment difficulties and academic problems:

> a disciplinary problem, or "I don't know how he does his math, the answer's right but it sure looks weird to me . . . I wish he would just learn to do it our way," or "he just doesn't get it," or "it's time to have a talk with this kid, he really has bad b.o. [*sic.*], don't they use deodorant where they come from?" . . . Why is it my job to talk to him? (C. Lam, 1996: 35)

As Cindy Lam writes, "[Rose's] point is that, no matter how trivial or mundane, ESL students are perceived to have their own problems and do not get much attention from non-ESL teachers. The ESL teacher is seen as a custodian of a wide, sometimes ludicrous set of problems" (1996: 36). Rose characterized herself as "[not just in the classroom,] all over the place really or I try to be as much as possible, and I also try to keep track of what my students are doing in other subject areas." In her interviews, she expressed ambivalence about this work, characterizing it as "good teaching," yet resentful that she was expected to compensate for other teachers' and administrators' inability or unwillingness to pay sufficient attention to non-mainstream students. Edgar also described running interference in cases where adults' limited understanding or attention resulted in some students "fall[ing] through the cracks," "wast[ing] their minds" or "[receiving] punish[ment] for things they have no control over."

Engaging in extended interactions with parents and providing interpretation and bridging between home and school across linguistic and cultural divides is a second dimension of these teachers' work on behalf of students beyond the classroom. The teachers responded to expectations that they engage in such work in a variety of ways. Mei described accountability to parents about student learning as an important dimension of her role; this understanding provided an impetus for careful observation and documentation of students' classroom activities. She expected and received "support, respect, and trust" from most parents, beyond the occasional negative response from a parent who doubted her competence as a teacher because she spoke English with an accent. She was comfortable with expectations placed on her, especially by Chinese parents, to teach their children "to listen to their mother and father . . . I fully understood what they were asking of me. Such a request, in fact, is the parents' way of showing trust and respect for a teacher" (M. Lam, 1996: 71). Mei saw herself as a two-way translator between cultures and generations, respectful of immigrant parents' culturally specific concerns and expectations and yet also taking the opportunity to explain, for example, that children's questioning is not always a sign of disrespect but may be an important critical thinking strategy. Rose, on the other hand, called upon by other staff to intercede between immigrant parents and school staff, resented being asked to serve as translator, not only for her students and not only for students and parents who spoke her native Cantonese, but for any Asian language. This, for Rose, was evidence of her colleagues' lack of sensitivity and understanding.

Work with Other Teachers

In school contexts where shared responsibility for students is not the norm (and where only responsibility for lower-status students such as non-native English-speakers and special education students are shared), teachers' relationships with other staff are particularly salient and challenging. The teachers dealt with such challenges in ways that were consistent with their personal histories, culturally relevant approaches to pedagogy and personal inclinations. Mei experienced her early years of teaching as a

> guest in [someone else's] house . . . I tried my best to observe the culture of the school in order to be accepted and respected by staff and students . . . I tried to do more, give more, and talk less, not only to live up to their standards, but also to do better because I am an immigrant. (M. Lam, 1996: 67)

But as she grew more self-confident and moved into a more comfortable school setting, she developed an understanding of her social role as requiring her to "fairly present my culture and my language. I accept this as the duty and obligation of a visible minority member in this country" (p. 73). When her Caucasian colleagues made "unintentionally racist comments" about Chinese students, for example, she attempted to reframe many of the traits they described as ethnically specific, as more universal. Her emphasis on similarities in her exchanges with colleagues parallels her classroom strategies:

> Although, for the most part, I try to blend in at work, I seize the opportunity when it is Chinese New Year to introduce Chinese customs to my students and staff. I try to be discrete and tactful in imparting my culture to others. If it is forced on them, it will invite rejection. The effect is minimal, but it is a start. (M. Lam, 1996: 72–3)

Edgar, who worked as a staff developer in his native Guyana and increased his expertise in literacy and multicultural literature over his years in Canada, was also interested in influencing and educating his colleagues. Through the relative flexibility of his ESL teaching assignment, he often spent time in other teachers' classrooms, reading stories or otherwise working with the class, attempting to provide subtle modeling of pedagogical strategies for other teachers. Occasionally, this work evolved into joint planning or even team teaching. Mentoring other teachers requires skills and sensitivity, the capacity to demonstrate sufficient expertise to allow entry into the previously unshared terrain of classroom practice and, perhaps paradoxically, a display of humility and deference, to minimize the extent to which teachers' autonomy or the presumption of egalitarian status among teachers is challenged (Little, 1990b). Focusing directly on curricular issues, Edgar shared materials and techniques, and demonstrated his expertise while taking care to portray himself as an equal, a colleague, another teacher. Describing his work with one teacher, he said:

> I want him to relax and enjoy his profession, enjoy working with children. So it's empowering the individual as a teacher, talking, lunching together, coffee, that helps break the ice and then he feels less threatened by me. I'm not an official consultant, I'm not a bureaucrat, I am a professional just like him. [I talk] about all the experiences I've picked up with my direct contact with kids . . . that's what makes me credible. (Bascia, 1996b: 89)

As a school counselor — as an educator a on par with teachers, but not in the classroom himself — Carleton attempted to sensitize teachers to the cultural content of their curriculum. As part of a school-level committee, he helped organize workshops once or twice a year, but he did not believe such efforts were particularly successful:

> [The teachers] would love that, the food and the dance and the costumes. But when it comes down to actually doing true multicultural education, where in the classroom you ask teachers to weave into their lessons and lesson plans considerations of the cultural traditions and values of other cultures — [there's] a lot of resistance. (Thiessen, 1996a: 112–13)

Attempting to influence colleagues' practice is a daunting task. Mei acknowledged that her collegial comfort was "based on certain relationships

. . . I try not to go into [certain topics] too deep" (Bascia, 1996a: 169). Diplomacy is crucial. If any of the teachers discovered that a student had been badly treated, they were much more likely to work behind the scenes to release the student from harm than to confront another colleague directly. Some researchers have suggested that teachers put themselves at social and political risk when they attempt to transcend professional norms of autonomy to broach pedagogical and programmatic issues with school colleagues (Campbell, 1994; Lichtenstein *et al.*, 1992; Little, 1990a, 1990b). Carleton would never directly challenge a colleague,

> because I don't want to be in a position of conflict of interest. For example, there have been opportunities when I could have gone into schools [in my own district] to set things right, but then I said, "Well you know, here I'm going to be face to face against a colleague, maybe questioning decisions he made . . . [It] could be very uncomfortable. (Thiessen, 1996a: 120)

In some contexts, teachers' behavior is so circumscribed that even autonomous activity may be construed as invasive if it runs counter to the norm. Cindy Lam writes that "a colleague once asked [Rose] to leave her conscience at home, fearing that her attention to and efforts at dealing with extra-curricular issues would set a precedent for expectations of other teachers" (C. Lam, 1996: 19). Other research suggests that positive influence on colleagues' behavior may be particularly elusive for minority teachers. Another teacher in the larger study, just completing his teacher training year and contemplating a possible teaching future, expected that, given both his own expectations for himself and the expectations placed on him as a black man,

> The energy [required for] trying to move that inertia is tremendous and I'm not sure I can succeed. And race has a lot to do with it, because what Black man in his right mind would go into a school now . . . and try to be a shit disturber. They're going to brand you and colour you . . . Plus it would probably kill me. (Bascia, 1996a: 170–71)

Rose and Edgar, in particular, perceived their advocacy of immigrant students as made more difficult by powerful beliefs and regulations that framed most teachers' responsibility almost exclusively in terms of delivering the standard curriculum. Rose believed that the lack of teachers with ESL training at her school, given the large immigrant student population, helped frame ESL as an organizational "problem." She perceived her colleagues' open disdain for multicultural and antiracist concepts (she described how they "guffawed" during staff development sessions) as resulting from a lack of organizational and administrative commitment. Experiencing their remarks as explicitly intended to hurt her and other minority teachers, Rose felt alienated and marginalized.

The lack of meaningful relationships with other teachers in their schools resonates as a powerful theme across some of the interviews. The teachers referred repeatedly to their work as intensely isolated. While professional isolation may be a norm in many schools (Lortie, 1975; Waller, 1932), several of the teachers believed they experienced a particular exclusion from professional and social encounters that might help them plan curriculum, refine their teaching skills, or access information, participate in organizational decision-making, and engender a more general sense of belonging. These teachers turned instead to colleagues outside of their schools for professional community, moral support, practical aid and intellectual stimulation. There are clear costs to an absence of professional community in school: nowhere but within their own schools can teachers assume shared responsibility for particular students, and share common working conditions and community contexts, and only at the school level are there opportunities for program planning, organizational decision-making, and the kinds of professional learning that would help meet the needs of their students.

Professional Work beyond the School

Edgar and Carleton, well into their careers, children grown, and fueled by a conception of teaching that included professional and political work beyond classroom and school borders, were also involved in attempts to influence educational policy, promote teacher welfare, and increase teachers' capacity to work with diverse students. These realms of activity beyond the school were not mentioned by Rose and Mei. In some circumstances these kinds of professional activities tend to be coded as masculine, inappropriate for or unattractive to female teachers (see Bascia, 1998; Bascia and Young, 1998). Our interviews certainly suggest Mei and Rose, at early career stages, were focusing more specifically on classroom-related issues; as young mothers, each also had very young children claiming their time and attention.

Carleton initiated a local Black Educators' Association, whose primary objective was:

> advocacy . . . to insure that the needs of the Black child are provided for in the system . . . That might mean trying to influence the government and school boards to change curriculum so that the contribution of Blacks in history are presented in the curriculum. Also it might mean accompanying parents to schools to talk to principals and teachers because some parents are intimidated by the whole idea of going into a school. It might also mean participating in the Junior Black Achievement Awards. We also want to get involved in publishing things about Black educators in Canada. (Thiessen, 1996a: 118)

Carleton and Edgar were both active in their local teachers' unions and found these activities personally and professionally important (see also Bascia, 1997). During the time of our interviews, Edgar produced a regular column for his local union newspaper and participated in a union-sponsored professional development initiative. Carleton described the educational significance of union work:

> With fellow-teachers, doing something that is different from teaching, [you are brought] into contact with people who are non-teachers, the union people, the other professional people whom you must talk to, such as those who represent the school board, people you have to talk to to get advice on what you are doing for teachers. I got a deeper understanding of the variety of influences in society that have an impact on what happens in school and what happens to teachers . . . One of the important things that I learned is that teachers should be aware of those influences and teachers should try to be part of the decision making that affects their work . . . Unfortunately the classroom teacher, because of a lack of time and not making the time, is not aware of these things. Very often they are distracted by things in the media, as the media begins criticizing the positions that teacher takes, the average classroom teacher panics because he (*sic*) really has not got the knowledge of everything that's going on behind the scenes and very often comes out against his own association because he's not sure that what they're doing is right because he does not have the information or the insights as to why these things are happening. (Thiessen, 1996a: 106–7)

Carleton's political activities were also rewarding because of the respect he received from other teachers because he was "doing a job . . . dealing with problems." But, like Edgar, he described his teachers' association involvement as "risky" in terms of his professional career in that it "annoyed the people who have to make the decisions that would lead to your promotion" (p. 108).

Edgar was keenly interested in providing support for other teachers' learning. He was often invited to present workshops for teachers on meeting the educational needs of immigrant children in settings beyond his school, regionally and even internationally, and he co-authored several articles on these topics. His work took him into other schools (and often other teachers' classrooms), sometimes during regular school hours, much to his principal's displeasure; eventually he was told that he could no longer participate in the initiative during school hours. In both types of staff development activities, respect for his expertise and his ability to negotiate the logistics and relationships far exceeded what Edgar was able to accomplish in his own school. Edgar spoke in the interviews about how mystified district administrators were about his interest in work that was not necessarily directly tied to district priorities and would therefore not result in administrative career advancement.

In the Community

Mei, Edgar and Carleton each worked with programs and associations directly or indirectly connected to the Chinese-Canadian (Mei) and

Caribbean-Canadian (Edgar and Carleton) communities. The teachers worked in a number of ways to help others adapt to the school system and other social institutions. Edgar and Carleton actively supported and represented the Caribbean community in its social and political endeavors. Despite the relevance of this community engagement to their work in and for schools, only Edgar deliberately wove this aspect of his life into his professional work.

Mei, Edgar and Carleton were *teachers* in the community. Mei taught Chinese heritage language classes on Saturdays, occasionally wrote columns on education for Chinese newspapers, and periodically assisted in projects to support and study the experience of immigrants in Canada. Through their many associations in the Caribbean-Canadian community, Edgar and Carleton provided counseling and training so that more people knew how to relate to and work within the various structures, procedures and policies that governed their lives. Carleton gave the following example of his efforts to create awareness and understanding of different values and traditions:

> I have been involved in workshops within the Black community over the last six months. These people are grappling with the influences on their thinking and their living, especially where their children are concerned, where children are coming in daily contact with other traditions and other values of the wider society. That is affecting the relationship between the kids and their parents. So in our workshop, what we're doing is trying to work with the parents to point out to them that this is a different world that your kids are growing up in. You have to accept the fact that your kids are not going to accept the values that you know so well because you were brought up with it totally . . . Cultural conflict occurs all the time and the parents, of course, are beside themselves when their teenagers insist on behaving in certain ways that they feel are totally inappropriate for that age group. (Thiessen, 1996a: 114)

In a role similar to the one they adopted with students in the classroom (*comparing difference*), the teachers stood facing both ways. They represented Canada to those immigrants who came from the same region of the world as they did and represented the lives of these immigrants to Canadian-born educators and students whom they met each day. By assuming this multiple and mutual perspective, they could create bridges for immigrants to travel back and forth across cultures.

The teachers were actively involved in helping their own children participate in the many opportunities available in their communities. Yet as they got more integrated into the mainstream of Canadian life, they were even more aware of their own cultural, ethnic and linguistic roots and their need to pass on their legacy: to assist their children in defining who they are, with due regard to their familial histories and diasporic realities. What was primarily a personal desire of respect for their differences was now an imperative for their families. Two teachers, Edgar and Carleton, extended this commitment to work in support of those who had emigrated from their homelands.

Edgar and Carleton tried to change those conditions which make it difficult for newcomers to Canada to have their differences treated with respect and equity. They worked in the community in ways which encompassed but went beyond reacting to situations which threatened these rights, or sought ways to negotiate greater social and political space for these rights to exist. They spoke out in public forums, lobbying for changes in regulations or conventions which disadvantaged those from the Caribbean-Canadian community, and developed advocacy organizations. Carleton, for example, was instrumental in the establishment of the British Columbia Afro-Canadian Cultural Society, the British Columbia Black Action Coalition, the Black Theatre West and the Black Educators' Association.

Both Edgar and Carleton traced their disposition toward community action back to their image of teachers and other professionals in their formative years in the Caribbean. Carleton explained:

> Professionals have a social responsibility to contribute to the growth of their own profession and also to contribute to the society that has given them this trust. To provide expert knowledge. There was this feeling that you do have a responsibility to make a contribution to your society. That's why I was oriented towards political action. The expectation of the community is that a teacher is a person with training and knowledge and he will know what to do and how to help us. (Thiessen, 1996a: 104)

Yet they differed on why and how this obligation to give back to the community matters to their work in Canada. Carleton situated his views within a concept of the kind of citizen one should be. In response to a question about how he would advize a group of Caribbean teachers who were considering emigration to Canada, Carleton provided the following lessons from his biography:

> As a teacher, it is important to be a competent person in the classroom, someone who is able to work with the students and teachers outside of the classroom, participating in activities not related to direct instruction, ones that would make a contribution or promote the life of the school as a social unit. The other important thing is the family. I would say that if you have a family, be a good family member. Spend time with your children and let the community see you as a person who is interested in his children, in his family, in doing things together as a family. It's going to give your kids a certain degree of confidence as well as send a message to the community at large that you're a competent parent, you're a parent who's quite willing to make a sacrifice and devote some time towards other aspects of community living, over and above just being a taxpaying citizen. In other words, you must be a vital part of your community and be recognized as such. Don't be afraid because you have a different skin color; there are going to be people who are going to be prejudiced against you because of your racial identification, but just charge ahead as a person who

is equal, who feels equal and is equal and acts as if he's equal. In that way, you can be an effective individual that way. You must participate . . . (Thiessen, 1996a: 121–2)

Contributing to the community was a significant but differentiated part of Carleton's life story. Edgar had a more integrated perspective where his efforts in the community were embedded in his "broad vision of the world as a teacher." He traced this image to his first teaching post in the Guyanese countryside where teachers were "powerful . . . [socially] respected, I became a community leader . . . I visited the home of every kid . . . I helped [families] deal with problems" (Bascia, 1996a).

Working the Margins

Though their dominant zones of action differed — Mei and Rose primarily in the classroom; Carleton in his professional work outside the school and in the community; and Edgar in classroom, corridors, community and other professional work — the four teachers shared a range of values. They embraced a view of their work that was profoundly political in its scope, intent and practice. What they desired professionally paralleled their wider conception of what they sought for both their students and themselves: a place where they could maintain and develop their ethnic and racial identities while simultaneously being involved in the development of Canadian society (an outcome Herbert, 1989, describes as integration). This intent compelled a disposition to the job that was culturally relevant, strategic, inclusive, boundary spanning and transformative. They exemplified, in short, what some educational scholars would identify as "teacher leadership": equating teaching with intellectual work, considering the broader social implications of their actions, and maintaining a deliberate sense of moral purpose (Fullan, 1992; see also Aronowitz and Giroux, 1991; Simon, 1992).

When working with students in the classroom or in the community, most of the teachers experienced few tensions or complications. They seemed to have considerable control over their roles and activities and to feel reasonably at home in both these realms: in the classroom because they could give full expression to their commitment to a diverse student population and in the community because they could reaffirm, and sometimes reconstruct, the traditions and values of their past and present lives. In their professional work inside corridors and outside school, however, the teachers faced struggles and dilemmas.

The schools the teachers worked in were neither particularly welcoming places nor hotbeds of reform; traditional structures were protected and innovations dismissed. Each teacher could recall occasions when their race, ethnicity or immigrant status was the object of misplaced concern in the workplace: a parent bothered by the alleged linguistic inferiority of a Taiwan-born teacher; a principal amazed by a Chinese teacher of French; or a colleague unable to sit at the same lunchroom table with a black teacher. Implicitly, teaching was understood as a job for "real Canadians." Being on the fringe often was experienced more like exile than opportunity.

Among colleagues who did not often appreciate or support their cultural and political orientations to teaching, the teachers experienced contradictory desires to influence the directions of their schools and school systems and to maintain their own senses of safety and security. Some preferred to mind their own business, to worry about their territory and location, to watch out for pending mistreatment, and to avoid controversy and conflict. Some questioned the advisability of long-standing routines; disagreed with decisions of colleagues, administrators or policymakers; ignored or circumvented cumbersome and disabling procedures; and pursued a different approach to a problem others could not see. Their tactics differed: Mei explored and elaborated what was possible; Carleton supported and deliberated what was feasible; Rose confronted and insisted on what was essential; and Edgar negotiated and advocated what was critical.

Each perceived his or her activities, especially those beyond the classroom, as constrained by their marginalization as an immigrant and a teacher of color in an overwhelmingly white occupation; as a teacher of immigrant students; by conceptions of teaching inherent to the administrative culture of their schools and school districts; and by the absence of collegial cultures within their own schools. While their activities exemplify what many policies and researchers characterize as teacher leadership, their stories illuminate some of the paradoxes of such work: teachers who elect or are willing to carry out teacher leadership activities are not necessarily broadly popular or charismatic, especially those who champion issues that are contentious, potentially threatening or lacking in social status. People with the experiential base and conviction to engage in teacher leadership work are not always well situated to bring about technical improvements or cultural changes in their organizations. These realities suggest the importance of establishing support networks and systems for such teachers outside of school settings (Lichtenstein *et al*, 1992; Lieberman and McLaughlin, 1992; Little, 1992, 1993). But although support groups and professional development activities are crucial to sustaining teacher leaders as individuals, it is hard to imagine how these extra-school communities and activities could bring about the sorts of educational change, such as the achievement of equity goals, that require the organizational response of whole schools. Without significant shifts in structural and normative conditions, it is highly unlikely that minority teachers could influence their colleagues to rethink their own practices. According to Rose Chu, "Just putting a green teacher in a school full of green kids does not make them happy green kids."

Note

1   The study was funded by a grant from the Social Sciences and Humanities Research Council of Canada.

References

Aronowitz, S. and Giroux, H. (1991) *Postmodern education*. Minneapolis: University of Minnesota Press.

Banks, J. (1993) *Multiethnic education: theory and practice*. New York: Allyn and Bacon.

Bascia, N. (1994) *Unions in teachers' professional lives: practical, social and intellectual concerns*. New York: Teachers College Press.

Bascia, N. (1996a) Inside and outside: the experiences of racial minority immigrant teachers in Canadian schools. *Qualitative Studies in Education*, 9(2), 151–65.

Bascia, N. (1996b) Teacher leadership: contending with adversity. In D. Thiessen, N. Bascia and I. Goodson (eds.), *Making a difference about difference: the lives and careers of racial minority immigrant teachers*, pp. 79–101. Toronto: Garamond Press.

Bascia, N. (1997) Invisible leadership: the roles of union-active teachers in schools. *Alberta Journal of Educational Research*, 43(2/3), 69–85.

Bascia, N. (1998) Women teachers, union affiliation, and the future of North American teacher unionism. *Teaching and Teacher Education*, 14(5), 551–63.

Bascia, N. and Young, B. (1998) Careers beyond the classroom. Unpublished manuscript. Edmonton: University of Alberta, and Toronto: Ontario Institute for Studies in Education of the University of Toronto.

Blackmore, J. and Kenway, J. (1995) Changing schools, teachers and curriculum: but what about the girls? In D. Corson (ed.), *Discourse and power in educational organizations*. Toronto: OISE Press.

Campbell, E. (1994) Personal morals and organizational ethics: a synopsis. *The Canadian Administrator*, 34(2), 1–10.

Clune, W. (1990) Three views of curriculum policy in the school context: the school as policy mediator, policy critic and policy constructor. In M. McLaughlin, J. Talbert and N. Bascia (eds.), *The contexts of teaching in secondary schools: teachers' realities*, pp. 256–70. New York: Teachers College Press.

Cochran-Smith, M. and Lytle, S. L. (1992) Communities for teacher research: fringe or forefront? *American Journal of Education*, 100, 298–324.

Comer, J. (1980) *School power*. New York: Free Press.

Cummins, J. (1986) Empowering minority students: a framework for intervention. *Harvard Educational Review*, 56(1), 18–36.

Cummins, J. (1993) Bilingualism and second language learning. *Journal of Applied Linguistics*, 13, 31–45.

Darling-Hammond, L. and McLaughlin, M. (1995) Policies that support professional development in an era of reform. *Phi Delta Kappan*, 76(8), 591–6.

Dei, G. (1996) The role of Afrocentricity in the inclusive curriculum in Canadian schools. *Canadian Journal of Education*, 21(2), 170–86.

Earl, L., Bascia, N., Hargreaves, A. and Jacka, N. (1998) *Teachers and teaching in a world of rapid change*. Report prepared for the Canadian Teachers' Federation. Toronto: International Centre for Educational Change, Ontario Institute for Studies in Education of the University of Toronto.

Fielding, M. (1997) Beyond school effectiveness and school improvement: lighting the slow fuse of possibility. *The Curriculum Journal*, 8(1), 7–28.

Foster, M. (1991) "Just got to find a way": case studies of the lives and practice of exemplary Black high school teachers. In M. Foster (ed.), *Readings on equal education Volume II: qualitative investigations into schools and schooling*, pp. 273–309. New York: AMS Press.

Foster, M. (1992) The politics of race: through the eyes of African-American teachers. In K. Weiler and C. Mitchell (eds.), *What schools can do: critical pedagogy and practice*, pp. 177–202. Albany, NY: SUNY Press.

Fullan, M. (1993) *Change forces: probing the depths of educational reform*. Bristol, PA: Falmer Press.

Hargreaves, A. (1994) *Changing teachers, changing times: teachers' work and culture in the postmodern age*. Toronto: OISE Press.

Herbert, J. (1989) *Ethnic groups in Canada: transitions and adaptations*. Toronto: Nelson Canada.

Irvine, J. J. (1992) Making teacher education culturally responsive. In M. E. Dilworth (ed.), *Diversity in teacher education*, pp. 79–92. San Francisco: Jossey-Bass.

Ladson-Billings, G. (1990) Like lightening in a bottle: attempting to capture the pedagogical excellence of successful teachers of Black students. *Qualitative Studies in Education*, 3, 335–44.

Ladson-Billings, G. (1994) *The dreamkeepers: successful teachers of African American children*. San Francisco: Jossey-Bass.

Ladson-Billings, G. (1995) Toward a theory of culturally relevant pedagogy. *American Educational Research Journal*, 32, 465–91.

Lam, C. (1996) The green teacher. In D. Thiessen, N. Bascia and I. Goodson (eds.), *Making a difference about difference: the lives and careers of racial minority immigrant teachers*, pp. 15–50. Toronto: Remtel/Garamond Press.

Lam, M. (1996) Of "scattered beads": reflections on my teaching career from the periphery of Canadian society. In D. Thiessen, N. Bascia and I. Goodson (eds.), *Making a difference about difference: the lives and careers of racial minority immigrant teachers*, pp. 51–78. Toronto: Remtel/Garamond Press.

Levin, H. M. (1987) Accelerated schools for disadvantaged students. *Educational Leadership*, 44(6), 19–21.

Lichtenstein, G., McLaughlin, M. W. and Knudsen, J. (1992) Teacher empowerment and professional knowledge. In A. Lieberman (ed.), *The changing contexts of teaching*, pp. 37–58. Chicago: NSSE Yearbook, University of Chicago Press.

Lieberman, A. and McLaughlin, M. W. (1992) Networks for educational change: powerful and problematic. *Phi Delta Kappan*, 73, 673–7.

Little, J. W. (1982) Norms of collegiality and experimentation: workplace conditions of school success. *American Educational Research Journal*, 19, 325–40.

Little, J. W. (1990a) The persistence of privacy: autonomy and initiative in teachers' professional relations. *Teachers College Record*, 91(4), 509–36.

Little, J. W. (1990b) The mentor phenomenon and the social organization of teaching. *Review of Research in Education*, 16, 297–352.

Little, J. W. (1992) Opening the black box of professional community. In

A. Lieberman (ed.), *The changing contexts of teaching*, pp. 158–78. Chicago: University of Chicago Press.

Little, J. W. (1993) Teachers' professional development in a climate of educational reform. *Educational Evaluation and Policy Analysis*, 15, 129–52.

Lortie, D. (1975) *School teacher*. Chicago: University of Chicago Press.

McLaughlin, M. W. (1993) What matters most in teachers' workplace context? In J. W. Little and M. W. McLaughlin (eds.), *Teachers' work: individuals, colleagues and contexts*, pp. 79–103. New York: Teachers College Press.

McLaughlin, M., Talbert, J. and Bascia, N. (eds.) (1990) *The contexts of teaching in secondary schools: teachers' realities*. New York: Teachers College Press.

Moses, Y. T. (1989) *Black women in academe: issues and strategies*. Washington, DC: Project on the Status and Education of Women, Association of American Colleges.

National Commission on Teaching and America's Future (1996) *What matters most: teaching for America's future*. New York: Teachers College, Columbia University.

National Education Association (1996) *Status of the American public school teacher 1995–1996*. Washington, DC: National Education Association.

Oakes, J. (1989) What educational indicators? The case for assessing the school context. *Educational Evaluation and Policy Analysis*, 11(2), 181–99.

Olsen, L. and Mullen, N. (1990) *Embracing diversity: teachers' voices from California's classrooms*. Oakland, CA: California Tomorrow.

Ontario (1993) *Antiracism and ethnocultural equity in school boards — guidelines for policy development and implementation*. Toronto, Ontario: Ministry to Education and Training.

Ortiz, F. I. (1982) *Career patterns in education: women, men and minorities in public school administration*. New York: Praeger.

Pollard, A., Thiessen, D. and Filer, A. (1997) *Children and their curriculum: the perspectives of primary and elementary school children*. London: Falmer Press.

Reynolds, C. (1990) Hegemony and hierarchy: becoming a teacher in Toronto, 1930–1980. *Historical Studies in Education*, 2, 95–118.

Rudduck, J., Chaplain, R. and Wallace, G. (1996) *School improvement: what can pupils tell us?* London: David Fulton Publishers.

Simon, R. I. (1987) Being ethnic/doing ethnicity: a response to Corrigan. In J. Young (ed.), *Breaking the mosaic: ethnic identities in Canadian schooling*, pp. 31–43. Toronto: Garamond Press.

Sleeter, C. E. and Grant, C. A. (1987) An analysis of multicultural education in the United States. *Harvard Educational Review*, 57, 421–44.

Smylie, M. and Denny, J. (1990) Teacher leadership: tensions and ambiguities in organizational perspective. *Educational Administration Quarterly*, 26, 235–59.

Thiessen, D. (1993) In the classroom, in the corridors, and in the boardroom — the professional place of Canada's teachers in future policy making. *Journal of Education Policy*, 8(3), 283–303.

Thiessen, D. (1996) "Look after your own interests": a thematic record. In D. Thiessen, N. Bascia and I. Goodson (eds.), *Making a difference about difference: the lives and careers of racial minority immigrant teachers*, pp. 102–22. Toronto: Remtel/Garamond Press.

Thiessen, D., Bascia, N. and Goodson, I. (eds.) (1996) *Making a difference about difference: the lives and careers of racial minority immigrant teachers.* Toronto: Remtel/Garamond Press.

Waller, W. (1932) *The sociology of teaching.* New York: Russell and Russell.

Wasley, P. A. (1991) *Teachers who lead: the rhetoric of reform and the realities of practice.* New York: Teachers College Press.

Weiler, K. (1993) Representation and life history narratives: reflections on writing the histories of women teachers. Paper presented at symposium at the American Educational Studies Association annual meeting, Chicago, Illinois, November.

Werner, W. (1991) Curriculum and uncertainty. In R. Ghosh and D. Ray (eds.), *Social change and education in Canada* (2nd edn). Toronto: Harcourt Brace Jovanovich.

9   Changing Schools in a Changing World

Benjamin Levin and J. Anthony Riffel

Almost everyone agrees that schools today are facing a world of change. The ability of schools to remain vital and important institutions depends on their ability to understand and cope with the changing world around them. We lack, however, empirical evidence on the ways in which the processes of understanding and coping occur. In school systems, where do ideas about what is happening in society come from? What sense do school board members and senior administrators have of what may be required in the face of external change, and how do their views affect the efforts of teachers and administrators in schools?

Our discussion of these questions draws on empirical work we have done on how people in leadership positions in school systems understand and respond to external change. After a brief description of our study, we look at how the educators who participated in the study viewed selected areas of social change and the responses being made to them by schools. The dominant sense in our study was of schools buffeted by changes that educators felt unable to manage effectively. We take the view that this situation could be improved, and conclude the chapter with suggestions for practice arising from our analysis.

The Study

The main empirical base for this chapter is our study called "Schools in a changing world" (Levin and Riffel, 1997).[1] Our work focused on developing an understanding of the ways in which school systems try to understand and manage social change.

Such an understanding is vital because the strongest drivers of change in schools are changes in the larger social environment. In the long run, the nature of schooling and the work of teachers are far more powerfully affected by changes in families, in the economy, in law or in technology than they are by any number of curriculum revisions or school board policies. For example, the changing role of women may be the most important social trend of the last century (e.g., Shakeshaft, 1999). It has reshaped the way teachers are recruited, paid and promoted; altered ideas about education leadership; led to significant changes in curriculum and teaching; and changed dramatically relationships between schools and families. Changes in work have been at least equally powerful. The dramatic increase in requirements for educational credentials has been a powerful force in extending formal education, shaping ideas about curriculum and teaching, increasing the training requirements for teachers, and lately in calling into question the purpose and value of secondary education (Levin, 1999). Many other examples could be cited, such as the increased recognition of individual rights, the growing recognition of cultural diversity, or changes in information technology. Hargreaves (1994) has a very good discussion of these changes.

Although understanding social change is a vital organizational task, it is not easily accomplished (Levin, 1993). Work in several disciplines emphasizes the limits of human and organizational capacity to adapt (e.g., Aldrich, 1979; Warriner, 1984). Some authors stress the ways in which organizations and managers fail — sometimes through oversight and sometimes deliberately — to be responsive and adaptive. Certainly a substantial literature in education points to the difficulties in creating meaningful and lasting change (e.g., Cuban, 1990; Sarason, 1996).

Meaning and action in organizations are affected by a multitude of factors both inside and outside the organization, including individual dispositions, training, roles, organizational history and communication patterns (McCall and Kaplan, 1985; Morgan, 1986). Dror's work (1986) is especially insightful in illustrating many "policy-making incapacities," both those inherent in settings or problems and those in human practices of understanding and action. Recent work in neo-institutionalism (March and Olsen, 1989; Wilson, 1989) shows that organizations are also strongly affected by long-established patterns of practice held in place by features such as professional associations, socialization through training programs, collective agreements, regulations set by external authorities and other features that lie outside any single organization. These elements interact in complex ways to create an organizational world-view, or perhaps more often multiple and competing organizational world-views.

In the last few years a growing literature on organizational learning (e.g., Dodgson, 1993; March, 1991) has emerged, concerned with the ways in which organizations construct their pictures of the world and with ways in which organizations can become more adaptive. Organizational learning is a broad concept, but it typically involves defined processes to focus on external demands and build an understanding of the larger social context. In education the movement toward teacher professionalism reflects a view that organizational change is also critically dependent on the learning and beliefs of those in the organization (Hargreaves, 1994).

All of these concerns shaped our approach to our research, which was primarily inductive. We wanted to learn about the ways in which people in leadership roles in school systems constructed and understood the world outside of schools. Although our data come from school board members (trustees) and administrators, we believe that they have important implications for everyone working in schools. Social change presses on the work of teachers in very direct ways. It is in large measure the work and actions of school boards and administrators that shape teachers' ability to cope with change as well. The recommendations we make at the end of the chapter also clearly involve teachers, since in our view the work of understanding social change must occur throughout the school system, not only at the managerial level.

Our main source of data involved case studies of five school districts in a Canadian province. The focus of these cases was to develop a description of the way school board members and administrators in each district saw and thought about their external environment as well as the approach they were taking in trying to deal with the challenges of social change. The five districts are diverse and represent most of the province in terms of size, location and socioeconomic context, including urban (some 30,000 students, many of them attending inner city schools), suburban (roughly 10,000 students in a rapidly expanding suburb of the same city), suburban-rural (5000 students in a rural district adjacent to the city), rural (1500 students over a large geographic area) and aboriginal (1000 students in a First Nations community in the province) jurisdictions. In each district we tried to map the kinds of social issues seen as important, sources of information about these issues, and the kinds of strategies districts were using to try to manage the issues.

Our data sources included documents, interviews and dialogue with trustees and senior administrators. We reviewed thousands of pages of documents such as board minutes, newspaper accounts of board meetings, press releases, working papers and policy documents. The document analysis was conducted before interviews took place, in the hope that we might get an initial picture of some of the external issues confronting the districts. This analysis was not as helpful as we hoped, and yet what we discovered was telling: the documents were either silent on issues important in the districts or were simply declarative, outlining a plan or stating a policy without illuminating the background thinking that must have been a part of planning and policymaking processes in the districts.

We conducted nearly fifty interviews with school board members, district administrators and school administrators — roughly equal numbers in each category. The interviews were lengthy and wide-ranging conversations structured around questions about what social changes they saw to be important, the effects of those changes on schools and school systems, how they saw their systems responding to the changes, and whether different social changes called for different responses in schools. Although we began the study with an interest in some issues that we saw as particularly interesting — in particular information technology, poverty and labor force change — we also tried to be as open as we could to the issues that people in the districts felt were important to them.

In the course of the study, we also held more than a dozen meetings with colleagues in the participating districts to discuss the research and some of the ideas that we were drawing from the information they had provided. We use the term "colleague" deliberately. We certainly did not see the people with whom we worked as "subjects." Nor did we envisage a study in which they were merely "informants" or "participants" in our work. Rather, we hoped for dialogue about social changes and their impacts on educational systems, and for a relationship which was collaborative and mutually beneficial. In practice this goal was achieved partially at best, and we feel that we were largely unable to make our work useful in the way we had hoped. Hereafter we use more conventional terminology to refer to the people in the districts. This too is telling.

We have struggled with how to present our observations and conclusions in a way that is fair to the educators in our study and does justice to the situations in which they find themselves and the constraints facing them. It is all too easy for academics to adopt an air of intellectual superiority or to tell others what to do and assume they can and should do it. Especially given the collaborative nature of our research, we have tried to find a stance that raises questions about practice, but does so sympathetically. In reporting on our interviews, we have tried to present the range of views we encountered and to note where there was considerable consensus among those with whom we spoke.

How Social Change Was Understood

When we began this study we believed that a (some would argue "the") central problem of educational organizations today is responding to external change, and that traditional approaches to sensing and then coping with change no longer seem adequate. We thought we might see some systematic approaches to studying the environment, some formal and open mechanisms for analyzing social change and considering its educational implications, some imaginative stretching of the boundaries of the present system, some processes for supporting and then disseminating information about educational responses to social change.

Instead, our conversations yielded a picture of school board members, superintendents and school administrators who feel bombarded by change. They recognize clearly that the world in which they work — and the world their students inhabit — is changing in important ways. Changes in information technology, families, employment opportunities available to young people, child poverty, government policy and attitudes toward authority were often mentioned as having powerful impacts on what happens in schools.

At the same time, many of those we interviewed felt uncertain about what these changes imply for structures and relationships within schools systems, as well as for the nature and purposes of public education. With only a few exceptions, there was a general tendency to focus on the negative aspects of change, a reluctance to see the changes as presenting positive opportunities for educational development, and an inability to think about education differently, in ways that would bring ideas about the nature and processes of schooling to greater congruence with significant changes in society.

This lack of fit between social and economic forces outside of school systems and organizational and educational forces within school systems is the dominant theme in the accounts that follow. The accounts are brief, and are intended to illustrate the main ways of understanding and responding to social change we encountered in the five districts. While there was some important variation within and among the systems we studied, the accounts seem to us to be typical of what we observed. Instead of reporting on all areas of social change, we summarize three that illustrate different modes of interpretation, again for the sake of brevity. Information technology was very much on these educators' minds and also an issue that we had identified at the outset of our study as being of interest. Poverty was an issue that we felt was vitally important to schools yet seemed to us to be under-emphasized and was seldom raised spontaneously in our interviews. Changes in families, on the other hand, were consistently raised as being especially important and difficult for educators to manage.

The accounts that follow show senior officials who were keenly aware of the pressures of social change, who recognized the need to respond somehow, who were very aware of the difficulties of doing so, and who had yet to perceive positive educational opportunities in the social changes around them. They were truly struggling to understand and cope with the world their schools were facing.

Information Technology

Nearly all of the administrators and school boards members believed that changes in information technology were important to schools. In all the school systems we studied, measures were being taken to provide students with more experience in using information technology.

The most frequently cited reasons for giving attention to technology were economic and political, and reflected assumptions about the impact of technology on work, the role of schools in preparing students for work, and the need to respond to student and parental pressures. For example:

> [T]he reality existing in the work world and the world of tomorrow is that without a knowledge, understanding and an awareness of technology, our kids cannot survive. It does have a direct impact on what we do. We are catching up with the kids. (Suburban principal)

It worked its way up, but there were a lot of outside forces too. It was probably one issue in which we got a lot of feedback from parents who have major concerns because they are seeing the need and the growing technology within their own work places. We are getting it both ends; from the parents, from the community and also from the system as a whole. (Suburban board member)

However, nearly everyone had misgivings about the costs and educational consequences of information technology.

It is always a problem to me because I ask whether computers are really the crux of education . . . justifying the expenditures seems horrendous sometimes. (Rural board member)

I see technology as an unproven bandwagon that demands dollars but has not demonstrated its contribution to student learning. There is public pressure to go the technology route in the sense that they feel that the kids need to become technologically literate in order that they have the skills necessary to be competitive in the work force . . . I ask why? In spite of all this talk about technology I think that only a small percent of jobs require moderate levels of skill in technology. (Suburban superintendent)

The worries about using technology were accompanied by a very hazy idea of what each district's educational goals were in this area.

I remember participating in a meeting eight or nine years ago when we were discussing computers in the school, and I asked what are we doing it for? What are we trying to achieve? Are we trying to achieve a generic standard of computer literacy for all of our students so that, for instance, all grade 10 students would have approximately the same level of computer skills? Or are we saying that we want this at a certain level, but we also want pockets available for those students who need to go further with their computer skills? . . . we didn't answer the question then, and I'm not sure if we have answered the question now. (Urban superintendent)

The most advanced systems seemed committed to doing a variety of experiments in the use of technology to support teaching and learning, but had no framework to guide their work. Most seemed to believe that efforts of committed volunteers represented an appropriate response to the demand for change.

Most often it's where you have a key principal who believes in the program, who will find the right people, and badger for resources. (Urban district administrator)

The reliance on the voluntary efforts of individual teachers and principals was not accompanied by a strategy for organizational learning, that is for transferring to the whole system what had been learned in individual projects. The strong sense of a need to do something in the area of technology despite the costs and problems generated a considerable amount of activity but did not seem to be matched by a clear sense of what to do or how to move the system as a whole forward.

Child Poverty

While technology was on the formal agenda of all of our partner districts, poverty was not at the top of the agenda of any. It was discussed, more widely in some districts that in others, but was not very much the subject of policy deliberations, perhaps because there were no lobby groups or high-status advocates to raise the political profile of the issue. Moreover, poverty was seen as a problem concentrated in specific communities and thus as a school-level rather than a system-wide problem.

The views expressed to us about poverty were shaped but not entirely determined by respondents' understanding of the social context of their division. In two districts — one urban and one aboriginal — poverty is a very visible presence.

> It's a disastrous affliction . . . We, and society, haven't managed it yet. We have a large amount of transience in this district, although it is down from what it used to be, so there has been some stabilization. But the level of poverty has not improved whatsoever and the economic situation hasn't helped one bit. Poverty is incredibly destructive. (Urban board member)

> I think it [high dropout rates] is due to the social situation here, the economic situation. There is really poor housing, there is no employment. That's what I think it is. (Aboriginal district board member)

In suburban and rural districts educators were aware of poverty, but saw it as a confined, though perhaps growing, phenomenon. For instance:

> It's hard to know how many of those farm kids are in bad shape, some of them are for sure . . . I don't see poverty as affecting a large number of our kids but I know it's an important thing for the small number of our kids that are in that spot. (Rural board member)

> Up until the last five to eight years, you probably could have identified which schools in the division would have children that would have poverty as an issue in their life. There were schools where that would not have been an issue at all. What we are seeing is that the issue of poverty and all of the concerns that come with it are becoming more prevalent in a number of our schools . . . Probably the majority of our schools have some element of that. (Suburban board member)

The dominant view of poverty was of a deficiency in individual students that needs to be remedied or compensated for in order to allow students to benefit from their schooling. Problems in families caused by poverty were often mentioned. Schools adopted measures such as making some financial assistance available to students, waiving fees for field trips or referring students to social agencies. Relatively few people, even in the urban and aboriginal districts, saw the schools as needing to change their own core practice in significant ways to respond to the needs of students in poor families.

> What our schools are attempting to do is to make it easy for them to identify themselves as being in need in a discreet manner, then we provide

them with support. If there are students who could succeed with a small amount of income, we try to help them find a part-time job. If there are students who are already working and simply don't have the wherewithal to pay all the expenses, we will attempt to find some assistance for them, maybe through a bursary fund. If some students come to the school hungry, they do know where to go for some food, which again is provided in a discreet manner through the school cafeteria or some other method. We also attempt to get the social services involved in supporting the students where we are aware of difficulties. We find that more and more students are identifying themselves to us, knowing that their cases are handled confidentially. (Urban principal)

We are very much aware that there is child poverty here. [We] have initiated a nutritious snack program because some of the students come to school without breakfast. At Christmas time last year, instead of giving the kids from Nursery to grade 6 toys and little trinkets, we gave them scarves, tunics, and gloves to help them keep warm . . . We also extended our incentive program to include students in grades 7 and 8 . . . We did this because I found out we were losing kids in grade 7 with regard to attendance and dropout. (Aboriginal district board member)

In contrast to the issue of information technology, our respondents often wondered if dealing with poverty should be a responsibility of the school.

I am required to respond to changes like feeding kids and developing housing registries. I don't think it is my function to do these; certainly I wasn't trained to do them. I am not sure that the public school should be doing half of what it is doing in terms of meeting social needs. I don't believe children should be fed out of education funds. I believe that is a social service function. I believe I am handicapped in doing my educational job by having to use my education funds to feed kids and employ people to develop housing registries. Those are societal functions that I think belong to other organizations. (Urban principal)

But others saw no way for schools to avoid the issue, even if they were troubled by it. For example:

For a long time schools were able and willing to take on more and more. Many teachers have a strong social conscience and they identified needs in a child and were determined to meet those needs. Other agencies have built on this pattern and said let's try to push a service on to the school system. On the other hand we've probably voluntarily taken on things like this. Maybe it was easier for us just to implement a program than it was for us to fight with somebody else to get them to take it on. (Urban superintendent)

In comparison with technology, poverty was given less priority and received less attention in almost every respect. It was seen predominantly as a community and local school issue whereas technology was seen as a matter requiring a system-wide response. The system-wide approaches on poverty issues typically involved additional resources for schools with high concentrations of poor families, although the urban district did have a set of programs in place that were intended at least to mitigate some of the impacts of low income on children.

Changes in Families

The definition of poverty as an important issue was ours rather than our colleagues'; they tended to talk much more about changes in families. Indeed, we were impressed during the interviews by the frequency with which these administrators and school board members spoke about the powerful impact on their schools of changes in family structures and expectations. These problems were seen to be more important, pervasive or system-wide than those associated with poverty. Whereas poverty was perceived as a deficit, or an obstacle to be overcome on the path to education, changes in families represented a more fundamental threat to the school systems and the authority of the people within them.

The dominant impression we received was a view of change for the worse, of single-parent families, of families under stress and of families without social supports:

> The family is not the same as it used to be and the influence that parents had on the children doesn't seem to be what it used to be. Perhaps that is because both parents are working outside of the home, and there is less family life being conducted in the home. At the same time, the churches are less influential on families than they used to be, and they have little relevance for young people. (Urban superintendent)

> The family unit is no longer the father and the mother and the children with the dad and mom working and all coming home at five o'clock to get together and share the day's events . . . I suspect that the number of single-parent families in our own school would be between 40 and 50 percent. That has had a major impact on our students. A lot of the students are facing stress. (Suburban/rural principal)

Family difficulty ("dysfunctional families" was a phrase used often) was seen as the cause of an increase in students with serious behavior problems. We also heard about growing levels of violence in schools, and of children living on their own.

> We are seeing more violence, more transient students in our schools and more disintegration within the family. We are seeing students that just do not have the family supports such as were in place even ten years ago. We are dealing with a lot of social, societal factors. (Rural principal)

> If we see a dysfunctional family, the situation is often far more serious than anything we were ever exposed to. I used to see kids getting beat up, but it was always one on one, if somebody went to beat up somebody it was

always you against me. Now it is usual to see groups, and someone really getting beat up badly. Baseball bats and those kinds of things are not unusual. (Suburban principal)

We do certainly have many of our students living on their own at the age of 16, 17 or 18. They work part-time, study part-time, and really live in a very difficult situation. (Urban principal)

In consequence, schools were required to play different roles than in the past. And once again educators reported uncertainty as to what can reasonably be expected of schools, where their responsibilities begin and end.

There seems to be almost a paradoxical public expectation that all kids should be educated and deserve to be in schools and at the same time the school should be an environment that does not tolerate violent behaviors. If parents believe, as they say, that all kids have the right to attend school, they will also have to understand that this right would also extend to kids who may have violent behaviors. We can't have it both ways where all kids have the right to education and we have zero tolerance. (Suburban superintendent)

I do not think the schools can do any more than they are doing. We often put the basic education on the back burner for a while and a lot of this stuff that we are trying to do preventive work for creeps in. I do not think it is right that we have to spend so much time in the school trying to solve all the problems that have happened outside of the school. That is exactly what we are faced with. (Rural administrator)

It is worth noting that the situation was seen quite differently in the aboriginal district. Even though it had the highest levels of poverty and unemployment, concern about aggressive and violent behavior was not high here, underscoring the view expressed to us that changes in families and resulting increases in unwanted student behavior are not in the first instance related to poverty.

Our people right now have a very nice community to live in — we don't worry about safety and things like that. I know that there are problems that come with development like happens in big cities, but being a small community, such problems don't affect us. (Aboriginal district superintendent)

Thinking about Change

We were struck throughout the research by the frequently negative tone of the comments we heard about social changes and their implications for schools and school systems. Perhaps it is to be expected that people will focus on the negative aspects of change, but we found few mentions of positive changes that had recently occurred. Nor did these administrators and school board members typically see educational potential in the changes. Technology, for example, has the potential to improve education in important ways. Greater attention to diversity in students, families and school populations offers the promise of moving marginalized groups into the mainstream. Greater parental interest and pressure is surely a positive outcome of education and a potential gain for schools. Yet our respondents tended to describe all of these pessimistically, as problems rather than as gains or opportunities.

Such worry and uncertainty could lead to more emphasis on understanding external pressures. Yet the five districts gave little formal attention to social change. The people we interviewed seemed perceptive and to have a good grasp of the organizational intricacies and political subtleties of their school systems. We had every reason to believe they were committed to improving education. Still, the structures and processes by which they directed their efforts were essentially inward-looking and appeared to constrain their thoughts and actions. It seemed to us that social changes surrounding schools raise fundamental questions about the purposes and organization of the school system, as well as the nature and processes of education. We did not see many signs that the districts had become engaged with such questions.

These views about social change were shaped to a very great extent by direct experience or the interpretation of the experience of others. We found little evidence of an analytic or data-based approach to understanding the environment of schooling. We heard many stories about individual students, parents or teachers, but little mention of research or data analysis of any kind. Sometimes particular stories were retold around a district until they become a part of the folk-wisdom even if they appeared to be quite atypical. Administrators relied on what teachers told them about children and parents while school boards and district administrators seemed often to be using third-hand information — what principals said that teachers said that students or families were doing or experiencing. In short, the information base for forming a picture of how school contexts are changing seemed to us narrow and constrained.

Nor did we see very much evidence that issues of external change were widely discussed in systematic ways. We found only rare mentions of these issues in any of the school board minutes, agendas, plans, budgets or other documents we reviewed. Almost all the official attention in meetings of school boards and administrators was given to the internal operations of the system. The school systems had created working groups on curriculum development or implementation or teaching methods, but not on issues of coping with changes in families. None of the systems we studied had conducted formal environmental analyses or had prepared what might be called a strategic plan. In the area of technology districts did have plans, but these focused largely on acquiring hardware and software rather than on educational purposes.

A result of such practices was that our districts did not always have an adequate analytic framework for identifying significant problems and understanding the dynamics surrounding educational issues; instead they seemed to respond when external pressure required it. The mainstream view of the purpose of schooling as largely to serve economic needs was widely mentioned, yet most educators with whom we spoke saw this perspective as too narrow to encompass everything schools need to do (e.g., Barlow and Robertson, 1994; Touraine, 1991). Although these educators perceived the need for school systems to respond to increasing social diversity — in ethnicity, gender, religion and class — very few provided us with an analysis at the level of fundamental change. Postmodernity, a term frequently used in many different ways in academic discourse (e.g., Hargreaves, 1994; Taylor, 1991), was not mentioned; nor were changes in such fundamental constituting elements of society as ideas of time and space, concepts of identity, approaches to politics and epistemological underpinnings. Based on our evidence, school administrators and school board members do not really use any of these analytical frames. They speak in experiential terms, telling stories of incidents and events rather than citing data or using conceptual language.

We might also expect that organizations feeling powerful external pressures might experiment with alternative forms of response to those pressures. Again, our evidence did not show that this occurs. We observed that school systems had tried to respond to change by doing more of what they already did — adding specialized staff, creating additional programs, or adding services. Given pressures on budgets, none of these is easy to do, which contributes to a sense of frustration. Perhaps this is why there seemed to be such a high reliance on the voluntary efforts of individuals as a way of responding to issues.

Still, in each system there were some indications that people were struggling to find new ways of thinking about education. There were questions about present practice, and various pilot projects which were bringing people to the brink of new approaches to education. The next steps, yet to be taken, are to incorporate these questions into the formal agenda and structure of the systems and to consider the projects as ways of learning about systems of education, which we take to be more than only organizations for schooling. If the school systems we studied are at all typical, then schools are likely facing continuing and perhaps increasing turmoil. Without a proactive response to change they run the risk of being buffeted endlessly by forces that are only dimly understood.

The Limits of Analysis

In making these comments, we are conscious of the dangers of a kind of academic rationalism, a view that the world can be understood and managed through processes of analysis. The limits of this view have been stated by others often and eloquently. It is not clear that change can be "managed" at all. As Kaufman (1985) notes, "organizations by and large are not capable of more than marginal changes, while the environment is so volatile that marginal changes are frequently insufficient" (p. 131). We know that standard models of organizational learning understate the complexity, diversity and uncertainty of many organizational processes. There is nothing simple about organizational functioning, especially in public organizations such as schools where goals are multiple and may be inconsistent.

Moreover, it is typical for organizational attention to be focused on day-to-day matters, crises and surprises, or immediate items with financial implications. Delays are inevitable, and partial or tangential responses to external pressures are sometimes unavoidable. At the same time, although external pressures can be important drivers of change, no simple or complete correspondence between external changes and internal adjustments should be expected, or wanted. Schools should be responsive to external changes, and also have their own evolving identity. Organizational learning is not just about change; it is also involves harmonizing education and social change, responding to change in educationally appropriate ways.

Schools are limited by external constraints. Much of what they do is determined by mandates imposed by others, notably governments that set curricula, timelines, and other features of the system. During the time of this study the provincial government announced several major policy changes that required considerable time and attention from school districts. Schools are also subject to multiple political pressures in their local communities. And of course every day thousands of students arrive in schools needing to be taught and looked after; the time and energy to think about large-scale change has to be taken from somewhere.

Still, to recognize the problems of improvement is not to say that nothing can or should be done. We believe that school districts could do more to understand and address social change. Many of the elements of a more systematic approach to organizational learning seem almost self-evident when considered abstractly: scanning the environment and placing external change on the districts' agendas; building district capacity for learning and planning; developing a knowledge base and collecting and distributing information about important external changes; professional development; integrating research into the policymaking process; seeking regular feedback from friendly and reliable critics; and promoting pilot schools or projects. The challenge is a practical one, to determine how to do these things in a concrete situation. As one of our colleagues remarked, "The big question is how to make things happen."

Some Suggestions for Practice

Our approach to the question of "how" concentrates on the intellectual side of learning in school systems. This emphasis is not to diminish in any way the considerable importance of interpersonal skill and political acumen in responding to environmental change. Still, the intellectual or conceptual side of organizational learning has been neglected in the literature and in educational practice.

Our suggestions focus on the ways in which school systems acquire and use information, as well as the ways in which innovation is fostered and sustained. They are analogous to the ways in which we would regard any problem of education, for participants at any level and in any role — as a combination of aquiring information, promoting discussion, and exploring ways of understanding and acting.

A first requirement is to place more emphasis on gathering and discussing information about the changing world. By this we do not mean only collecting information or research in the usual sense, although these would certainly be involved. Successfully relating the external perspective to an understanding of the internal workings of the system — linking analysis and reflection — involves treating a number of questions as a set. What is happening in the environment? How are these events and trends related to the system and its ability to achieve its main purposes? How might the system respond? Does the system need to change in order to achieve its purposes? Are there practices in parts of the system which are promising and should be generalized to the whole? Hannah Arendt called this "to think what we are doing" (1978: 4). In schools this will require more deliberate and sustained attention to social change so that it is accepted as the frame for what schools do instead of being seen as an interference with organizational purposes. One consequence of such inquiry would be to look for the educational possibilities in social change, rather than focusing only on its problematic aspects.

An important dimension of the intellectual side of organizational learning is creating the conditions which make systematic analysis and reflection more likely. There is a tendency to concentrate on the role of official leaders, but the formal leader is not the only source of either external perspective or internal reflection. All leaders are heavily dependent on others, and in this sense their interpersonal skills and political acumen might be used to support a more intellectual approach to how school systems respond to social change.

More specifically, leaders need to exemplify this approach to learning. If we want people to seek out friendly criticism, to express differences of opinion respectfully, to listen to others, to question, to participate in active inquiry, model building and exploration, and to engage in dialogue and debate over time, we need to acknowledge that these will not happen if the senior personnel of a school system neither value nor model them. Traditional hierarchical notions of schooling, in which teachers are seen as the implementors of plans made on high, will not work because in schooling the understanding and commitment of people are fundamental to what happens, regardless of what may have been written in a policy or plan. Everyone in the organization — students, parents and teachers as well as administrators — will need to have skills of dialogue, empathy and conflict resolution. Educational ideals will need to be part of our total practice, not just something that we apply to curriculum (Levin, 1998).

Possessing information about social change and the skills to talk about it will only be useful if social change is on the official agenda of schools and school boards. For this to happen, school administrators and school boards will have to find other ways to deal with the issues, items and working assumptions which now crowd out social change. There are many reasons why a school board might be preoccupied with financial items, to the neglect of education and social change. For example, board members might understand financial matters as their realm, with education being the purview of professionals; they might suspect the financial judgement and political prudence of the superintendent; they might be experiencing a tax-payer revolt of sorts; or they might be deeply divided on educational philosophy, and so avoid discussing it. When budgets are under pressure, of course, these tendencies are exacerbated. Changing the agenda, then, is not trivial. Nor is it just a matter of changing priorities or superimposing new priorities on old ones. It requires reconsidering the personal habits, administrative logic and political assumptions reflected by the current agenda.

Putting social change on the official agenda could help school systems to become more outward looking. Just as important is widening the range of people with whom educators talk. This may mean bringing visitors into staff meetings and staff rooms, changing the kind of people who are involved in professional development days or circulating different sorts of reading material. Because educators' views are greatly influenced by their personal interaction, talking with people is an important step in the development of ongoing linkages and relationships. People in schools need to hear from other people to get their stories and experiences. However, changing who we talk to does not just mean dialogue with professionals in fields such as justice and social services. We strongly believe that those in our society who are relatively powerless are too seldom heard, yet our data indicate that these groups are typically seen as people to be helped, not people to be heard. We found very few mentions of working with students or parents as opposed to trying to manage them. If our concern is with poverty we should talk at least as much with people who are poor as we do to other professionals who provide the poor with social and educational "services." Need we also observe that students have perhaps the strongest interest in the adaptation of schools to a changing environment, but perhaps the least influence over the course of educational change?

Another important requirement is to link the current reliance on volunteers and projects to ongoing development of the entire system. In the systems we studied, the connections among schools were generally weak, and the relationships between schools and the board offices sometimes uncertain. School systems need better ways not only of encouraging innovation but of learning from and making use of it as it occurs. Because administration and governance systems are not well organized to understand and respond to social change, teachers and principals are likely to face continuing demands without the tools or supports to help them respond effectively, and without the frameworks which will help them know where their projects and initiatives fit in a larger scheme of things. Most of the people at the system level valued the initiatives of teachers and principals, and waited for them. At the same time, they said little about encouraging initiatives, channeling them in particular directions, or using them as part of a process of system-wide organizational learning. The result is that successful educational change is likely to be restricted to a few sites and very difficult to sustain. Projects, which are the common response in schools to change, are important. Attaching some larger significance to them may well be a way to rescue educational change from the project syndrome. Getting more value from projects means organizing processes for sharing experiences, disseminating successes, learning from disappointments. Teachers are critical to this effort.

Finally, we believe that a fundamental obstacle to coping with change lies in the tyranny of the standard model of schooling. The educators in our study could see clearly the limits of current practice, but could not always see what else they might do. It was as if they recognized that the boat they were in was listing badly, but had nothing else to turn to. Despite recent discussions of "full-service school," education as a whole lacks alternative models that might envisage schools as, for example, economic development agencies, true community learning centers or collegial enterprises organized around community needs. Although conditions vary greatly from locale to locale, schooling everywhere looks much the same. Dramatic changes in communications patterns, information handling and human interaction will need to be reflected in quite different ways of organizing our institutions. It seems evident to us that schools designed for the conditions of the nineteenth century will not do justice to educational needs in the twenty-first century. Until parents and educators consider alternative forms of education that might look very different, schools are unlikely to be able to cope with the changes being thrust upon them.

Note

1   The study is outlined in detail by Levin and Riffel (1997). A number of other papers have been published arising from the study; readers are invited to contact the authors for a complete list.

References

Aldrich, H. (1979) *Organizations and environments.* Englewood Cliffs, NJ: Prentice Hall.

Arendt, H. (1978) *Thinking: Volume II, The life of the mind.* New York: Harcourt Brace Jovanovich.

Barlow, M. and Robertson, H.-J. (1994) *Class warfare.* Toronto: Key Porter.

Cuban, L. (1990) Reforming again, again, and again. *Educational Researcher,* 19(1), 3–13.

Dodgson, M. (1993) Organizational learning: a review of some literatures. *Organizational Studies,* 14(3), 375–94.

Dror, Y. (1986) *Policymaking under adversity.* New York: Transaction Books.

Hargreaves, A. (1994) *Changing teachers, changing times: teachers' work and culture in the postmodern age.* New York: Teachers College Press.

Kaufman, H. (1985) *Time, chance and organizations: natural selection in a perilous environment.* Chatham, NJ: Chatham House.

Levin, B. (1993) School response to a changing environment. *Journal of Educational Administration,* 31(2), 4–21.

Levin, B. (1998) The educational requirement for democracy. *Curriculum Inquiry,* 28(1), 57–80.

Levin, B. (1999) Schools and the labour market: a research agenda. Paper prepared for the Pan-Canadian Education Research Agenda Colloquium, Ottawa, February 1999.

Levin, B. and Riffel, J. A. (1997) *Schools and the changing world: struggling toward the future.* London: Falmer Press.

McCall, M. and Kaplan, R. (1985) *Whatever it takes: decision makers at work.* Englewood Cliffs, NJ: Prentice Hall.

March, J. (1991) Exploration and exploitation in education, *Organizational Science,* 2(1), 71–87.

March, J. and Olsen, J. (1989) *Rediscovering institutions.* New York: The Free Press.

Morgan, G. (1986) *Images of organization.* Newbury Park, CA: Sage.

Sarason, S. (1996) *Revisiting the culture of school and the problem of change.* New York: Teachers College Press.

Shakeshaft, C. (1999) The struggle to create a more gender-inclusive profession. In J. Murphy and K. Louis (eds.), *Handbook of research on educational administration,* pp. 99–118. San Francisco: Jossey-Bass.

Taylor, C. (1991) *The malaise of modernity.* Concord, ON: Anansi Press.

Touraine, A. (1991) A world that has lost its future. In A. Touraine (ed.), *Facing the future: young people and unemployment around the world,* pp. 1–41. New York: Orient Longman.

Warriner, C. (1984) *Organizations and their environments: essays in the sociology of organizations.* Greenwich, CT: JAI Press.

Wilson, J. (1989) *Bureaucracy.* New York: Basic Books.

IV   PROSPECTS FOR CHANGE

10 Inside–Outside Change Facilitation: Structural and Cultural Considerations

Wayne Seller and Lynne Hannay

Schools world-wide are facing significant challenges to rethink the learning opportunities they provide for students, their leadership practices and their operational structures. Schools and even school districts cannot achieve these mammoth tasks alone; they need support from outside agencies. Yet the reform experiences of the last thirty years document that, regardless of financial investment, outside agencies cannot facilitate sustained change by themselves. Clearly there is a need to investigate systemic collaborative relationships between school personnel and external agencies — whether foundations, governmental agencies or universities — to help them work together to initiate and sustain school change.

Part of the difficulty in inside–outside partnerships has been a lack of research attention to an integrated and embedded approach to school reform. As Fullan suggests:

> An external change agent cannot represent "one more project." To be effective, the dual preoccupation of external reformers should be to focus on the elements of implementation of the program or initiative in question, but to do so in a way that actively and explicitly helps *integrate* the work of the school. Internal capacity building is a coherence-making proposition which cannot be done from the inside acting alone. (Fullan, 1997: 40; italics in original)

Partnerships between school systems and universities provide a natural possibility for an integrated approach to facilitating reform, but maintaining such relationships has been problematic because of structural and cultural incompatibilities. In this chapter, we explore one type of school–university relationship that has existed across Ontario, Canada, for thirty years. Our intent is not to advocate that every university or outside agency adopt this model verbatim but to identify the characteristics that might form the cultural and structural bases for effective means of supporting inside–outside educational reform partnerships.

School–University Collaboration

Schools need universities and universities, particularly schools or faculties of education, need schools. In our current reform-minded culture, the need for such relationships is especially self-evident. Yet also self-evident is the lack of examples of sustained school–university partnerships that have made a difference to both the schools and the universities.

First, schools need universities. School-based personnel often lack the knowledge to assess reform initiatives adequately and yet the literature suggests schools which successfully deal with reform operate from a data base within a culture of inquiry (e.g., Darling-Hammond and McLaughlin, 1995; Hannay and Ross, 1997a, 1997b; Kruse *et al.*, 1995; Lieberman, 1995). The change literature and other chapters in this book suggest that the changes being faced by schools today are complex (e.g., Fullan, 1999). The complexities involved in such reform initiatives, in terms of both process and impact, are subtle and develop over a lengthy time period. University faculty members have the skills to assess the effectiveness of change efforts but this can only be useful if the process is ongoing, rather than a "drive-by assessment." Faculty members can also help school personnel make links with other schools involved in similar reform initiatives and to the reform literature.

Universities also need schools. Academics in education need to understand the evolving realities of schools in order to prepare prospective teachers to enter that world and to help students who are already teachers and administrators to understand their world better. By developing relationships and increasing mutual understanding, university faculty members can counter the perception that they are out of touch (Sachs, 1997). Members of faculties of education also need contact with schools in order to engage in research and development activities not only that meet their academic requirements but through which they can contribute to the educational knowledge base.

While relationships between schools and universities are obviously beneficial to both parties, there are few examples of sustained partnerships. Certainly, school–university collaborative networks are a recent growth industry that is having a documented impact on individual schools and on our knowledge about educational change (e.g., Lieberman and McLaughlin, 1992). However, many networks, while valuable, tend to focus narrowly on specific areas of practice and are often led by an "idea champion," a factor which Lieberman (1988) suggests is a potential Achilles' heel. If the idea champion leaves, the project can collapse (see also Hannay and Smyth, 1996). Professional development schools (PDS) are another increasingly popular form of school–university partnership (see Darling-Hammond, 1994; Ross, 1995). As with networks, Whitford and Metcalf-Turner (1999) argue that PDS partnerships rarely achieve an organic partnership that is critical for sustained success. Experience with these sorts of partnerships suggests that if school–university collaboration is to be a means of supporting educational reform, then the process needs to be sustained, and this requires that it be embedded in educational organizations. Yet this is difficult, because schools and academic institutions differ in their orientations (Brookhart and Loadman, 1992; Goodlad, 1988; Ross, 1995). According to Fullan, "On their worst days schools are 'fire, fire, fire' and universities are 'ready, ready, ready'" (1993: 121).

The structures and cultures are different for each kind of institution. Public demand and governmental policy increasingly pressure personnel in schools and school systems to initiate significant change. Encapsulated within traditional bureaucracies more attuned to the modern rather than the postmodern world (Hargreaves, 1994), school personnel often respond by looking for a guru or quick-fix solution, and fail to address root issues (Hannay, 1994). When they turn to a university for possible assistance, they run into structures and cultures that militate against quick response even when individual university faculty members want to assist. Traditional research paradigms, time lines, and tenure and promotional criteria of a university tend to militate against the levels of response that schools desire (Goodlad, 1994; Hannay and Smyth, 1996; Heckman, 1988; Keating and Clark, 1988; Lieberman, 1988; Sinclair and Harrison, 1988).

For school–university collaboration to go beyond a superficial project level, structural and cultural changes are required — new structures and cultures that recognize and support the different needs and aspirations of school system and university educators. Achieving an organic partnership requires direct attention to the mainstream structures and cultures of all organizations that participate in the collaborative effort (Whitford and Metcalf-Turner, 1999). Indeed, Howey and Zimpher (1999) argue that the foundation of school–university partnerships is an organic partnership based on both institutional and programmatic change. Achieving this organic partnership is problematic because of the differing purposes of the organizations. As Watson and Fullan (1992: 218) explain, "universities have as part of their primary mandate the production of knowledge, while schools by the very nature of their mission are more concerned with day-to-day practical issues." Perhaps the crux of these differences is rooted in the meaning of knowledge itself. Hargreaves (1996) suggests the issue might demand a blurring of the boundaries between university knowledge, which is "abstract, generalized, propositional, and detached from the everyday life of teachers" (p. 106) and a more practical focus on reflective practice, personal practical knowledge, pedagogical content knowledge and teacher research. Tensions in school–university relationships build unless the needs of all parties are achieved (Goodlad, 1988, 1994; Watson and Fullan, 1992).

Not surprisingly, Howey and Zimpher (1999) suggest that a reculturing of practices and partnerships is necessary if forms of school–university partnership are to be established and maintained. In this chapter, we explore an ongoing and evolving school–university collaboration that began over thirty years ago. This model, the Field Centre Model of the Ontario Institute for Studies in Education at the University of Toronto (OISE/UT), exemplifies school–university relationships which are essentially a hybrid culture that spans the worlds of schools and universities (Hannay and Smyth, 1996).

The Field Centre Model

When the Ontario Institute for Studies in Education was created in 1965, its mandate was not only to fulfil traditional graduate-level university teaching and research responsibilities but also to work directly on improving educational practice in Ontario schools. It was originally assumed that such support for school reform could be provided through the central Institute in Toronto, but this strategy proved to be "of little help to school [districts] and little interest to competent university personnel" (Leithwood *et al.*, 1975: 4). The Institute began to experiment with alternative forms of school–university collaboration. In 1968, a small number of Field Centres were created and very quickly expanded to a network of Centres to service the vast geographical space and diversity of Ontario.

From the inception of the Field Centre Model, the guiding philosophy has been one of partnership. The Centres are typically housed in school district facilities at little or no charge for the space. Centre faculty members, one or two individuals, work with school districts to support locally initiated change efforts at little or no charge for their services. While Field Centre faculty members do work similar to their more traditional academic colleagues, teaching graduate courses and conducting research through funded and unfunded projects, they also are actively involved in field development in schools and school districts. All of these functions operate in ways that ground the work in practical reality. As faculty members are housed in the Centre and are not just guests on a rotating basis, they develop long-term partnerships and relationships that embed school–university collaboration deeply into the regional educational landscape.

The experiment with Field Centres as a model of school–university collaboration has lasted for over thirty years. The required modifications to both the traditional university culture and its structure have provided many challenges. Over the three decades, especially in fiscally tight times, the continuation of the Field Centres has been questioned by traditional university faculty members who did not understand their value. School district personnel, on the other hand, have been consistently enthusiastic about the Field Centres (see Smyth and Hannay, 1993; Hannay and Smyth, 1996 for details) and senior university administrators have actively supported their continuation because of the obvious political benefits for the university. The long-term existence of the Field Centres has necessitated modifications in tenure, promotion and merit pay for involved faculty. The importance of the embedded modifications has been apparent with the recent merger with a larger university with more traditional promotion and tenure criteria.

This chapter provides a glimpse into the underlying practices of the collaboration between Field Centre faculty and practitioners. The thirty years of experience, grounded in real practice, provide insights for individuals interested in promoting and supporting school change through externally based technical support grounded in an organic partnership. Four case studies, representing typical Field Centre projects, are provided. The commonalities apparent across the case studies are then discussed. These commonalties can help others begin to understand how to provide effective external change agent roles of their own.

Case Studies

Lake Superior

Lake Superior School District is a small school district encompassing four separate and distinct communities spread over a geographic area of approximately 150 kilometers (90 miles) from end to end. As a small jurisdiction with few students, the district lacks personnel to assist schools with implementing educational reforms either at the central office or in the schools.

Over the years, the regional Field Centre faculty members have acted as external consultants and researchers on many occasions both to district administrators and trustees and to individual school principals and staffs. When a new reform initiative is introduced by government policy or considered by local practitioners, the school system tends to contact the Field Centre for advice or ideas, or to request that Centre faculty join a locally formed committee or to work with schools to plan implementation strategies. At other times, the Field Centre staff are asked to act as evaluators with respect to an initiative in order to provide a formative evaluation of progress. Conversely, if the Field Centre staff are conducting a funded research study, and if the subject of the research is of interest to the school system or to particular schools, the Lake Superior School District and its personnel are often invited to participate. Such invitations are inevitably accepted and the results often contribute to further change initiatives within the school district.

It was with this background that the Field Centre was asked to work with the district's Administrative Council to help rethink the role of the principal and the introduction of school councils (sometimes referred to as parent councils). Besides overseeing the common administrative duties involved in operating the schools, this Administrative Council also formed the professional development committee for principals.

The faculty member who worked with the council was personally known to almost all council members and came to the present situation with a detailed knowledge of the school system based on fourteen years of personal involvement. His role with respect to the current reform initiative was multifaceted. He would sit on the professional development sub-committee of the Council and help create the professional development program for the principals. Since he was known to have expertise in professional development program design and development as well as an ongoing interest in the role of the principal, he would also be asked to conduct some professional development sessions. In the second stage of the project, which involved implementing school councils for each of the schools, the faculty member would become a researcher, gathering information on implementation progress and on the further training and informational needs of both principals and school council members.

While this project was entering the second stage, the Field Centre, along with two other Field Centres, obtained a research grant to study the implementation of school councils more broadly. The faculty member brought this information to the Council and asked if they would like to participate in the study, through which they would obtain information on their own situation as well as comparative data from a cross-section of other jurisdictions engaged in the same reform initiative. Three schools became part of the research study. The Field Centre faculty member's involvement with this school district with respect to this reform issue spanned four years and resulted in changes in how local educators understood and managed school council policy.

Lakehead

External assistance to practitioners dealing with educational change can take many forms. Sometimes the influence of such assistance is not immediately recognizable and, indeed, it is not always clear that the external agent is providing any concrete assistance at all. This may be especially true when a specific educational reform is not central to the interactions between the field developer and the local practitioners.

As several other chapters in this book suggest, all school districts in Ontario had been struggling to implement a number of reform initiatives. School effectiveness and school improvement research was being promoted as a way of identifying desirable changes in school administration and classroom practice. This put pressure on school districts to provide new and improved forms of professional development for their staff. Special education services were changing and the integration of special needs students into regular classrooms was mandated. New curriculum guidelines were issued across elementary and secondary grades. Secondary school reform became a priority across the province. The formation of school councils was first recommended, then required, for all schools.

While such changes were being initiated externally, the Lakehead School

District had identified needs of its own. Reduced funding had led to a severe reduction in central office staff available to assist schools in dealing with the initiatives they faced. The district also recognized that the way professional development programs had been organized and delivered to staff was no longer adequate, effective or efficient. And there was a recognized leadership crisis developing in the school district: almost half of the school administrators were due to retire over a short period and there did not appear to be a cadre of potential leaders within the system to fill the gaps. The system's ability to cope with massive change was severely compromised.

The Field Centre was directly involved with various local practitioners in several activities. District staff charged with revamping the professional development system worked with Centre faculty to design a new system and then monitor its effectiveness. The Centre also worked with schools, studying the change initiatives and attempting to determine the best way of implementing them. Faculty members were asked to sit on system-wide work groups to help design evaluation components to gauge the effectiveness of the work done by these groups; this would be followed up by helping the groups interpret the results.

Field Centre assistance also extended beyond these concrete examples. The district Director of Education understood that the system's capacity to deal with change, especially such massive change, was hampered by an organizational structure which had been developed in another time and under other circumstances and sought the critical ear of the Field Centre faculty. They met informally several times a year; during these meetings, the Director would explain what he had done, what changes he had made and was contemplating making, and what he hoped to accomplish in making progress toward his ultimate goal. The faculty member listened, took notes, and when feasible, teased out some ideas.

When the district's organizational structure reached a level of relative stability, a research project was established to link the current structure to appropriate theory and research and provide a grounded rationale for what had been done. The research also served as a formative evaluation of the structure's success in meeting organizational goals.

In this case, external assistance has taken many forms, ranging from active participation to passive observation, and has been directed toward many different change initiatives that have occurred simultaneously. The impact of Field Centre participation is apparent in the design of several present school district undertakings and in the approach being taken toward different initiatives by various practitioners.

Northumberland-Clarington

While Field Centre personnel realize that "one-shot" presentations do not usually advance an educational reform agenda, sometimes they will make such presentations to share their learnings about one site with another, or because they have come to understand that they may provide the seeds that will grow into a project. One example that resulted in a multifaceted and long-term project can be found in the Northumberland-Clarington School District. In this instance, school district personnel had requested a presentation on research on secondary school change that had been conducted in other Ontario districts (Hannay and Schmalz, 1995). The presentation quickly developed into a field development project with the Field Centre faculty providing ongoing advice and additional presentations. As the Centre continued to support this school district in its early exploration of restructuring, reculturing and retiming its secondary schools (Fullan, 1997), it became apparent that what the district was attempting was unique and that it offered an opportunity for cutting-edge research on secondary school reform. Consequently, Field Centre faculty proposed a research partnership to investigate the district's efforts.

The original "one-shot" presentation has resulted in six years of multifaceted collaboration between the school district administration, the teachers' federation (union) and two university faculty members. The research project focuses on the school district's efforts to empower secondary school staffs to create new organizational structures that will heighten learning opportunities for students. District consultants and teachers have helped collect and analyze data. University faculty members have worked with district personnel to help them consider their options, to try to understand why some schools are changing more quickly than others and to support all schools in their efforts. They have also contributed to ongoing professional development in terms of presentations and in planning the nature of the professional development. Field Centre faculty also responded to a challenge by senior administration to create an on-site graduate program focused on secondary school change. The research program in this district has yielded statistical evidence that the school system has grown significantly in its capacity to deal with ongoing change as well as qualitative data that provides some indicators on why the system is changing (Hannay and Ross, 1997a, 1997b, 1999; Ross *et al.*, 1998). The system and the school teams have employed these data to make action decisions and the research reports themselves are a key component of the professional development program as schools review and apply the research. Inquiry has been incorporated into the culture and practices of the system and of individual schools.

Because Field Centre faculty members are considered full and active partners with the district, they have had access to the insider perspective that is often denied to educational researchers, including insights into planning and decision-making processes at the system and school levels. The partnership between the two original field developers and school district personnel was extended to another university faculty member who has access to sensitive information on the collective bargaining process that would not be available to most external researchers or change agents.

Through this research program, Field Centre staff have learned a great deal about the complexity of secondary school change and some of the elements that enable or constrain school-based change. This knowledge has been in demand. In addition to professional and academic conference presentations, presentations were made in at least twenty different Ontario districts in a two-year period. As university faculty, Field Centre staff fulfil the academic mandate of creating and sharing knowledge through numerous professional and refereed published articles, often co-authored with school district partners.

The partnership has resulted in research that is deeply embedded in the real experiences of the schools. The embedded knowledge is perceived by practitioners in other jurisdictions as being legitimate and useful and is being used as a starting point in other situations.

Nipissing

Since 1988, because of their particular areas of expertise, two Field Centre faculty members were invited to participate in projects in this school district which was outside their immediate regional jurisdictions. The first invitation was made to a faculty member to be involved in facilitating peer coaching in a traditional professional development program. The other began when the initiative was expanded to a district-wide peer coaching training program. The involvement around peer coaching lasted three years. Several years later, one of the faculty members was part of a team investigating the possibilities of using action research as a means of professional development across the province. Because of the past history of collaboration, the Nipissing School District was invited to be part of this project. The faculty member worked in this district for two years to develop and implement a professional development program to facilitate school-based use of action research.

Throughout this period, a superintendent and the faculty member discussed the possibility of using action research as a teacher-controlled means of performance appraisal. These conversations eventually led to the district funding a small pilot project with teachers and administrators volunteering to participate. Field Centre faculty with expertise in performance appraisal joined the project and a new stage in this intermittent collaboration began.

This example of collaboration between Field Centre faculty and a school district is different from the others used in this chapter as both faculty members were far away from their geographical jurisdictions, but there were several similarities to the other projects. First, there was a local Field Centre whose faculty member was respected within the school district, and the Field Centre concept was an integral component of the educational community. Second, while the Centre initially responded to the local agenda, it then invited the district to join a project that emerged from its own research interests. Third, right after the initial involvement, a superintendent who had worked with both faculty members elsewhere was hired by the school district (indeed, Centre faculty had provided a reference for him), and brought with him a past history of collaboration. Fourth, the collaborative history led to a mutual exploration of new ideas which seemed like a natural extension of eight years of work in this school district. The long-term partnership evolved to meet the needs of all parties. Throughout this process, the faculty members and school district personnel challenged each other about possibilities and ideas, enriching their understanding of professional growth and change processes. The outputs of this long-term project included several sustained professional development programs that supported the school district's concept of teacher leadership and collaboration. The university faculty received support to try new concepts and generate research about the use of those new concepts within a trusting and supportive partnership.

Successful Inside–Outside Collaboration for Educational Change

The cases outlined above contain important elements for consideration by external agents who work with practitioners engaged in change activities. Although these cases are diverse in their settings and foci, they exhibit similar characteristics which help to explain what we have found to be a mutually productive model of field development. In this section, we include direct quotations collected during a recent review of the OISE/UT Field Centres as well as serendipitous comments made in data collected or in other research studies by individuals in many professional roles and from all regions of Ontario.

Continuity

Each of the cases represents one point in time in an ongoing relationship between university faculty and practitioners. This is a complex relationship in several ways. In some situations, the same faculty member has been integral to the partnership, while in others the faculty member involved in the specific initiative described is the beneficiary of a relationship built by others. Each initiative described in the cases represents a multiyear interaction between the faculty member and practitioners. While a clear beginning point can be identified for each initiative, the length of time required to reach a natural end is often uncertain until work is well underway.

In Lake Superior and Lakehead, the Field Centre faculty member had worked with school district personnel for eighteen years. But he was also able to draw on the involvement of the Centre with school districts that extended back another ten years beyond his personal experience. In

Nipissing and Northumberland-Clarington, the faculty members working with the practitioners on the described reform initiatives originally became involved through work each had done in other regions, but in both cases they were able to build on a relationship which had been maintained by other faculty members in other Field Centres.

This continuity of contact marks the Field Centre approach to university –school collaboration as different from the sporadic and short-term approach typical of most external change facilitators. While one or two years is considered to be a long-term involvement for other university-based projects, this is generally considered short-term involvement by Field Centre faculty.

The ongoing nature of Field Centre work with local practitioners fosters a sense of trust based on a history of experience. According to a superintendent, "As a teacher, a principal, a resource person, now as a superintendent, the Field Centre has always been there — any role that I have played in the board." As demonstrated in Nipissing and Northumberland-Clarington, this trust can be extended to other Centre personnel. While in both cases the faculty members had to establish their own "credentials," they were given the opportunity to do so in large part because of practitioners' past experience with Field Centre staff. Since change involves risk and risk involves the potential for failure, trust in the external person is crucial to the potential impact.

The relationships and experiences of the practitioners with Field Centre faculty over time also establishes the credibility of the faculty members. A Director explained:

> Relationships are really important. Everyone around the table has mentioned their personal connectedness with [a Field Centre faculty member]. The stability of staff, even though we are talking about flexibility and change, that building of personal rapport, becomes a great strength.

In some projects, this might begin with low levels of impact brought about by relatively low-risk initiatives, but over an extended period of time success with riskier initiatives will be remembered. Even projects that do not achieve desired ends can build credibility and trust. In such situations, Field Centre staff are remembered as people who did not disappear and leave local practitioners to pick up the pieces, but rather tried to determine what went wrong and what could be done to correct it.

Multifaceted Projects

One direct result of the ongoing nature of the relationship between field development faculty and practitioners is the evolution of project foci. While Field Centre members are often sought by practitioners looking for specific knowledge or skills, the initial reasons for the request do not usually act as restrictions on what might be accomplished. Rather than remaining fixed on only one small part of the whole process of change, the projects appear to evolve in relation to the reality of life in school systems. As the field developer works with practitioners, the focus changes and the work of the faculty member also changes. A Director describes the ebb and flow that shaped the involvement with the local Centre:

> [The faculty] came in and started doing the one-shot deal on school improvement. I am [now] looking five years later and people are talking about how to improve, where do we go, how do we build from here. That is because [the involvement] was over five years, a lot of ongoing contact, visits, on site. Since then there is monitoring but as soon as the faculty member arrives for monitoring, there comes the invitation because I [the Director] want to move to the next step.

The faculty member's history with a local site provides an intimate knowledge of the school and the system and a context for understanding the logic of a particular focus. Such knowledge and experience with the local situation is not possible for an external agent who enters the situation for a single purpose.

Collaborative Agenda Setting

The Lake Superior, Lakehead, Northumberland-Clarington and Nipissing cases each began because local practitioners identified a need and called upon Field Centre faculty to provide assistance. Similarly, the multidimensional characteristics of the projects emerged because of local requirements. But these situations differ from requests often made of other external change agents in two ways. First, the practitioners already knew what interests and expertise the faculty members were able to bring to the situation. They were also aware of the faculty members' needs to be involved in knowledge creation through research and to publish what they learned in scholarly journals. In other words, the practitioners were aware of the local agenda of the Field Centres and considered that part of their own agenda.

When schools districts seek the assistance of other external agents, their work tends to be very specifically targeted (for example, a single workshop or set of workshops). While the knowledge or expertise of such agents is well known, they usually cannot legitimately influence the course of the project. If the focus changes, so does the agent. The locus of control stays firmly with local practitioners.

Conversely, when university faculty go uninvited into a school system to conduct research, even if that research is directed toward answering pressing questions asked by the practitioners, the agenda is perceived as university-based. The practitioners do not feel that they have the right or ability to alter that agenda. A field development and Field Centre approach to effecting change in a school system combines these two local agendas. It is the respect for the local agenda connected with unique solutions that is important. A district superintendent:

It is always a shaping, a partnership that it is not a laid on program. Taking something that is grounded in research, modifying and adapting it, meet the particular needs of the group. That has been really appreciated.

The local practitioners establish and shape their own agenda, but the Field Centre research agenda is also considered and helps shape the outcomes. The university agenda evolves over time because of this involvement. Since both parties have a vested interest in the reform efforts, they each have an intrinsic motivation to be successful in their efforts. Because the practitioners realize the importance of the project to a faculty member, faculty members' credibility is enhanced and the work stands a better chance of having a direct and positive impact.

Unique Solutions

The centrality of the local agenda ensures that local needs are addressed directly and the outcomes are solutions to problems which may be unique to the local context. Since the university faculty member's agenda is developed around professional interest and expertise as well as the needs of the local system and practitioners, these local solutions are beneficial to all parties.

While there are obvious benefits to the local system, there is a double benefit for the faculty member. If this is the first time s/he has been able to study an issue, then strategies developed in this situation become available for use later. When the issue being addressed has been a dimension of other projects s/he has been involved with, there is an opportunity to study the usefulness of strategies developed elsewhere in a different context. In other words, working with practitioners on local problems and solutions ultimately allows the faculty member to contribute to new knowledge in the area under study. In the process of developing local solutions the field developer is expected to play a dual role. Previously established credibility and acceptance enable the faculty member to be considered a member of the local problem-solving team. In this capacity, s/he cannot be a totally objective outsider; rather, s/he is expected to be sensitive to and knowledgeable about the particular factors that might affect the implementation of any solutions that come from the group's work. On the other hand, the faculty member is expected to bring to the discussions a knowledge of solutions tried elsewhere and to possess a broader scope of knowledge than the practitioners.

Northumberland-Clarington is an example of how the roles of the faculty member operate in the development of local solutions. In this case, the faculty member was originally invited in because she had knowledge of secondary school reform. She became an integral part of the team whose task was to develop a local solution through a combination of external knowledge about possible strategies, insider information about the system accumulated through continued involvement and interaction with the local team. The field developer was able to contribute significantly to the shape of the local change strategy. As noted by an involved teacher:

> I think it's been absolutely invaluable to the success of the Northumberland-Clarington restructuring initiative that [the Field Centre staff] have been involved in it. It gives authority to what we are doing. It provides, I think, the foundation of the research that supports what we are doing. We're not simply making changes for the sake of making changes. We're doing it for a reason and that's taught a lot of us a lot of things about what we're doing and how we should be doing it.

Transferability of Knowledge

A prominent feature of field development is the ability to transfer knowledge into and out of local situations. Practitioners expect knowledge associated with university faculty activities to be brought to bear on local issues. As noted by a school administrator, this results in "The popularization of research — somehow it is more usable when it flows through the Centre." Another superintendent claimed that "Research is no good *per se*, the research has to be put into practice. One of the most effective ways we have seen it put into practice is through the Field Centres that bring the research to the field." It is expected that this knowledge will be delivered in a language and format that is understandable and usable by practitioners. For Field Centre faculty, this type of dissemination is a job expectation.

Field Centre faculty members are involved in knowledge creation through the continuous creation of contextually specific solutions to problems which can be identified in a much broader educational population. Through simultaneous participation in several field development projects, they can transfer knowledge continuously, and with each iteration such knowledge is refined and made more generalizable. Practitioners tend to lend more credence to such knowledge than they do to knowledge which is couched in academic language and presented through journal articles or university-style lectures.

All of the cases presented in this chapter are examples of knowledge creation, transfer, adaptation and evolution. In Nipissing, for example, knowledge of peer coaching and action research was brought into the local situation. The peer coaching model particularly was changed as a result of the work done there and was applied in other locations in its evolved form within months. The action research component led directly to new knowledge and ways of thinking about performance assessment and this new knowledge was disseminated at an international conference and through publications. The Northumberland-Clarington project not only used existing knowledge of secondary school change, but contributed significantly to the general body of knowledge through the research program. In all of these cases, the faculty members were able to disseminate and create knowledge and to study its application through the cooperation of practitioners. By both bringing knowledge to bear on the local situations and demonstrating through ongoing activities how knowledge could be refined and transported elsewhere, these faculty members are able to influence change on a continuous basis.

Partner Equality

The relationship between the Field Centres and schools or school systems is a partnership of equals. Each party contributes and receives value. School systems and their personnel receive access to resources and expertise they cannot afford to maintain on their own. There is often a residual benefit for the school systems in the form of additional skills and knowledge which can be used in future situations. Field Centre faculty gain knowledge and ongoing access to real-world educational practice: besides research results, there is continual information about practitioners' current concerns, how they cope with policy changes and other initiatives, and their general practices in a variety of areas. These understandings can be incorporated into teacher training, other professional programs and graduate courses; as a result, as a consultant suggested, "the courses are more grounded in reality."

In this relationship, both partners are learners, problem solvers and representatives of various areas of expertise. Faculty members can extend their learning around previous research and how the applications from that research may be made more effective, as well as identifying where there is a lack of research information which should be pursued. Both parties focus on solving problems of both immediate and longer-term significance. This aspect results in far richer understandings for everyone, since, in the process, different perspectives are constantly being applied to the problem.

Politics

Field Centres exist within a political context but these politics are muted because of factors explored earlier in this section. Continuity and partnership equality are particularly essential in allowing the Field Centres to overcome political agendas which might otherwise derail collaborative efforts. Long-term Field Centre regional presence allows relationships with specific school districts to simmer when senior school district administration opts for directions incompatible with the Field Centre mission. Even when the Field Centre is not actively involved, long-term partnerships with individuals at all levels of the system ensure that contact is maintained, and more intense collaboration resumes. Long-term involvement and the resulting trust means that gaining entry is not as traumatic as it often is in other school–university relationships.

The recent turmoil in the Ontario educational system provides specific examples. School boards were required to amalgamate with other boards to create much larger organizational units. While this political mandate caused the affected school boards to focus on internal issues and to initiate few collaborative projects with the Field Centres, intimate knowledge of the school boards involved and trust established through multi-faceted projects enabled faculty members to listen and advise as the parties struggled to create new organizations. Field Centres were then well positioned to begin new collaborative projects when school districts were ready to launch new initiatives.

On another plane, amalgamation between OISE and the University of Toronto has placed Field Centres themselves in the midst of organizational restructuring and reculturing. Initially, at least, many of the political tensions inherent to school–university collaboration reported by the literature emerged as issues for the Field Centres themselves (Goodlad, 1994; Hannay and Smyth, 1996; Heckman, 1988; Keating and Clark, 1988; Lieberman, 1988; Sinclair and Harrison, 1988). Yet OISE's organizational history of modifying criteria and expectations for tenure and promotion and its longstanding commitment to field development are impacting on the practices of the new organization. This certainly suggests that ongoing involvement and attention to the needs of all parties must be embedded for sustained school–university collaboration to survive political turmoil in both school districts and universities.

Lessons Learned

The Field Centre model for external agents' involvement in local change initiatives suggests that university faculty members can provide a positive influence on the direction and form of the local implementation of change initiatives. A primary lesson of this model concerns the need for adequate time. Beyond the need for time to implement a change initiative, which is well known and documented in the literature on change and implementation, the ability of an external agent to influence change requires time to develop trust and credibility.

When undertaking a project which has the potential to result in significant changes to practice, educators often feel uneasy and unsure that what they are doing is going to be successful. There is a strong element of risk involved and the possibility of failure. Experience with past change initiatives may have planted the seeds of doubt about the efficacy of imported solutions and skepticism with respect to the claims made by external people about the merits of these solutions. Each locality perceives itself as possessing conditions and needs that are not the same as those found anywhere else. Practitioners require time to develop an understanding that the external person does not give advice or make suggestions for personal gain or aggrandizement. The practitioners also need to know that the external person does not view the local situation as a laboratory in which radical interventions can be made that could significantly raise the chances of failure and permanent damage.

The cases discussed in this chapter also suggest that the time required to establish this level of trust and credibility can be nurtured by, and accrue to, an institution: while individuals must ultimately earn the respect and trust of the practitioners, the past history of the institution and its relationship with the field can lay a strong foundation for relationships with individuals. In the Field Centre model, this time investment is made by maintaining the Centres across the province and ensuring that the institution is present through both times of turbulence and change and times of relative calm.

A second important lesson taught by the Field Centre model is that external agents need intimate knowledge of local contexts. This can only be gained over time through ongoing involvement and interaction with practitioners. With this knowledge base, which comes from personal experience as well as through the reports and project records of other Centre faculty, the external agent's ideas and suggestions are more likely to be consistent with the locality's history, especially its experiences with change initiatives. This leads to a third lesson provided by the Field Centre model. Imported solutions should be considered as starting points for assisting educators, not as final solutions. The time invested and the accumulation of local knowledge will provide direction for how solutions to similar problems developed elsewhere should be adapted to fit the local context. This adaptation can be valuable for the external agent because the revised solution is more flexible and adaptable for future applications. The practitioners, having seen and been part of the adaptation, are more likely to commit themselves to seeing that it does indeed work. A solution that has been obviously adapted and extended to meet local reform needs has a better chance of being adopted than a solution which attempts to adapt local needs to fit a preconceived solution.

A final lesson is that an external agent will have a greater chance of success in influencing change if the situation is one in which everyone wins by achieving substantive benefits from the project. The motivation for the external agent must be intrinsic in nature rather than for personal gain and this must be recognized by the practitioners. In part, this lesson is an extension of the first lesson and relates to the external agent's credibility. But it also acknowledges previous experiences of practitioners with external agents. Experiences with other external agents who were not seriously interested in the success of the project can create a poor impression: researchers who provided an intervention, collected their data, wrote their report, and then did not share their results or help the practitioners understand what the results meant for them; someone who had a model or solution who convinced the practitioners to use it without adaptation, then left without accepting any responsibility for the results.

The Field Centre model teaches that there can be benefits for all parties and that these benefits do not have to be gained by one partner at the expense of the other. This model supports organic partnerships (Howey and Zimpher, 1999; Whitford and Metcalf-Turner, 1999) that can span cultural and structural chasms to blur the boundaries between research, policy and practice (Hargreaves, 1996). While money may change hands and models and solutions that the external person thinks are useful can be tried, the primary reason for involvement is neither money nor the application of a solution. The Field Development model suggests that the investment of time and energy must be extended beyond a short series of events directly related to the initiative, and the agent, as well as the practitioners, must be learners in the process of understanding and designing change.

References

Brookhart, S. and Loadman, W. (1992) School–university collaboration across cultures. *Teaching Education*, 4(2), 53–68.

Darling-Hammond, L. (1994) *Professional development schools*. Teachers College Press: New York.

Darling-Hammond, L. and McLaughlin, M. (1995) Policies that support professional development in an era of reform. *Phi Delta Kappan*, 76(8), 597–604.

Fullan, M. (1993) *Change forces: probing the depths of educational reform*. London: Falmer Press.

Fullan, M. (1997) Broadening the concept of teacher leadership. In S. Caldwell (ed.), *Professional development in learning-centered schools*, pp. 34–48. Oxford, Ohio: National Staff Development Council.

Fullan, M. (1999) *Change forces: the sequel*. London: Falmer Press.

Goodlad, J. (1988) School–university partnerships for educational renewal: rationale and concepts. In K. Sirotnik and J. Goodlad (eds.), *School–university partnerships in action: concepts, cases, and concerns*, pp. 3–31. New York: Teachers College Press.

Goodlad, J. (1994) *Educational renewal: better teachers, better schools*. San Francisco, Jossey-Bass.

Hannay, L. (1994) Strategies for facilitating reflective practice: the role of staff developers. *Journal of Staff Development*, 15(3), 22–6.

Hannay, L. and Ross, J. (1997a) *Secondary school reform: developing new structures to enhance student learning*. Ministry of Education and Training, Ontario, Block Transfer Grant to OISE/UT, Kitchener, Ontario: The Ontario Institute for Studies in Education of the University of Toronto, Midwestern Centre.

Hannay, L. and Ross, J. (1997b) Initiating secondary school reform: the dynamic relationship between restructuring, reculturing, and retiming. *Educational Administration Quarterly*, 33 Supplement, 546–603.

Hannay, L. and Ross, J. (1999) Department heads as middle managers? Questioning the black box. *School Leadership and Management*, 19(3), 345–58.

Hannay, L. and Schmalz, K. (1995) *Examining secondary school change from within.* Ministry of Education and Training, Ontario, Block Transfer Grant to OISE/UT, Kitchener, Ontario: The Ontario Institute for Studies in Education of the University of Toronto, Midwestern Centre.

Hannay, L. and Smyth, E. (1996) Defining school–university collaboration: from being experts to being partners. In *The Second International Conference, Teacher Education: Stability, Evolution and Revolution*, pp. 851–60. Netanya, Israel.

Hargreaves, A. (1994) *Changing teachers, changing times: teachers' work and culture in the postmodern age.* Toronto: OISE Press.

Hargreaves, A. (1996) Transforming knowledge: blurring the boundaries between research, policy, and practice. *Educational Evaluation and Policy Analysis*, 18(2), 105–22.

Heckman, P. (1988) The southern California partnership: a retrospective analysis. In K. Sirotnik and J. Goodlad (eds.), *School–university partnerships in action: concepts, cases, and concerns*, pp. 106–23. New York: Teachers College Press.

Howey, K. R. and Zimpher, N. L. (1999) Pervasive problems and issues in teacher education. In G. Griffin (ed.), *The education of teachers*, pp. 279–305. Chicago: University of Chicago Press.

Keating, P. and Clark, R. (1988) Accent on leadership: the Pudget Sound educational consortium. In K. Sirotnik and J. Goodlad (eds.), *School–university partnerships in action: concepts, cases, and concerns*, pp. 148–68. New York: Teachers College Press.

Kruse, S., Louis, K. S. and Byrk, A. (1995) An emerging framework for analysing school-based professional community. In K. S. Louis and S. Kruse (eds.), *Professionalism and community perspectives on reforming urban schools.* Thousand Oaks, CA: Corwin Press.

Leithwood, K., Hedges, H., Robinson, F., Russell, H. and Stinson, R. (1975) Field development at the Ontario Institute for Studies in Education. Unpublished manuscript, The Ontario Institute for Studies in Education, Trent Valley Centre, Peterborough, ON.

Lieberman, A. (1988) The metropolitan school study council: a living history. In K. Sirotnik and J. Goodlad (eds.), *School–university partnerships in action: concepts, cases, and concerns*, pp. 69–86. New York: Teachers College Press.

Lieberman, A. (1995) Practices that support teacher development: conceptions of professional learning. *Phi Delta Kappan*, 76(8), 591–6.

Lieberman, A. and McLaughlin, M. (1992) Networks for educational change: powerful and problematic. *Phi Delta Kappan*, 73(9), 673–7.

Ross, J. (1995) Professional development schools: prospects for institutionalization. *Teacher and Teacher Education*, 11(2), 195–201.

Ross, J., Hannay, L. and Brydges, B. (1998) District-level support for site-based renewal: a case study of secondary school reform. *Alberta Journal of Educational Research*, 44(4), 349–65.

Sachs, J. (1997) Renewing teacher professionalism through innovative links. *Educational Action Research*, 5(3), 449–62.

Sinclair, R. and Harrison, A. (1988) A partnership for increasing student learning: the Massachusetts coalition for school improvement. In K. Sirotnik and J. Goodlad (eds.), *School–university partnerships in action: concepts, cases, and concerns*, pp. 87–105. New York: Teachers College Press.

Smyth, E. and Hannay, L. (1993) School–university partnerships: an examination of the OISE Field Centres. Paper presented at the annual meeting of the Canadian Society for the Study of Education, Ottawa.

Watson, N. and Fullan, M. (1992) Beyond school district–university partnerships. In M. Fullan and A. Hargreaves (eds.), *Teacher development and educational change*, pp. 213–42. London: Falmer Press.

Whitford, B. L. and Metcalf-Turner, P. (1999) Of promises and unresolved puzzles: reforming teacher education with professional development schools. In G. Griffin (ed.), *The education of teachers*, pp. 257–78. Chicago: University of Chicago Press.

11   Professionals and Parents: A Social Movement for Educational Change?

Andy Hargreaves

> Parent–teacher work has usually been directed at securing for the school the support of parents, that is, at getting parents to see children more or less as teachers see them. But it would be a sad day for childhood if parent–teacher work ever really succeeded in its object.
>
> (Waller, 1932: 69)

Introduction

Teachers experience more anxiety about their relationships and interactions with parents than almost any other aspect of their work (Hargreaves and Fullan, 1998). While the rhetoric that teachers should treat parents as partners in their children's education is widespread (Epstein, 1995; Sanders and Epstein, 1998; Vincent, 1996a; Webb and Vulliamy, 1993) and while more than a few positive partnerships exist in practice, the more pervasive reality is often very different. In his masterly work on *The sociology of teaching* in 1932, Willard Waller was characteristically blunt about the matter.

> From the ideal point of view, parents and teachers have much in common in that both, supposedly, wish things to occur for the best interests of the child; but in fact, parents and teachers usually live in conditions of mutual distrust and enmity. Both wish the child well, but it is such a different kind of well that conflict must inevitably arise over it. The fact seems to be that parents and teachers are natural enemies, predestined each for the discomfiture of the other. (p. 68)

The task of establishing strong partnerships between teachers and parents is, indeed, riddled with problems. These include:

- *The problem of the unit of concern.* Parents are primarily concerned about their own individual child, their most treasured possession, whereas teachers must be concerned about and balance the needs of all children in a group (Sikes, 1995).
- *The problem of subjects superseding students.* Conventional structures of secondary school specialization entail teachers having to teach too many students to be able to know most of them well (Meier, 1998; Sizer, 1992).

Teachers are therefore likely to minimize or avoid interaction with parents when their limited knowledge of each parent's "most treasured possession" might expose and embarrass them.

- *The problem of time and scope.* Especially in subject-based secondary schools with specialized, compartmentalized curricula, it is hard for teachers to find time within existing structures to interact meaningfully with all parents of the many students they teach. After-school time is often taken up with reform requirements, implementation demands, increased paperwork and a proliferation of meetings. As a result, teachers' capacity to forge relationships with large numbers of parents is squeezed even more (Hargreaves, 1994).

- *The problem of professional distance.* While many of the core activities of teaching and learning require close emotional understanding between teachers, parents and students (Denzin, 1984; Hargreaves, 1998), "classical" professionalism modeled on the traditionally male preserves of medicine and law requires professionals to avoid emotional entanglements with their clients' problems and to maintain professional distance from them (Grumet, 1988). While teachers are supposed to care for their students, they are also expected to care in a somewhat clinical and detached way — to mask their emotions with parents and control them when they are around students, especially at the secondary school level (Hargreaves, forthcoming).

- *The problem of social distance.* Teachers are not only professionally distanced from their students' parents; they are often socially distanced from them as well. Coming predominantly from lower-middle and upper-working-class backgrounds (Lindblad and Prieto, 1992), in a profession that is overwhelmingly WASP (NEA, 1986; Reynolds, 1990), teachers often find themselves teaching "other people's children" (Delpit, 1993). The attitudes, orientations and lifestyles of these students' parents are often incomprehensible or even offensive to them (Burgess *et al.*, 1991).

- *The problem of isolation and uncertainty.* Traditionally, teaching has been characterized by chronic uncertainty (Jackson, 1986). Many of the effects of teaching on students are long term, and among all the other things influencing children, teachers' specific impact is unclear to them. Working alone in their classrooms, without the benefit of collegial reassurance and feedback, teachers can feel inwardly unsure about the value of their teaching and assessment strategies, and feel threatened by the prospect of external adult scrutiny (A. Hargreaves, 1994; D. Hargreaves, 1980; Little, 1990; Lortie, 1975; Rosenholtz, 1989).

- *The problem of unworldliness.* Teachers spend much of their working lives with children or with teachers of children. More than a few of them are, therefore, regarded by parents as unworldly in some respects. One of the characters in David Storey's (1976) prize-winning novel *Saville* describes teachers as "men among children and children among men." In prestigious communities especially, such apparent unworldliness can be a professional liability.

- *The problem of unpreparedness.* Few teachers are trained how to interact and work effectively with adults in general and with parents in particular (Hargreaves and Fullan, 1998). They are unprepared to deal with the conflicts, crises and general emotional turmoil that parent communication and criticism can throw at them.

- *The problem of pedagogical ordinariness.* Having spent 13,000 to 15,000 hours of their lives in classrooms (Rutter *et al.*, 1979), most parents do not see teaching as being particularly extraordinary. Teaching seems to be something that most people, with effort and attention, might reasonably be able to do (Labaree, 1999). Anyone can be an expert on it! Although seemingly simple lessons, like making apple-sauce for example, can often get children to learn quite extraordinary skills and understandings (Clark, 1995; Elbaz, 1991), none of this may be self-evident to parents. In teaching, the project of professionalism can easily be defeated by the apparent ordinariness of the work.

- *The problem of abstruseness.* The opposite problem can be just as self-defeating for teachers. If teachers artificially elevate the expertise and language of teaching far above the seeming ordinariness of the work, its resulting abstruseness in school reports or teachers' talk can quickly open teachers up to ridicule (Nespor, 1997).

- *The problem of client anxiety.* In a world where many people's standards of living are being eroded, and their children's futures seem precarious (Castells, 1996), parents can be prone to status panic (Mills, 1951) about their family's loss of position in society. Where schooling is organized around principles of school choice and the workings of the market, or around high-stakes systems of accountability, parents can play out these anxieties through their children — putting pressure on those teachers who seem to hold their children's futures in their hands.

- *The problem of increased accountability.* Increased accountability makes many parents more aware of and attentive to their educational rights. Teachers can find themselves under inordinate pressure to explain and justify what they do, rather than being treated as trusted, "classical" professionals who exercize their judgement as they best see fit.

These obstacles to building successful partnerships between teachers and parents are formidable, but they are by no means insurmountable (Epstein, 1995). With so many students at risk academically and the quality of state education itself in jeopardy, the necessity for strong teacher–parent partnerships is so great that the problems cannot be allowed to defeat us. This chapter therefore explores three broad kinds of parent–teacher partnership: silent partnerships, partnerships involving mutual learning and support, and activist partnerships that form the foundation of a social movement for educational change.

Silent Partnerships: Discrete Distance and
Unquestioning Support

It is widely acknowledged that involving parents in their children's education, especially during the early years of schooling, can significantly improve their learning (Henderson, 1987; Sanders, 1997; Villas-Boas, 1993). As Bastiani (1989) puts it, parents are their children's first educators. By helping their children to learn at home — reading them stories and hearing them read aloud; taking an active interest in their schoolwork; ensuring that homework obligations are met and that appropriate space is set aside for completing them; and generally cultivating values of diligence, perseverance and willingness to defer gratification — parents can prove to be great assets in their children's education (Sanders and Epstein, 1998). Epstein (1995) has outlined numerous strategies that parents can use to help their children in this respect.

In many Asian families, for example, these parental values and virtues appear to exist in abundance. Through the encouragement they offer to and pressure they place upon their children in the home, many Asian parents are effectively their school's and its teachers' *silent partners*. Where the goals of learning are shared between home and school, and where the technology of teaching is relatively straightforward and familiar (in terms of whole-class teaching, seatwork and question-and-answer routines), then parents become the teacher's ideal silent partner — pushing the student to work harder at home while maintaining a respectful distance from the teacher and his or her expertise at school (Biggs, 1996; Shimahara and Sakai, 1995).

In most North American and many European communities, however, the conditions for these silent partnerships between home and school do not seem to apply. In fact, the goals of learning are increasingly disputed and the pedagogies of schooling are no longer straightforward or uncontroversial. What children need to learn and teachers must teach is changing. A schooling system that excessively emphasizes basic skills, memorization and recall of factual knowledge cannot develop the capacities for creation and innovation that are essential to living and working successfully within informational societies (Schlechty, 1990).

The tacit agreement on learning goals that often existed between homes and schools in pedagogically simpler times is collapsing. As the explosion in pedagogical science impacts more and more on schools — in areas like cooperative learning, literacy strategies, constructivism, metacognition and portfolio assessment — parents are becoming and will become increasingly bewildered by these developments, especially if teachers use the language of classical professionalism to defend and distance their expertise in relation to the ordinary language and understandings of parents (Nespor, 1997).

Silent partnerships are not sustainable when the goals of learning and strategies of teaching take such dramatically new directions. Teaching parents as well as students about these new developments in learning is one way of encouraging a new professionalism to promote partnerships between home and school. Developing parents' understanding and alleviating their anxiety by communicating new concepts in plain language, explaining learning targets accessibly, demonstrating new teaching strategies through workshops, making students' work and learning more visible through the use of portfolios and exhibitions, setting shared homework assignments to be completed with a family member, and opening schools and classrooms up to parent observation are just some of the ways in which the value of new approaches to teaching and learning can be made more transparent to parents. Similarly, teachers have much to learn from many parents about areas such as information technology, for example. The learning to be undertaken does not all run in one direction.

Learning Partnerships: Mutual Learning and Support

In addition to the challenge of explaining new learning and teaching goals and strategies to parents, teachers also have to relate differently to parents and communities beyond their school because of the increasingly multicultural nature of many of the world's towns and cities and the impact of changing family structures on the work of teachers.

More and more children come from cultures that are different from and unfamiliar to those of their teachers. Students' families are changing in their structure and form. They are more postmodern and permeable (Elkind, 1997). They comprise single-parent families, blended families, families with parents who spend much of their lives apart, families without parents at all, and busy families entrapped in what Hochschild (1997) calls the "time bind" where they engage in *emotional downsizing* (persuading themselves that their children are more independent than they really are and can do without them more than they really can) and *emotional outsourcing* (passing across much of the emotional work of child-raising, playing and even party-planning to contracted individuals).

In addition to coming from different cultures and families, today's youth also lives in a world of what Castells (1996) calls *real virtuality* — of Sony walkmen, cell-phones, VCRs, multi-channel TV, MTV, computers, video-games and even virtual pets! For the youth of today, a profusion of images *is* their most insistent reality, and this affects *what* they learn, *how* they learn and *how well* they learn, in home and school alike.

What all this signifies for many teachers whose mean age is well into the 40s in most Western countries (OECD, 1998) is that their students today are, in Bigum and Green's (1993) words, "aliens in the classroom." Likewise, their students' parents are "aliens in the community." All too often, teachers look at students and parents with growing incomprehension. They just do not know where they are coming from anymore.

The changes that teachers see are not in their imaginations. Behavior in classrooms is more problematic, learning styles are more variable, and what teachers teach can no longer be taken for granted. Sadly though, in many cases, instead of engaging with students' cultures and families and really trying to understand them, many educators see changes in parents and communities as largely (and sometimes exclusively) changes for the worse. Their assumptions and expectations about parental interest and support are often socially or ethnoculturally biased — misconstruing problems of poverty as problems of single-parenthood (Levin and Riffel, 1997), regarding failure to attend meetings or other officially organized events as parents' failure to support their children or the school (Central Advisory Council for Education, 1967), and measuring all parenting of young children or "sensitive mothering" (Vincent and Warren, 1998) against a yardstick of practice that is culturally skewed toward middle-class norms (Burgess *et al.*, 1991). In all too many cases, teachers see only obstacles in the changing lives and cultures of their students, families and communities, rarely opportunities. My own research repeatedly points to this.

For example, when my colleagues and I asked focus groups of teachers in every Canadian province and territory about how social changes had affected their work, the responses were consistently negative and critical. They depicted all change in families and communities as a problem; none of it as an opportunity (Earl *et al.*, 1999). The following quotations are typical:

> Many of our students have family problems — divorce, separation, alcohol, gambling, etc.

> The extra baggage that kids bring to school — more single parents, poverty, breakup of the family, hunger and the spin-off in violence and anger in young people — necessitates social programs to help them.

> There has been a blurring of school and home responsibility with a shared responsibility for social and emotional development. The incursion of non-educational issues into schools means less time for teaching.

> Teachers have become "multi-service providers" who provide the services that used to be provided by support staff. We're expected to be teachers, social workers, psychologists, professors and disciplinarians. It's demoralizing.

> Students' poor work ethics, lack of respect for school property, disdain for teachers and their emphasis on rights without responsibilities parallels the change in societal values.

> Teachers are doing a lot of what families should do and would have done ten years ago.

> Students are assuming less personal responsibility. They are not encouraged at home to take responsibility and expect everything to be handed to them.

In a separate study on the emotions of teaching and educational change where my colleagues and I interviewed fifty-three teachers and asked them (among other things) about positive and negative emotional incidents with parents, teachers reported being angry with parents who expected too much of them; afraid of parents who "blew up," were "livid" and "leaped all over" them; annoyed with parents who thought "they're experts in education" and questioned teachers' professional judgement; frustrated with parents who appeared not to care about their children's absences, bad behavior or poor work habits (and would even lie to protect them); exasperated by parents who would believe their child's word before the teacher's; and bitter about parents who constantly criticized the system. In comparison, teachers experienced positive emotion when parents thanked them, supported them or agreed with them. On no occasion did teachers cite a source of positive emotion with parents when they had actually learned something from them.

Vincent's (1996b) research shows that most teachers want parents to work with the school as *supporters* or *learners*. They enlist parental support in terms of raising funds, organizing special lunches, preparing materials, mixing paints, hearing children read and so on. This approach to partnership leaves existing versions of the teacher's professional authority intact. What teachers do not seem to want, says Vincent, are partnerships with parents where they learn as much from parents as parents do from them; where communication, learning and power run between teachers and parents in two directions, not one. This is exceptionally important where students and their parents are from cultures and communities that are very different from the teacher's (Moore, 1994; Ogbu, 1982).

This issue is highlighted in baseline interview data from ten teachers in one of four secondary schools with which my colleagues and I are working in a school improvement project. This school had changed from being in a small village to having a large, diverse multicultural population move into its area of rapidly expanding housing development.

What we found was that while teachers in special education, in administrative positions or who were parents themselves tried to reach out to the busy and diverse parent body, and work with it effectively, other teachers found establishing relationships a struggle. Contacts were episodic and invariably teacher-initiated — on parents' nights or when teachers phoned home to discuss a problem (most often, a problem of attendance). "If I don't initiate it," one teacher said, "I don't often hear from parents." "Although parents are very supportive when necessary," another teacher said, "I don't see the parent involvement that I would like to see or that other teachers would like to see." At "Meet the Teachers" night, this teacher recalled, only one parent of her ninety students turned up. Another teacher tried "to bring parents in and to involve them more in the life of the school" by, for example, phoning all parents of ninety students at the beginning of the school year. But the poor response led him to conclude that "parents are really stressed and . . . sort of abdicating their responsibility of educating the kids to an institution."

In the emotions of teaching project I described earlier, we also found that the positive emotions which secondary teachers experience with parents occur almost exclusively in episodic events like parents' evenings and one-to-one conferences. By contrast, only one teacher in fifty-three mentioned how positive emotions occurred in more casual circumstances when the teacher met a parent within their own community (this was in the one rural secondary school in our sample). Meanwhile, negative emotions in secondary school between parents and teachers was reported as occurring largely on the telephone or in writing — usually in relation to issues of behavior or attendance. There is little chance for developing any kind of intellectual or "emotional understanding" (Denzin, 1984) between parents and secondary school teachers, when encounters between them are normally so formal, infrequent and episodic.

Second, we found that teachers generally developed the purposes and mission of the school themselves, as a set of professionals, without the involvement of students or parents. It was the teacher's job to explain the school's purposes to students and parents, through the parents' council, parents' night, the school handbook, the barbecue for the families of incoming Grade 8 students, "messages that go home" and "printed material that goes out with the report cards." It was not seen as the teachers' job to include parents themselves (or students either) in developing the school's purposes.

Third, when we asked teachers about the political skills they needed in their work, they identified quite different skills as being necessary for working with colleagues and parents respectively. Working with colleagues entailed largely passive skills of tact, understanding, patience, being yourself, listening, modeling and compromising. Working with communities involved more active, even directive skills of communicating, marketing, publicizing, telling one's story, presenting information and advocating. Collegial skills involved working *with* people. Community skills involved working *on* them. Treating parents and the public as partners to learn *from*, and not just people to persuade and present *to*, was a leap of political imagination that our case study teachers had not yet made.

Given the postmodern families and societies in which many children now live, it is exceedingly important that partnerships between professionals and parents allow and encourage teachers to learn about their students' lives, families and cultures which shape their prior knowledge, frame what is important and motivating for them, and influence how they learn best. Yet, especially at the secondary level, evidence suggests that most partnerships remain ones of support (either silent or active) in which little professional learning among teachers from parents is evident or even wanted.

This form of relationship where parents are active or unquestioning supporters of what teachers do keeps teachers in a state of classical professionalism which distances them, intellectually and emotionally, from the learning and lives of the increasingly diverse and demanding students whom they teach (as well as from their families). This makes it harder for teachers to help their students.

New forms of more principled professionalism (Goodson, 1999) are needed, where teachers engage with parents in relationships of reciprocal learning that are more open, interactive and inclusive in character. As Willard Waller (1932) said in the opening quote to this chapter, it would be a sad day for childhood if we ever really did get parents to see children the way that teachers see them — even more so in the diverse communities of today.

None of this is to suggest that all parents are virtuous and that teachers are simply insensitive villains in the partnership drama. We should avoid idealizing partnerships representing all parents (or indeed teachers) as being altruistic and perfect. Parents can be a pain sometimes — they can try and get special deals for their children (lenient grades, assignment to the best teacher, movement out of mixed ability tracks, etc.) (Oakes *et al.*, 1997), or rummage through papers on the teacher's desk when he or she is out of the classroom (Acker, 1999). Some parents neglect their children, or abuse them, or barely know how to relate to them through their alcohol-clouded stupor. Other parents are excessively inclined to live their lives through their children, are prematurely ambitious for them, want their children's futures to compensate for their own lifetime disappointments, or vicariously pursue their own goals and dreams through the education of their children. Such parents can be especially difficult and demanding for teachers to deal with.

Schools can, and many do, offer parents with social, emotional and psychological difficulties vital services and support through collaboration with community agencies. Sanders and Epstein (1998) cite a wide range of international studies that point to specific strategies for involving low-income parents especially in their children's education, such as workshops and home visits (Villas-Boas, 1993).

It is even and especially when parents are critical, suspicious and difficult that these partnerships are most essential. Teachers must move toward the danger here, rather than closet themselves away (Hargreaves and Fullan, 1998; Maurer, 1996). It is in teachers' own interests to treat even seemingly problematic parents not just as irritants or as targets for appeasement, but as the most important allies teachers have in serving those parents' own students and also, as we shall see, in defending themselves against political assaults on their professionalism.

Combating Nostalgia

Making the new realities of classroom practice more transparent, and building relationships with diverse parents that are open, reciprocal and inclusive in nature, is also essential if educators are to combat the parental nostalgia that so often defeats school change and improvement efforts that are designed to benefit all students. In an age of uncertainty, when parents are anxious for their children's futures, and school innovations can seem obscure to them, they may be inclined to cling on to the comfortable recollections of real classrooms and "real schools" — with single teachers, in separate classrooms, teaching a standard curriculum to homogeneous groups — that are familiar to them from when they were school-children (Metz, 1991). Such nostalgia drives parents to press teachers to return to and reinstate "real schooling" for their own children. Dramatic innovation efforts, especially in new schools, often founder because no one acknowledges or engages with this nostalgia (Fink, 1999; Sarason, 1982). In their history of failed educational reforms, Tyack and Tobin (1994) catalogue how innovations have repeatedly collapsed because uncomprehending communities were excluded from their development.

When parents long for stronger standards, simpler teaching and better times this is not just the result of memory, of their recalling something better. It is the product of nostalgia. As Christopher Lasch (1991: 80–82) elegantly argued, nostalgia differs from memory because

> the emotional appeal of happy memories does not depend on disparagement of the present: the hallmark of the nostalgic attitude. Nostalgia appeals to the feeling that the past offered delights no longer attainable. Nostalgic representations of the past evoke a time irretrievably lost and for that reason, timeless and unchanging. Strictly speaking, nostalgia does not entail the exercise of memory at all, since the past it idealizes stands outside time, frozen in unchanging perfection.

"Nostalgia," Lasch tells us, used to refer to a medical condition: a pathological sickness brought about by estrangement from one's own homeland. Yet, as the title of Thomas Wolfe's (1940) classic novel proclaims, "You can't go home again!" When you return to the physical place that once was home, it has changed — and so have you (Schutz, 1973). So when we actually act on nostalgia, disappointment very frequently follows. When the past is demystified, the present may no longer seem so bad after all. In the 1960s Canadians used to prescribe their homesick English immigrants what they called the $1000 cure. One flight back home and a dose of bad weather, poor service and an endlessly complaining populace quickly dispelled most people's nostalgic illusions.

The best cure for nostalgia, then, is reality. This means confronting the myths of the past with the realities of the past. Educationally, this can be achieved by helping parents to uncover (often painful) memories of their own past experiences of schooling — by sharing stories in focus groups, for example (Beresford, 1996). At the same time, as I argued earlier, it is important that teachers open up the realities of the present to parents by making their work more transparent, through portfolios, shared homework assignments, three-way parent interviews, questionnaires sent home about how their students are learning and so on. There is no one strategy. Indeed, the strategies will be more effective when they are multiple and diverse

(Hargreaves and Fullan, 1998). And most will be effective not when they comprise time-consuming additions to the already overburdened nature of teachers' work — through more one-off, episodic meetings, phone calls and other events — but when existing meetings, report cards, interviews and assessments are handled quite differently, so that trust and understanding can be developed and learning can flow between parents and teachers in both directions.

Activist Partnerships: Professionals and Parents as Social Movements

Building partnerships with parents and others within a new, more principled professionalism means more than showing greater individual empathy toward and understanding of parents. Creating a more principled, open and inclusive professionalism is a *public project*, not just a private one. Following Goodson (1999), and Hargreaves and Goodson (1996), such a principled professionalism includes being open to, inclusive of and actively learning from others (especially parents) who have a stake in children's education and children's futures; and it takes an activist stance (Sachs, 1999) beyond the classroom as well as within it to defend and develop public education on which teachers' own long-term effectiveness and the good of all children ultimately rests. The feasibility of such a principled professionalism rests on teachers being open to, engaging with and developing understanding among parents and the public on whom the future of teaching and state education ultimately depend.

The public is yet to be convinced that teachers need more time for activities other than working with students. It has, in large part, yet to understand how and why teaching has changed since the time most parents were themselves at school. It is not yet persuaded to commit to the kinds of tax increases that would benefit the public education system and the quality of those who teach in it. For too long, much of the public has been prone to nostalgia in an age of uncertainty, impressionable in the face of political and media-driven derisions of schools and teachers today, and too easily bought by the market-ideology of parental choice which helps them believe that in times of chaos, at least their own private, individual choices can benefit their own children in their own schools (Crozier, 1998). It is now vital that the teaching profession works in partnership with the public, to become a vigorous social movement (Touraine, 1995) of acting subjects who work together to improve the quality and the professionalism of teaching, rather than a set of fragmented individuals who act as clients only in their families' private interest.

When I describe the contributions of the teaching profession to a wider social movement, what I have in mind is similar to the environmental, peace or women's movements. Such social movements are neither driven by the self-serving market nor entirely provided by the sometimes dependency-creating state. They are not managed through official organizations or political representation (like Parent–Teacher Associations) but may be supported by such things. Social movements may begin through reaction and resistance (like the Zapatistas in Mexico) but can and, at their best also do, become extremely proactive (like the environmental movement). In both cases, they challenge the existing order of things. Social movements have a wide-ranging repertoire of strategies incorporating informal networks, lobbying, protest marches, media campaigns, lifestyle choices, sometimes formal bodies and much more. Relationships are at the heart of them.

As Byrne (1997) argues, "Social movements are expressive in that they have beliefs and moral principles and they seek to persuade everyone — governments, parents, the general public, anyone who will listen — that these values are the right ones." They are rooted not in self-interest but in a clear moral purpose which ultimately benefits the universal good of all. Despite many differences and conflicts within social movements (for example among different feminisms), this high level of unity of purpose is what drives the movement and holds it together. In that sense, social movements are uncompromising — their principles must remain unadulterated and not be compromised for short-term tactical gains (Byrne, 1997). Lastly, social movements are embedded in what Lash and Urry (1994: 243) as well as Castells (1996: 126) call *glacial time* — in the creation of and commitment to a long-term future that does not protect and preserve the interests of one single group but advances the good of all our children and grandchildren for generations to come.

Social movements arise in response to the fragmentation of consumer society, the abstractness of globalization and information technology, and the exhaustion and emptiness of official politics. Globalized economies erode the capacity of governments to exercise national policy control and reduce such governments to the electronically monitored and digitally massaged politics of opinion polls, focus groups, personal style and public scandal (Castells, 1996). Social movements provide ways beyond these official politics for people to find meaning and hope in projects the values of which resonate with groups and individuals far beyond them.

Social movements are empowering for their adherents. They acknowledge that those who stand aside from social change are "those who consume society rather than producing and transforming it [and] are subordinate to those who are in charge of the economy, politics and information" (Touraine, 1995: 233). They are "purposive collective actions whose outcome, in victory as in defeat, transforms the values and institutions of society" (Castells, 1996: 3–4).

These social movements, says Castells (p. 361), are "the potential subjects of the Information Age"; they are perhaps our best hopes for a democratic, sustainable and socially just future. It is in these diffuse and subtle networks that our best hopes for positive change may rest — even when the possibilities for such change seem most remote. As Touraine (1995: 241) puts it:

> It is in moments of solitude and desolation, and in the face of a seemingly inevitable future, that the consciousness of certain individuals comes to feel itself responsible for the freedom of others.

What better candidate for a social movement than public education? When democracies are threatened by military dictatorships, teachers are often the first to be tortured, be killed or go missing. When General Franco took control of Spain, Catalan teachers were immediately removed from their region's schools so that children would no longer speak their own language (Castells, 1996). Many systems have dealt teachers such a bad hand in that the profession is now experiencing severe crises of recruitment as its image spirals continually downwards. Even the sons and daughters of teachers are being advised not to follow their parents into an increasingly devalued profession. Do we have to wait for teachers to go missing or recruitment supply lines to dry up to grasp how important teachers are to democracy and public life? Does life have to be like Joni Mitchell's lyrics that "don't it always seem to go, that we don't know what we've got till it's gone"?

When the arteries of communication to government are blocked — as they are where governments remain under the sway of neo-liberal market ideologies, and have minimal commitment to public education and public life — then teachers must build a bypass around governments, and capture the public imagination about education and teaching today, on which governments and their electability ultimately depend. Developing a principled professionalism that opens schools and teachers up to parents and the public — one classroom, one school at a time — where learning runs authentically in both directions, is most likely to build the capacity, trust, commitment and support for teachers and teaching on which the future of their professionalism in the postmodern age will depend.

We will know that such a social movement for defending and developing state education is truly under way and that principled professionalism is a significant part of this:

- when the public joins teachers in protests against state or national governments that try to restrict teacher professionalism by reducing teachers' classroom and curriculum discretion, cutting back on their time to learn, think, reflect and develop away from students, or overloading them with excessive implementation demands
- when teachers and their unions do not just protest against government changes that they oppose but also argue passionately in favor of changes they support that will benefit all students — even if this requires new learning and practices among many of their members
- when teachers do not stand back, retreat from or overreact to unfounded

criticism, but stand up and respond to it with grace, calm and authority — in a concerted effort to gain the respect of those who criticize them most

- when teachers have the confidence and maturity to acknowledge criticism that is fair, indeed to actively seek it out, in a quest to maximize their own learning and to push their standards of practice and professionalism even higher

- when parents acknowledge that their own child's teacher is not an heroic exception to the parlous state of state schooling that is frequently depicted in the media, but that many teachers are as exceptional as their own child's teacher is

- when media campaigns that defend teachers and teaching against government attacks move beyond the high-cost, glossy public relations initiatives of teacher unions, to extensive letter-writing to the press by individual parents and members of the public, and to more proactive moves by schools to feed positive stories to the media about the success of what they do

- when, after the failure of waves of reform, and quick-fix solutions in an economic climate of run-down investment in public education, governments are made to face their responsibilities in having contributed to low educational standards — as seen in the spate of litigation against failed systems now spreading across the United States

- when campaigns to increase awareness and appreciation of public education and of those who do its work spread beyond small, professional minorities to include a broad range of public groups and constituencies

- when more and more teachers make lifestyle choices to live (and not merely work) in or near their school's community, to build solid and trusting informal relationships with members of that community, and to become more worldly by participating actively in the work of the wider community — for it is only through these relationships that deep understanding of the work of teaching and the world of students and their families will ever be truly achieved

- when more and more parents make lifestyle choices that attend to all children's good, not just their own; that are made as if their child is everyone's child and everyone's child is their own; and that, especially in inner cities, recommit parents of all classes to the project of public education and public life rather than contracting out their children's education to the self-interested advancement of the private sphere

- when educators open the doors of their schools and their systems to public celebrations of teaching and learning through performances, exhibitions, teach-ins and entire Education Weeks — as in the Education Week that takes place annually throughout all the schools of Western Australia and which is a prime focal point for the media; or as in one of the schools in our improvement project which staged a "This Is How We Do It" day to show itself off to the community

- finally, when teachers treat every parents' evening, every report card, every piece of homework and every conversation at the school gates as a "teachable moment" when parents can be engaged and influenced about the work of learning and teaching.

We are now in a time where teachers deal with a diverse and complex clientele, in conditions of increasing moral uncertainty, where many methods of approach are possible, and where more and more social groups have an influence and a say. This age may see exciting and positive new partnerships being created with groups and institutions beyond the school. It may see teachers learning to work effectively, openly and authoritatively with those partners in a broad social movement that protects and advances their professionalism. On the other hand, it may witness the deprofessionalization of teaching as teachers crumble under multiple pressures, intensified work demands and reduced opportunities to learn from colleagues. Moreover, it may see discourses of derision that shame and blame teachers for their shortcomings, sapping their morale and their spirit. None of this is yet fully settled, though. This future should not be left to "fate" but should be shaped by the active intervention of all educators and others in a social movement for educational change which really understands and advances the principle that if we want better classroom learning for students, we have to create strong professional learning and working conditions for those who teach them.

The conditions for such a social movement to grow and flourish are starting to take shape. The teacher demographics are favorable — a bulge of imminent retirements (hastened by teachers' demoralization with the effects of educational reform) is leading to a crisis of teacher recruitment (and an opportunity for teacher renewal) in many parts of the world. Governments are consequently having to make strides (often small ones at first) to improve the public image of teaching so as to attract more people into the profession — by, for example, holding impressive commissions on the future of the profession in the USA (Darling-Hammond, 1997), and on the status of teaching in Australia, and by committing to higher pay rises than usual in New Zealand or devising schemes to reward advanced skills teachers in England and Australia. While some of these specific policies miss the mark, it is clear that governments are nonetheless beginning to bend. The public demographics are also favorable — with the aging boomer generation seeing their own offspring leave home, and starting to become involved in their later years less with their own private interests and their own families, and more with volunteering and participating in the wider community (Foot and Stoffman, 1996). Opportunities are emerging that can be seized and turned to the educational good of all.

The forces of deprofessionalization in teaching have already cut deep. But the objective prospects for a reinvigorated, principled professionalism, and the creation of a broad social movement that would support it, are strong. If teachers want to become professionally stronger, they must now open themselves up and become more publicly vulnerable and accessible. They must move toward the danger. That is their paradoxical challenge in the informational age of today.

References

Acker, S. (1999) *Realities of teaching: never a dull moment.* London: Cassell.

Bastiani, J. (1989) *Working with parents: a whole school approach.* Windsor: NFER-Nelson.

Beresford, E. (1996) How do we provide effective education/training for staff related work with parents? Paper presented at the Education is Partnership Conference, Copenhagen, November.

Biggs, J. B. (1996) Misperceptions of the Confucian-heritage learning cultures. In D. A. Watkins and J. B. Biggs (eds.), *The Chinese learner: cultural, psychological and contextual influences*, pp. 110–28. Melbourne: Comparative Education Research Centre, Hong Kong Faculty of Education, Hong Kong and Australian Council for Educational Research.

Bigum, C. and Green, B. (1993) Aliens in the classroom. *Australian Journal of Education*, 37(2), 119–41.

Burgess, R., Herphes, C. and Moxan, S. (1991) Parents are welcome: headteachers and mothers' perspectives on parental participation in the early years. *Qualitative Studies in Education*, 4(2), 95–107.

Byrne, P. (1997) *Social movements in Britain.* New York: Routledge.

Castells, M. (1996) *The rise of the network society.* Oxford: Blackwell.

Central Advisory Council for Education (1967) *Children and their primary schools.* London: HMSO.

Clark, C. M. (1995) *Thoughtful teaching.* New York: Teachers College Press.

Crozier, G. (1998) Parents and schools: partnerships or surveillance? *Journal of Education Policy*, 13(1), 125–36.

Darling-Hammond, L. (1997) *Doing what matters most: investing in quality teaching.* New York: National Commission on Teaching and America's Future.

Delpit, L. (1993) *Other people's children: cultural conflict in the classroom.* New York: The New Press.

Denzin, N. (1984) *On understanding emotion.* San Francisco: Jossey-Bass.

Earl, L., Bascia, N., Hargreaves, A. and Jacka, N. (1999) *Teachers and teaching in changing times: a glimpse of Canadian teachers in 1998.* Report prepared for the Canadian Teachers' Federation. Toronto: International Centre for Educational Change at OISE/University of Toronto.

Elbaz, F. (1991) Research on teachers' knowledge: the evolution of a discourse. *Journal of Curriculum Studies*, 23(1), 1–19.

Elkind, D. (1997) Schooling in the postmodern world. In A. Hargreaves (ed.), *Rethinking educational change with heart and mind*, pp. 27–42. Alexandria, VA: Association for Supervision and Curriculum Development.

Epstein, J. (1995) School/family/community partnerships. *Phi Delta Kappan*, 76, 701–12.

Fink, D. (1999) *The attrition of change.* New York: Teachers College Press.

Foot, D. with Stoffman, D. (1996) *Boom, bust and echo: how to profit from the coming demographic shift.* Toronto: MacFarlane, Walter and Ross.

Goodson, I. (1999) The crisis of educational change and the paradox of progressivism. Paper presented at the International Conference on "The New Professionalism in Teaching: Teacher Education and Teacher Development in a Changing World," Hong Kong, January.

Grumet, M. R. (1988) *Bitter milk: women and teaching.* Amherst: University of Massachusetts Press.

Hargreaves, A. (1994) *Changing teachers, changing times: teachers' work and culture in the postmodern age.* Toronto: University of Toronto Press.

Hargreaves, A. (1998) The emotional politics of teaching and teacher development: with implications for educational leadership. *International Journal of Leadership in Education,* 1(4), 315–36.

Hargreaves, A. (forthcoming) Beyond anxiety and nostalgia: building a social movement for educational change.

Hargreaves, A. and Fullan, M. (1998) *What's worth fighting for out there?* Toronto: Ontario Public School Teachers' Federation.

Hargreaves, A. and Goodson, I. (1996) Teachers' professional lives: aspirations and actualities. In I. Goodson and A. Hargreaves (eds.), *Teachers' professional lives,* pp. 1–27. London: Falmer Press.

Hargreaves, D. (1980) A sociological critique of individualism. *British Journal of Educational Studies,* 28(3), 187–98.

Henderson, A. (1987) *The evidence continues to grow: parent involvement improves student achievement.* Annotated Bibliography. Columbia, MD: National Committee for Citizens in Education.

Hochschild, J. (1997) *The time bind.* New York: Metropolitan Books.

Hoffman, J. (1998) New report card stinks [Letter to the Editor]. *Toronto Star,* December, p. A25.

Jackson, P. W. (1986) *The practice of teaching.* New York: Teachers College Press.

Labaree, D. F. (1999) The peculiar problems of preparing teachers: old hurdles to the new professionalism. Paper presented at the International Conference on "The New Professionalism in Teaching: Teacher Education and Teacher Development in a Changing World," Hong Kong, January.

Lasch, C. (1991) *The true and only heaven: progress and its critics.* New York: W. W. Norton.

Lash, S. and Urry, J. (1994) *Economies of signs and space.* London: Sage.

Levin, B. and Riffel, J. A. (1997) *Schools and the changing world.* New York: Falmer Press.

Lindblad, S. and Prieto, H. (1992) School experiences and teacher socialization: a longitudinal study of students who grew up to be teachers. *Teaching and Teacher Education,* 8(5–6), 465–70.

Little, J. W. (1990) The persistence of privacy: autonomy and initiative in teachers' professional relations. *Teachers College Record,* 91(4), 509–36.

Lortie, D. (1975) *Schoolteacher: a sociological study.* Chicago: University of Chicago Press.

Maurer, R. (1996) *Beyond the wall of resistance.* Austin, TX: Bard Books.

Meier, D. (1998) Authenticity and educational change. In A. Hargreaves, A. Lieberman, M. Fullan and D. Hopkins (eds.), *International handbook of educational change,* pp. 596–615. Dordrecht: Kluwer.

Metz, M. (1991) Real school: a universal drama amid disparate experience. In D. Mitchell and M. Gnesta (eds.), *Education politics for the new century. The twentieth anniversary yearbook of the politics of education association.* Philadelphia: Falmer Press.

Mills, C. W. (1951) *White collar.* New York: Oxford University Press.

Mitchell, J. (1969) Big yellow taxi. On *Ladies of the Canyon* [Record]. Reprise Records.

Moore, S. (1994) Culturally diverse classrooms: teacher perspectives and strategies. Paper presented at the Canadian Society for Studies in Education, University of Calgary, AB, June.

National Education Association (1986) *Status of the American public school teacher 1985–86.* Washington, DC: National Education Association.

Nespor, J. (1997) *Tangled up in school: politics, space, bodies and signs in the educational process.* Hillsdale, NJ: Lawrence Erlbaum Associates.

Oakes, J., Wells, A., Yonezawa, S. and Ray, K. (1997) Equity issues from detracking schools. In A. Hargreaves (ed.), *Rethinking educational change with heart and mind. The 1997 ASCD yearbook,* pp. 43–72. Alexandria, VA: ASCD.

OECD (1998) *Failure at school: problems and policies.* Paris: Organisation for Economic Co-operation and Development.

Ogbu, J. (1982) Cultural discontinuities and schooling. *Anthropology and Education Quarterly,* 13(4), 290–307.

Reynolds, C. (1990) Hegemony and hierarchy: becoming a teacher in Toronto, 1930–1980. *Historical Studies in Education,* 2(10), 95–118.

Rosenholtz, S. (1989) *Teachers' workplace.* New York: Teachers College Press.

Rutter, M., Maughan, B., Mortimore, P., Ouston, J. and Smith, A. (1979) *Fifteen thousand hours.* London: Open Books.

Sachs, J. (1999) Towards an activist view of teacher professionalism. Paper presented at the International Conference on "The New Professionalism in Teaching: Teacher Education and Teacher Development in a Changing World," Hong Kong, January.

Sanders, M. G. (1997) *Building effective school–family–community partnerships in a large urban school district.* Report No. 13, Center for Research on the Education of Students Placed at Risk, Baltimore, MD.

Sanders, M. and Epstein, J. (1998) School–family–community partnerships and educational change: international perspectives. In A. Hargreaves, A. Lieberman, M. Fullan and D. Hopkins (eds.), *International handbook of educational change,* pp. 482–502. Dordrecht: Kluwer.

Sarason, S. (1982) *The culture of the school and the problem of change* (2nd edn). Boston: Allyn and Bacon.

Schlechty, P. (1990) *Schools for the twenty-first century.* San Francisco: Jossey-Bass.

Schutz, A. (1973) The stranger: an essay in social psychology. In B. R. Cosin, I. R. Dale, G. M. Esland and D. F. Swift (eds.), *School and society: a sociological reader,* pp. 32–8. London: Routledge and Kegan Paul.

Shimahara, K. and Sakai, A. (1995) *Learning to teach in two cultures: Japan and the United States.* New York: Galard Publishers.

Sikes, P. (1995) *Parents who teach.* London: Cassell.

Sizer, T. (1992) *Horace's School: redesigning the American high school.* Boston: Houghton Mifflin.

Storey, D. (1976) *Saville.* London: Cape.

Touraine, A. (1995) *Critique of modernity*. Oxford: Blackwell.

Tyack, D. and Tobin, W. (1994) The grammar of schooling: why has it been so hard to change? *American Educational Research Journal*, 31(3), 453–80.

Villas-Boas, A. (1993) The effect of parent involvement in homework on student achievement. *Unidad*. Winter, Issue 2. Baltimore Center on Families, Communities, and Children's Learning, Johns Hopkins University.

Vincent, C. (1996a) Parent empowerment: collective action and inaction in education. Paper presented at the Annual Meeting of the American Educational Research Association, April, New York.

Vincent, C. (1996b) *Parents and teachers: power and participation*. London and Bristol, PA: Falmer Press.

Vincent, C. and Warren, S. (1998) Becoming a "better" parent? Motherhood, education and transition. *British Journal of Sociology of Education*, 19(2), 177–93.

Waller, W. (1932) *The sociology of teaching*. New York: Wiley.

Webb, R. and Vulliamy, G. (1993) A deluge of directives: conflict between collegiality and managerialism in the post ERA primary school. *British Education Research Journal*, 22(4), 441–58.

Wolfe, T. (1940) *You can't go home again* (4th edn). New York: Harper.

Index

ability/intelligence 78–80, 93, 139, 145
ability grouping *see* tracking
academic rationalism 189–90
Accelerated Schools 30
accountability 7; increased 219
Acker, S. 16, 132, 151, 225
action research 205, 210–11
activist partnerships 227–32
adaptation 179
administrators, teachers' view of 118
Advanced Placement 84, 89
advocacy 164–5, 168, 171
African-Americans 73, 82, 85, 86, 90
aging of staff 40–1
agency: assumptions about teacher
    agency 131–2; change agents and
    detracking 72–96; collaborative
    agenda setting 208–9; external
    197–216
agenda: collaborative agenda setting
    208–9; official 192
alienation 159–60
ambiguity 106–8
analysis: analytical frames 188–9; limits
    of 189–90
Anderson, G. 13
anxiety 59; parents' 219
Apple, M. W. 117, 120, 132, 151
Arendt, H. 191
Aronowitz, S. 8
asserting difference 162–3
assessment 7, 97–111; blending
    conceptions 106–8; folk pedagogies
    100–6; hardest part 99–100
Astington, J. W. 101
attrition of change 29–51

Baioğlu, A. 61
Ball, S. J. 66, 133, 134, 150
Bascia, N. 6, 9, 115, 163, 166, 167,
    172
Bastiani, J. 220
beacon schools *see* lighthouse
    schools
Bearfield Middle School 75, 77, 79, 80,
    82, 85, 86–7, 88, 90, 93
Beck, L. 52
Begley, P. 60
Belenky, M. 101, 102
Bereiter, C. 101
Beresford, E. 226
Bernstein, B. 17
Berry, B. 133
Beyond Sorting and Stratification Study
    73, 136–7
Bigum, C. 221
Black, R. 144, 145
Black Educators' Association 168, 171
Blackmore, J. 157
Blase, J. 13
Boesse, B. 54
Bond, Ward 32–3, 36, 45
bracketing difference 161–2
British Columbia Afro-Canadian
    Cultural Society 171
British Columbia Black Action Coalition
    171
Brookdale school 60–5
Bruner, J. S. 102
budgetary restraints 121–2
bureaucracy 123–4
Burgess, R. 218, 222
Byrne, P. 228

Caribbean-Canadian community 169–72
Carlson, R. 54
Carnegie Turning Points middle school
    model 76, 143–4
case study methodology 136–7
Casey, K. 132, 151
Castells, M. 19, 219, 221, 228, 229
Central High School: detracking 80,
    82–3, 86; gender politics 135, 137–43,
    149–50
Central Lifetime Achievers (CLA) 137–8
'Challenge' projects 78–9
Chandler, M. 101
change agents 7, 72–96; achievement
    of 87–90
child poverty 182, 184–6
Chinese-Canadian community 169–70
Chu, Rose 158, 159–61, 162, 167, 168,
    173; entitlement 163; role of ESL
    teachers 164, 165
Clark, C. 120
class 80–1, 91–2; confronting political
    pressures around 81–7, 92–4
classroom-oriented policies 125
classroom teaching 158–63
Clay, M. 97
climate for learning 11, 93
Clune, W. 113
Coalition of Essential Schools 30, 76,
    133
Cohn, M. 119
collaboration 8; attrition of change 33,
    38, 40; *see also* partnerships
community 34; gender politics and loss
    of 148–9; professional community
    and lighthouse schools 33, 34–5, 46,
    47; professional–parent partnerships
    224, 230; and sustainability of
    change 47; work of racial minority
    immigrant teachers 169–72
comparing difference 162, 170
competing ideologies 131–5, 150–1
Comprehensive Tests of Basic Skills
    (CTBS) 86–7
Connell, R. 116–17, 120
constructor, mind as 100–1, 101–2,
    103–6, 110
consultants 120–1
container, mind as 100–1, 103–6, 110

context of change 15–20, 116–19
continuity: inside–outside collaboration
    206–7; survival and 41–3
continuous professional learning 7–8;
    see also professional development
Cooper, R. 74
cooption strategies 59
coping strategies, teachers' 62–5, 67–8
corporate-funded projects 3, 9
Cousins, J. B. 60
creativity 31–6
credibility 207, 209, 212–13
Creemers, B. 52
criticism, teachers and 229–30
Crozier, G. 227
Cuban, L. 32, 119
Culver, E. 158, 160–1, 163, 164, 167,
    168–9, 173; curriculum 162; work in
    the community 169–72; work with
    other teachers 166, 169
Cunnison, S. 141
curriculum: adapting 162; and
    assessment 109–10

Darling-Hammond, L. 52, 231
Datnow, A. 6, 84
Day, C. 61
Delpit, L. 218
democratic deliberation 93–4
Demsey, V. 133
Denzin, N., 10, 11, 224
'deserving', privilege as 82–4
deskilling 119–20
detracking 72–96; achievement of
    change agents 87–90; challenging
    normative regularities 77–81;
    confronting political pressures
    around race and class 81–7; gender
    politics 138, 144, 144–5, 149;
    inventing new structures 75–7;
    lessons from detracking schools
    90–4; social justice 73–5
Dewey, J. 101–2, 112
DeYoung, A. J. 119
difference: with acceptance 56; racial
    minority immigrant teachers and 160,
    161–3
Differentiated Staffing Fund (DSF) 32,
    38

digital approach to assessment 108
dimensions of teaching 4–14;
  intellectual 7–9; socioemotional
  10–12; sociopolitical 13–14; technical
  4–7, 19
direct instruction 5
distance: discrete 220–1; professional
  218; social 218
district administration: and detracking
  86–7; principal rotation and 67
Doremus, R. R. 30
Dror, Y. 179

Earl, L. M. 5, 7, 8, 14, 67, 157;
  assessment 102, 104; social change
  222
Eastabrook, G. 32
education: ideologies of 139;
  philosophies of 145–8; of principals
  by teachers 62–3, 64–5, 67–8; tyranny
  of standard model of schooling 193
educational change/reform 3–4; context
  of change 15–20, 116–19; integrated
  approach to school reform 197;
  mandated *see* mandated change;
  practice of school change 92–4;
  predictable failure of 4; process of
  119–23; theories of school change
  90–2; trajectories and tragedies of
  14–20
elite classes 84, 89
Elkind, D. 10, 221
Elmore, R. 131
emotional labor 12
emotional understanding 11
emotions: learning partnerships 222–4;
  socioemotional dimension of
  teaching 10–12
empowerment 228
enrollment decline 39–40
entitlement 163; detracking schools
  82–4
entropy 39–41
Epstein, J. 219, 220, 225
equality, partner 211
equity 72–96; tracking as a structural
  barrier to 74–5
ESL teaching 164, 167
evaluation 33

exclusion 159–60, 167–8
exemplary schools *see* lighthouse
  schools
expectations of teachers 116–17
experience 188–9
experimentation 31–6
Explorer Middle School: detracking
  85–6, 86, 89; gender politics 135,
  143–50
external agents 197–216
external constraints 190
external influences, intrusiveness of
  19
extra-classroom work 164–5

families, changes in 182, 186–7, 221,
  222
Field Centres 200–14; *see also*
  inside–outside partnerships
financial assistance 184–5
Fink, D. 45, 48
flows and networks 16–17
folk pedagogies 100–6; teachers' 103–6,
  108–9
Foot, D. 231
Foster, R. 138, 142, 143
Foster, M. 132
foundation-funded projects 3, 9
Fullan, M. 10, 16, 19, 32, 131, 204, 227;
  anxiety 59, 217; external agency 197;
  government policies 9; intractable
  systems 123; Learning Consortium
  30; mandated change 120; school
  culture 68; teacher resistance 112,
  115; university–school collaboration
  199; unpreparedness 219

Galton, M. 5, 6
Ganz, H. J. 53
Gardner, H. 101–2
Garner, P. 41–2
gender politics 131–55
Giddens, A. 16
gifted pupils 78, 89
Giroux, H. 8
Gitlin, A. 124, 132, 151
Gleick, J. 16
globalization 228
goals of teaching 10

Goffman, E. 115
Gold, B. A. 46
Goleman, D. 10
Good Old Boys 137, 139–43, 150, 152
Goodson, I. 225, 227
Gramsci, A. 8
Grant High School 74, 75, 79, 86, 89, 94
Green, B. 221
Green Valley School 78–9, 81, 83, 86, 89
Greenfield, T. B. 67
Grey, B. 37–8, 38–9
Griffen, J. 74–5, 85, 86
Grumet, M. R. 218

Hall, G. E. 14
Hallinger, P. 6
Hannay, L. 199, 200, 204
hardening of school culture 55–60
Hargreaves, A. 11, 15, 40, 57, 97, 179, 214, 227; anxiety 59, 217; context of change 18, 19, 20, 117; emotions 10; government policies 9, 16; model schools 43, 48; planning 7; principal rotation 67; problem of time 218; professional development 8; school culture 68; teacher resistance 112; university–school collaboration 199; unpreparedness 219
Hart, A. 53
Helsby, G. 9, 12
Henley, M. 119
heterogeneous grouping 144–5; *see also* detracking
higher education 84
Hochschild, A. 12
Hochschild, J. 72, 221
Hopkins, D. 30
hostility, professional 34–5
houses, instructional 145–9
Howey, K. R. 199
Hoy, W. K. 53
Hoyle, E. 133–4
Huberman, A. M. 39, 115–16
Huberman, M. 132, 151
Hunt, D. 123–4
Hunter, M. 5

idea champion 198
Idea Team 138–43
ideology: competing ideologies and gender 131–5, 150–1; gender politics and ideological diversity 139–43, 144–9, 149–50
immigrant teachers *see* racial minority immigrant teachers
Improving Quality Schools for All project 30
inclusion 161–2
individualized approach to learning 88
information 19–20; organizational learning 191–3
information technology 182–3
innate intelligence 78, 80
innovative schools *see* lighthouse schools
inquiring into own practice 8
inside–outside partnerships 9, 197–216; case studies 201–6; collaborative agenda setting 208–9; continuity 206–7; Field Centre model 200–1; lessons learned 212–14; multifaceted projects 207–8; partner equality 211; politics 211–12; school–university collaboration 198–200; successful inside–outside collaboration 206–12; transferability of knowledge 210–11; unique solutions 209–10, 213
integrated approach to school reform 197
intellectual approach to organizational change 190–3
intellectual dimension of teaching 7–9
intelligence/ability 78–80, 93, 139, 145
isolation 218; racial minority immigrant teachers 159–60, 167–8

Jackson, P. W. 218

Kaufman, H. 189–90
Kelly, B. 41–2
Kentucky Education Reform Act 5–6
Kenway, J. 157
King Middle School 80, 89
knowledge: folk pedagogies and 101, 102; local contexts 213; transferability

of 210–11; universities and schools 199
Kottkamp, R. 119

Labaree, D. F. 219
Ladson-Billings, G. 161
Ladwig, J. 30
Lake Superior School District 201–2, 206, 208
Lakehead School District 202–3, 206, 208
Lam, C. 159, 162, 163, 164, 167
Lam, M. 158, 159–61, 166–7, 168, 169–70, 173; inclusion 161–2; relationship with parents 165; work with other teachers 165–6
language: immigrants and alienation owing to problems with 159–60; and power 135
large-scale reform 3–4
Lasch, C. 226
Lash, S. 228
Latino community 73, 80, 86, 137
leadership 8; attrition of change 32–3, 36; organizational learning 191; scaling up and lighthouse schools 44–5; teacher leaders 69, 172–3; women's 45–6
leadership succession 52–71; stages of 60–5
learning: climate for 11, 93; detracking and 87–8, 93; goals and silent partnerships 220–1; organizational learning 179, 190, 190–3; parents and early learning 220
Learning Consortium 30
learning partnerships 221–7
Leithwood, K. 14, 52, 60, 200
LeMahieu, P. G. 5, 14, 102, 104
Levin, B. 178, 179, 192, 222
Levin, H. 30
Liberty High School 74, 75–6, 82, 86
Lieberman, A. 117, 198
life cycle of new schools 31–43; creativity and experimentation 31–6; overreaching and entropy 36–41; survival and continuity 41–3
lifestyle choices 230

lighthouse schools 3, 29–51; life cycle 31–43; scaling up 30, 35, 43–6, 47–8; sustainability 47–8
Lindblad, S. 218
literacy 6
Little, J. W. 8, 52, 166
Lo, L. 18, 20
local knowledge 213
local solutions 209–10, 213
long-term collaboration 211–12
Lord Byron High School, Ontario 30–48
Lortie, D. 3, 116
Louis, K. S. 36

Macmillan, R. 52, 57
management of change 189–90
mandated change 5–6, 7, 29, 112–28; context of change 116–19; marginalization 114–16, 123; process of change 119–23
Manitoba School Improvement Project 30
Manning, Carleton 158, 162, 166, 167, 173; political activities 168–9; work in the community 169–72
marginalization 6, 172–3; mandated change 114–16, 123; teachers and principal rotation 62, 64–5, 66, 67–8; *see also* racial minority immigrant teachers
Margonis, F. 124, 132, 151
Mason, R. 3
McCall, B. 77, 93
McLaughlin, M. 15, 119
McNeil, L. 117
McQuillan, P. 132, 133, 151
media campaigns 230
Mehan, H. 134, 135
men teachers 151; *see also* gender politics
mentoring 166
Menzies, T. 52
Metcalf-Turner, P. 198, 199
Metz, M. H. 34, 47, 226
micropolitics *see* politics
middle schools model 143–4
Miles, M. 36, 39, 46, 115
Miller, L. 78, 117

Mills, C. W. 219
mind as constructor 100–1, 101–2, 103–6, 110
mind as container 100–1, 103–6, 110
mission, school's 224
mixed production style 108
model schools *see* lighthouse schools
Mothers of Excellence 82
motivation 79
multifaceted projects 207–8
multiple forms of intelligence 78–80
Muncey, D. 132, 133, 151
Murphy, J. 6, 52
mutual learning and support 221–7
Myrdal, G. 72

National Schools Network (Australia) 30
Native Americans 85–6, 143
'native' intelligence 78, 80
negative views of change 181–2, 187–8, 221–2
negotiation 62, 63–4, 65, 67–8
Nespor, J. 16–17, 219, 220
nested system 15–16
networks 16–17; school–university collaboration 198; support networks 8, 29–30, 173; for systemic change 29–30
New American Schools Network 30
Newmann, F. 13
Nias, J. 132, 134
Nipissing School District 205–6, 206–7, 208, 210
Noblit, G. 133, 134
Noddings, N. 10
norms 92–4; challenging in detracking schools 77–81
Northumberland-Clarington School District 203–5, 207, 208, 209–10, 211
nostalgia, combating 225–7

Oakes, J. 83, 92, 136, 152, 225
official agenda 192
Olson, D. R. 100, 102
Ontario 9, 212
Ontario Institute for Studies in Education (OISE) 200, 212
ordinariness, pedagogical 219

organic partnerships 199, 214
organizational learning 179, 190; intellectual side 190–3
organizational world-view 179
orphaning of mandated programs 122
outcomes-based reporting 99
overreaching 36–9

paradigm-breaking schools 43–6
parent councils (school councils) 201–2
parent–professional partnerships 217–35; activist partnerships 227–32; learning partnerships 221–7; obstacles to 217–19; silent partnerships 220–1
parents 14; attrition of change 34, 47; and detracking schools 74–5, 82–6, 89–90, 94; difficult 225; and work of racial minority immigrant teachers 164–5; *see also* parent–professional partnerships
participation: democratic deliberation and detracking 93–4; involvement of teachers in change 124–5; organizational learning 191–2
partnerships 125; equality in 211; inside–outside 9, 197–216; parent–professional 217–35
patriarchal culture 139–43
Pauley, E. 124–5
Payne, E. 74, 75
pedagogy: culturally relevant 159–61; problem of pedagogical ordinariness 219
peer coaching 205, 210
Phillips, D. 102
Plainview High School 79, 80, 81, 85, 88, 89
planning 7
policy: government 9, 156–7; regional 45
political maneuvring 142–3
political skills 224
politics: confronting political pressures around race and class 81–7, 92–4; inside–outside partnerships 211–12; racial minority immigrant teachers

and political action 168–9, 171–2; of
representation 134–5; sociopolitical
conception of teaching 13–14; *see
also* gender politics
Popkewitz, T. 17
portfolio innovation 17
poverty 6, 182, 184–6
power 150; empowerment 228;
language and 135; micropolitics of
school change 133–4, 151–2; silence
of the less powerful 85–6;
sociopolitical conception of teaching
13–14
Power House 145–8
Prieto, H. 218
principals 120; rotation of 52–71
principled professionalism 225, 227,
229–32
privilege, protecting 82–4
process of change 119–23
professional community 33, 34–5, 46,
47
professional development 7–8, 45, 169,
205–6; mandated change 120–2
professional development schools
(PDS) 198
professional distance 218
professional–parent partnerships *see*
parent–professional partnerships
professional work beyond the school
168–9
professionalism, principled 225, 227,
229–32
progressive teachers 144–5, 147, 149
protest 229
public, education of the 227–32
public celebrations 230
purposes, school's 224

race 91–2; confronting political
pressures around 81–7, 92–4;
confronting racial stereotypes 80–1
racial minority immigrant teachers
156–77; in the classroom 158–63; in
the community 169–72; professional
work beyond the school 168–9; work
beyond the classroom 164–5;
working the margins 172–3; work
with other teachers 165–8

Ray, K. 84
reactive response to change 188–9
recruitment crisis, teacher 231
reform *see* educational change/reform
renewing organization 124
representation, politics of 134–5
research: teachers and quality of 119;
university–school research program
204–5, 211
resistance to change: gender, ideology
and 132, 139–43, 144–9, 150–2;
leadership succession 61, 62, 63–5,
65–6, 68; mandated change 112,
113–16, 120
resources 8
Reynolds, D. 5, 14, 52
Riffel, J. A. 178, 222
Riseborough, G. F. 115, 132
Rites of Passage curricular model 147
Robertson, H.-J. 19
Rollinghills Middle School 74–5, 78,
84–5, 86, 90
Ropes House 145–8
Ross, J. 204
rotation of principals 52–71
Rowan, B. 7
Roxborough school 35, 39–40, 42, 43
Rudduck, J. 120
Rutter, M. 219

Sachs, J. 198, 227
Sanders, M. 225
Sarason, S. 3, 4, 91, 123, 131
scaling up 30, 35, 43–6, 47–8
Scardamalia, M. 101
Schlechty, P. 10, 220
Schmalz, K. 204
Schön, D. 59, 60
school boards 192
school councils (parent councils) 201–2
school culture 132; hardening of 55–60;
leadership succession and 52–71;
patriarchal 139–43; and structure
139–40
school districts *see* district
administration
school–university collaboration
198–200; *see also* inside–outside
partnerships

Schutz, A. 226
scope 218
self-assessment 105
sense-making strategies 62–5, 67–8
Sergiovanni, T. 6, 57, 60
Serna, I. 78
sexist discourse 141–2
sexual harassment suits 142
Shanker, A. 137
Shapiro, M. 134
Shulman, L. S. 7
Sieber, S. 65
Sikes, P. 39, 132, 157, 217
Silberman, C. E. 112
silence of the less powerful 85–6
silent partnerships 220–1
single-parent families 186
Sirotnik, K. 152
Siskin, L. S. 38, 134
Sizemore, J. 32, 35, 36, 37, 46
Sizer, T. 30
Slavin, R. 5, 29, 30
Smith, L. M. 15
Smyth, E. 200
social change 178–94, 221–2; changes
    in families 182, 186–7, 221, 222;
    child poverty 182, 184–6; information
    technology 182–3; limits of analysis
    189–90; suggestions for practice
    190–3; thinking about change 187–9;
    understanding 181–2
social class *see* class
social distance 218
social justice 73–5; *see also* equity
social movements 227–32
social problems 17–18
socioemotional dimension of teaching
    10–12
sociopolitical dimension of teaching
    13–14
solidarity of purpose 56–7, 60–1, 67
Soltis, J. 102
Spain 229
special education programs 42
specialization 38, 217–18
staff development *see* professional
    development
staffing 32
Stamp, R. 37

stereotypes: confronting racial
    stereotypes 80–1; gender roles 141
Stiggins, R. 105
stigma-theory 115
Stoffman, D. 231
Stoll, L. 45, 48
Storey, D. 218
stress 186
Stringfield, S. 30, 131
student-centered philosophy 44–5
students: consequences of teacher
    resistance for 116; excluded from
    educational change decisions 14;
    liberty at Lord Byron 37–8; problem
    of subjects superseding students
    217–18; teachers' work with and on
    behalf of, outside the classroom
    164–5; whole-child orientation 160–1
Success for All program 5
succession, leadership *see* leadership
    succession
supervision 63
support: mutual 221–7; unquestioning
    220–1, 224–5
support networks 8, 29–30, 173
survival 41–3
sustainability 47–8
systemic reform movements 29–30
systems: nested 15–16; ongoing
    development 192–3; unchanging and
    mandated change 122–3

Talbert, J. 15
teacher agency: assumptions about
    131–2; *see also* agency
teacher-initiated change 124, 151
teacher leadership 69, 172–3
teacher teams 144
teachers: and assessment *see*
    assessment; attrition of change 32–4,
    37–8, 40–1; culture and leadership
    succession 52–71; expectations of
    116–17; impact of detracking on
    87–8; impact of mandated change
    see mandated change; inquiring into
    own practice 8; judgements 5;
    parent-teacher partnerships *see*
    parent–professional partnerships;
    recruitment crisis 231; relationships

of racial minority immigrant teachers with other teachers 165–8; resistance *see* resistance to change; role of 139; 'streaming' of 163–4

teaching: dimensions of 4–14; goals of 10

teaching strategies 117–18; detracking and 87–8, 93

technical dimension of teaching 4–7, 9

technology 221

Thiessen, D. 120, 162, 166, 168, 169, 170, 171–2

198–200; *see also* inside–outside partnerships

Urry, J. 228

values: racial minority immigrant teachers' work in the community 170; teachers' work 117–18

Villas-Boas, A. 225

Vincent, C. 222, 223

violence 186–7

Vygotsky, L. 97

Waller, W. 217, 225

rren, S. 222

tson, N. 199

hlage, G. 13

lls, A. S. 78, 136

eatley, M. J. 16

ite flight 84–5

itford, B. L. 6, 7, 198, 199

ole-child orientation 160–1

liams, E. 74

liams, R. 86

lis, P. 116

dak, R. 135

lcott, H. 119

lf House 145–8

lfe, T. 226

men, changing role of 178–9

men's leadership 45–6

ng, K. 6, 7

ods, P. 10

k, changes in 179

, R. 136

ezawa, S. 86

hner, K. 116

pher, N. L. 199